DESTINED FOR GREATNESS

YOU HAVE WHAT IT TAKES TO SUCCEED

DANIEL O. ONDIEKI

authorHOUSE®

AuthorHouse™ UK
1663 Liberty Drive
Bloomington, IN 47403 USA
www.authorhouse.co.uk
Phone: UK TFN: 0800 0148641 (Toll Free inside the UK)
    UK Local: (02) 0369 56322 (+44 20 3695 6322 from outside the UK)

Published by AuthorHouse 12/12/2022

ISBN: 978-1-6655-8833-1 (sc)
ISBN: 978-1-6655-8834-8 (hc)
ISBN: 978-1-6655-8333-6 (e)

Print information available on the last page.

"Becoming more to do more is the secret of greatness".

I will praise You, for I am fearfully *and* wonderfully made; Marvelous are Your works, And *that* my soul knows very well.
My frame was not hidden from You, When I was made in secret,
And skillfully wrought in the lowest parts of the earth.
Your eyes saw my substance, being yet unformed. And in Your book they all were written, The days fashioned for me,
When *as yet there were* none of them.

—Psalm 139:14–16

This book is dedicated to my Heavenly Father, who loved us so much that He gave us His unspeakable, indescribable, and incomparable gift – His one and only Son, Jesus Christ. Our Father, You are the greatest Giver of all time. You are wonderful and excellent in Your guidance!

"For God so loved the world that He gave His only begotten Son, that whoever believes in Him should not perish but have everlasting life" (John 3:16).

Thank You, Father, for the Lord Jesus Christ, and thank you for the Holy Spirit and Your Word. Thank You for the body of Christ—one body, one church. Thank You for all the nations of the world. You love us unconditionally. Thank You for your angels who watch over us! I am forever grateful to know You. Knowing You is eternal life (John 17:3).

CONTENTS

FOREWORD

Destined for Greatness is an excellent book for anyone who desires a life of good success and wants to accomplish amazing things by turning a burning passion into a brave reality. In other words, this book is for those with a desire for greatness. You can be that someone. *Destined for Greatness* will show you how to change your life for the better by guiding you on your journey to your destiny of desire.

Pastor and coach Daniel O. Ondieki has authored a book relevant to both today's and future Christians that will challenge and encourage believers worldwide to rise up and be salt and light.

You are destined for greatness! God created you in His image and likeness, and He fully equipped you at birth with extraordinary abilities. You have the capacity, capability, and unlimited potential to achieve anything your heart desires—as long as you are willing to work diligently with all your heart, soul, and body.

You're designed for greatness. That's not an idea, proposition, empty claim, or fallacy. It is a fact that the Bible, the holy book of the Christian faith, confirms in many ways throughout the scriptures—from Genesis to Revelation.

God created all of us equal. No one is more fortunate than anyone else. Your race, colour, gender, country of origin, career, and so on are great, but they do not reveal your true identity or determine your destiny. God does! Jeremiah 29:11 confirms that God has great plans for your present and future life.

Unfortunately, many people have been deceived and accepted the lie that their value is lower than that of others. As a result of their acceptance of this fallacious belief, they miss the destiny God intended for them, and they have nothing great to look forward to. While they would have been extraordinarily successful individuals, many live hopeless lives and die without achieving greatness or making the world a better place than how they found it.

Is it possible that anyone whether born-again Christians or true worshippers of God, can change course, overcome the ugly scenario of heading nowhere great, change their attitude, and overhaul their belief system to start a new journey to a great destiny? Is it possible to achieve greatness? Are there principles, road maps, spiritual guides, tools, spiritual resources, and wise counsellors who can help you discover or refine your God-given talents, gifts, and opportunities?

The answer to these questions is a resounding yes! *Destined for Greatness* proves that we are all destined for greatness. In this book, first-time author Daniel Ondieki demonstrates that, for anyone who chooses to believe that all things are possible with God—and in doing so, changes the course of their life—it is possible to fulfil their life's purpose and reach a destiny of desire. Daniel is highly authentic, credible, skilled, mature, and experienced. He is an anointed preacher, coach, mentor, and teacher of the Bible. I have known Daniel as a brother in Christ and as a personal friend for over thirty years. He and I have shared intimate moments and had many intense discussions on different topics, including some that are shared in this book.

Before Daniel migrated to Germany and I to America in the 1990s, we spent a lot of time praying together, seeking God and asking Him to give our lives clarity and direction. At the time, both Daniel and I were facing difficult challenges, and our futures seemed unpromising. We were both concerned about our destinies and wanted desperately to change course. We had no money, no godfathers to help us, and no good jobs. The only things we had going for us were faith, hope in God, comfort in the Holy Spirit, courage to dare for the seemingly impossible, and confidence to aim high and touch the sky.

We aren't quite there yet, but we have certainly made significant progress in our respective journeys. God has been on our side, giving us countless victories all along the way. Thanks be to God, who always gives us victory through Jesus Christ, our Lord and Saviour (1 Corinthians 15:57).

Daniel, a man of unquestionable character, humble background, powerful testimony, admirable credentials, and wide knowledge and experience in Christian ministry, has helped thousands of people around the world. It is well worth reading his informative, inspiring, compelling and timely message in *Destined for Greatness*. In this book, you will hear Daniel's voice, recognize his passion for excellence, and encounter his impeccable integrity. He is a servant leader with outstanding credibility. It has been my great joy and pleasure to see Daniel grow up in many areas of his life and become the man he is now! This great book is my reward for the many years I spent coaching and mentoring him. To God be the glory, honour, and praise!

Destined for Greatness is a powerful spiritual, mental, and professional tool that will change lives on a grand scale across the globe. You are very fortunate to own a copy of this book. If you read it and digest it slowly, its message will fill your whole being. Your life and future will never be the same. The book's message will transform you and help you realize God's purpose and priorities for your life.

Great destiny is just a wish and a prayer away. Unleash your passion, and pray passionately. Work hard and smart until you reach the peak of your highest mountain of good success. Anything is possible! Don't wait until tomorrow. Make a difference in your life today, and change the world. Start reading *Destined for Greatness*, and depend on it as one of your most valuable spiritual guides. After all, you will need a guide while on the journey to your destiny of desire. Daniel, through this book, has made it easier for you to become a success at anything worthwhile that you're doing now or may wish to do in the future.

In this book, you will be inspired, motivated, and challenged by the many testimonials shared by ordinary people like you who have been impacted and transformed by Daniel's teaching, preaching, coaching, and mentorship. These individuals are now making a difference and adding value to many others! You could be next in line to share your testimony!

I now leave you with Daniel, who will talk to you personally—heart to heart and one on one. When you hear his heart and stories, you'll hear your own. The power that changed him and lifted him higher continues to lead him to great victories, and it will do the same for you. Believe the message and the messenger, and you may become Daniel's friend for life as you receive his teachings, coaching, mentoring and guidance.

Boaz B. Olang, Ph.D. is former adjunct professor of Business Management at the Dutchess Community College of the State University of New York. Dr. Olang is a scholar and researcher in the field of organizational leadership and management and is the founder of Christ for All Worldwide Church and Marriage Mirror Digest. He serves as marriage and family counsellor, consultant, and speaker to diverse audiences in conferences and churches. Boaz is a resident of New York State but currently lives in his native country Kenya with his wife Jane.

A WORD FROM THE FIRST EDITOR

In this book, Pastor Daniel Ondieki skilfully details how to prosper the soul. The prosperity of your soul determines the prosperity of all things. As 3 John 1:2 says, "Beloved, I pray that you may prosper in all things and be in health, just as your soul prospers." The soul consists of your conscience, mind, will, emotions, and intellect. Your soul is like a garden that you have to constantly work on until you know how to walk and work in a renewed mind.

This book equips you with tools and strategies for living a victorious and exceptional life. It also reminds believers of who they are in Christ Jesus and the power and resources they have to change their world.

Pastor Daniel Ondieki has spent over 21 years pastoring and ministering to broken-hearted and hurting people. He has captured the essence of what a Christian requires to fully overcome their past, walk in a renewed mind, and be in good health and victory today.

Each chapter highlights Pastor Daniel's insights and includes practical ways to maintain a personal life of victory. Pastor Daniel does not stop there, however; he goes on to explain how healed Christians can influence their society. This is significant for the times in which we live today. Drawing upon cases from the Bible, Pastor Daniel illuminates spiritual principles that can help the reader to practically navigate today's crises. Furthermore, Pastor Daniel explains how Christians can become blessings as he reveals the various opportunities available to them in society.

Pastor Daniel's passion for believers can be felt throughout the pages of this book. Every Christian should arise in the authority and power of Jesus Christ to influence their world for good. "Investing in people's lives" is Pastor Daniel's motto. Transformational leadership begins from the inside out. When people develop spiritually, personally, and economically while also making sure to develop their communities, the world becomes a better place!

It has been an honour to edit and prepare this book for print. I highly recommend it to every Christian who desires to stand strong, grow, and move beyond their past to eternally influence their world for the kingdom of God.

Pastor Funbi Oni-Orisan
Kingscourt Leipzig
Germany

A WORD FROM EDITH ONDIEKI

My husband Daniel is a source of inspiration to me. He has taught me to be aware of my internal dialogue. Whether we know it or not, we are always experiencing internal dialogue in our hearts. This can be positive, constructive, or destructive. We need to have this awareness and be intentional in the kinds of thoughts and conversations we allow into our hearts and minds.

Daniel is not only my husband, but he is also a great friend and mentor. Not only does he teach, father, coach, and mentor many lives, but he walks the talk. Daniel calls things which do not exist as though they do, and through this revelation, on the authority and dominion that God has given us (see Genesis 1:26 and Romans 4:17), we as a family have witnessed countless miracles and breakthroughs. It is common practice for Daniel to begin his day by speaking words of affirmation to himself based on the Word of God. He has also been instrumental in calling those things that were not in my life as though they were. Needless to say, I am not the same person he married 24 years ago. Indeed, God has used him to call those attributes that I did not have into being, for which I give all the glory to God.

I have seen Daniel burning the midnight oil, investing many hours and significant effort into the writing of this book. As you read, you will discover how you can bring changes to your life, family, and situations through basic principles based on the Word of God. *Destined for Greatness* is not just a book—it's a tool that you can use in real-life situations to get tangible and undebatable results. I am overjoyed to see that Daniel has finally put together these truths in the form of a book; I am sure this book will be of great help and bring transformation to many people's lives. Investing in people's lives is one of Daniel's top priorities.

The testimonials shared in this book are real, inspiring, and motivational. They will challenge you to become more in order to do more. Happy reading!

Edith Ondieki

ENDORSEMENTS

Pastor Daniel has been the international pastor of our church of over 70 different nations for many years. Not only is he a great leader and globally travelled teacher, but he is also an excellent pastor and mentor to many, many people from many countries.

Pastor Daniel has created a permanent home and place of service in our church. He oversees the English-speaking groups and the international ministries. I have learned a lot from him not only during our trip to India, but also through his innovative leadership style.

While we German pastors didn't even know the word "zoom" years ago, Pastor Daniel was already training countless leaders around the world via social and digital media.

If I had to describe Pastor Daniel in one sentence, I would say, "He is not only a modern hero of the future, but he is also a hero maker."

Pastor Mario Wahnschaffe,
The former Pastor of the International Church in Bonn, CLW-Centrum Lebendiges Wort. www.clwbonn.de

Daniel is my younger brother. I was given the opportunity to listen to him ministering and counselling when I visited his congregation in Germany. I noticed his unique anointing that prompted deep insights inspired by the gift of the Holy Spirit. You come to appreciate the talent in Daniel's skilful approaches to counselling, consulting, coaching, and mentoring. He breaks down complex concepts for easy application and real results.

I believe each chapter of *Destined for Greatness* will transform the lives of its readers, as this book is based on real-life experiences and deep revelations inspired by the Holy Spirit.

Dr. Victor Swanya Ogeto, BSc, MBA, LLB (Hon-UoN) Dip. Law (KSL), AClArb (Commercial Mediator-UK), Advocate

I know Pastor Daniel from a two-year mentorship period. I was then the assistant pastor having quite a challenging time when he offered me an opportunity to coach and mentor me. During that time, he helped me sharpen my perspective on the events I was going through and challenged me to ask God for a clearer vision for my ministry.

His most outstanding trait is probably his encouraging way of speaking. Daniel understands the power of words, and he uses his words with purpose. You almost can't leave an appointment with him without feeling encouraged in one way or another.

I look forward to reading his book!

Pastor Matthias Reinartz
Family Pastor of the International Church in Bonn, CLW

Pastor Daniel's mentoring and coaching are powerful reminders of what is truly important in life. He equips you with the necessary tools for ongoing success and awakens your spirit so that you can begin living a prosperous and fulfilling life. I know his coaching and mentoring will transform your life and make you realize that greatness has always been within your grasp—it simply waits within you until you water and nurture the correct seeds. Thank you, Pastor Daniel.

David Robinson
Opera Singer, Mexico City

The content of this illuminating book brings out truth, wisdom, and inspiration to empower you forward to greatness. It provides proven and timeless principles, methods, and counsel that you can put into practice to dramatically improve your life. What makes the book a must-read is the seamless blending of spiritual principles and the contemporary realities of life, as well as how you can apply this combination to navigate towards greatness.

I have known Pastor Daniel Ondieki since high school. He practices the same principles that have made him so inspiring. I have immensely benefited from his counsel and guidance. Let him hold your hand through this transformative book, as I am sure you will find it worth your investment. I recommend it as must-read for all.

Dr. Benson Momanyi
International Consultant in Strategic Management and Member of Governing Council, Maasai Mara University, Kenya

INTRODUCTION

True greatness is a lifelong journey that requires that you know the One who created you. His name is I AM WHO I AM—the Lord God Almighty, the Creator of the heavens and the earth.

Knowing Him will help you to better know yourself. Knowing yourself will help you to discover your true purpose in life. Knowing your true purpose in life will help you to know the priorities of your purpose. Knowing your priorities will protect your time, energy, and God-given resources, and it will help you to manage these things well. That is what I call true greatness.

Greatness is knowing and defining your God-given vision.

What is your vision? It is your picture of your future. It is the perspective that you have in your mind and heart. It is a blueprint of your life, family, ministry, business, career, profession, organization, and all that you may wish to be and do. King Solomon, the wisest man who ever lived, said, "Where there is no vision, the people perish: but he that keep the law, happy is he" (Proverbs 29:18).

In other words, where there is vision, people prosper, succeed, break through, and become more effective, fulfilled, and significant. A vision enables you to add value to others, make a difference, and ultimately make the world a better place.

King Solomon goes on to say, "but he that keeps the law, happy is he." What does that mean? He who keeps the given instructions and disciplines of life, family, business, and everything else will be happy. A God-given vision gives you direction, provision, protection, providence, and much more.

According to Dr Myles Munroe, "Purpose is when you know and

understand what you were born to accomplish. Vision is when you see it in your mind and begin to imagine it"

(Quotefancy.com).

Vision, good disciplines, and great values bring happiness, joy, and gladness into your life.

Greatness can also be compared to a precious seed, inside of which are treasures that are beyond description. If this seed is planted in good soil, nurtured, watered, and protected, it will bring forth sweet and healthy fruits.

Greatness follows a specific process before real fruits can be seen. Many people love to be great, but they don't want to go through the process of attaining greatness. The majority love the events of greatness but not the process of it, and hence, they fail to achieve it.

As receiving follows giving, even so greatness follows humility and service to others. Jesus said, "Yet it shall not be so among you; but whoever desires to become great among you, let him be your servant" (Matthew 20:26). Servant leadership leads to greatness.

Greatness is knowing and writing down your core values in life and leaning on these values at all times. The vision, mission, or strategies may change, but your values always remain to work for and protect you. Your core values make you valuable, and for those in business, they can be your assets and marketing agents for your products and services. Treasure and practise your values in private and in public. They are the foundation of your work.

Greatness is a choice. It requires a burning desire, determination, and commitment.

It takes love, hope, and faith in God. You are where you are today because of the choices, decisions, and actions you took yesterday. It is amazing what good beliefs, decisions, and actions can do for you. One of the greatest gifts they can give you is eternal life. They can give you a blessed and great life here on Earth and in the life beyond.

Great people are developed in different places. Moses, a great leader, was raised in a palace for four decades. For the rest of his 80 years, his development occurred in the wilderness. God may choose to train you at a Bible school, at home, in the community in which you live, or outside of your country.

In my case, He chose to take me to India, where I received incredibly challenging training for four-and-a-half years. Ten years later, He sent me to Germany. Over twenty years, I have received training in many different cities, and indeed, I have learned a lot from the German people and other nationalities in both our community and Europe as a whole.

There is a particular place where my training is hardest, and that place was Wüstenrot. In English, this name means "desert." I was very humbled in this community. I am grateful for the wonderful congregation that loved and took care of us, and blessed us in many ways for ten years. I learned many things. All that I am doing today—seminars, counselling, coaching, and mentoring—began in that beautiful community. I am forever grateful that my real ministry started in Wüstenrot.

Abraham had to leave his country, family, and father's house to go to the unknown land that God would show him.

Now the LORD had said to Abram:

"Get out of your country,
From your family
And from your father's house,
To a land that I will show you.
I will make you a great nation;
I will bless you
And make your name great;
And you shall be a blessing.
I will bless those who bless you,
And I will curse him who curses you;
And in you all the families of the earth shall be blessed."

So Abram departed as the LORD had spoken to him, and Lot went with him. And Abram *was* seventy-five years old when he departed from Haran. (Genesis 12:1–4)

The greatness of Abraham required faith, courage, and obedience. God had promised him that He was going to make him a great nation and bless him. In the course of time, Abraham became a friend of God. God was so pleased with Abraham's obedience that He introduced Himself to Moses as "I am the God of your father—the God of Abraham, the God of Isaac, and the God of Jacob" (Exodus 4:6).

Greatness requires you to surround yourself with like-minded people who will help you to grow into your calling and assignment here on Earth. King Solomon wrote in Proverbs 13:20, "He who walks with wise men will be wise, But the companion of fools will be destroyed." Be intentional in choosing good companions.

The assets of greatness are love, faith, patience, and self-control. King Solomon wrote, "Whoever *has* no rule over his own spirit, *Is like* a city broken down, without walls" (Proverbs 25:28). Be emotionally intelligent as well as diligent. You need both of these skills. Emotion management and leadership require self-control at all times.

Above all, true greatness requires the Holy Spirit of the true, living God and His Word within you. The Holy Spirit is your greatest Mentor and the Coach for your greatness. He will point you to God's Word, which has all the secrets to greatness. Get to know Him better and better.

Greatness is what we leave in people. It involves caring about others, doing things for them, loving them, and showing up for them consistently.

Greatness means moving from personal success and significance to inspiring others to become what they were created to be. It means wanting others to do more than you have done. Jesus said to His disciples in John 14:12, "Most assuredly, I say to you, he who believes in Me, the works that I do he will do also; and greater works than these he will do, because I go to My Father." Jesus, having trained His disciples, wanted them to do more than He had done. That is true greatness.

What does the title of this book, *Destined for Greatness*, mean? The word *destined* means that you are set apart for a certain purpose. You are intended for something special or designed for a specific task or responsibility that no one else can do. It means you are heading towards a specific destination. You are the only one who can carry out that particular assignment. You have the marks that distinguish you for greatness, love, humility, integrity, excellence, and diligence. Having said all that, I must remind you that this comes at a high price. If you are willing to pay that price, you will eat the good of the land. There is a promise from God in Isaiah 1:19, which says: "If you are willing and obedient, You shall eat the good of the land" (Read Isaiah 1:18–20). Willingness and obedience will usher you into greatness. They will bring you into the goodness of the Lord that is in the land.

What other price am I talking about? I'm talking about your time, energy, discipline, and willingness to do what others are not willing to do. Your destiny will also cost money. Nothing is free; everything has a cost. Ecclesiastes 10:19 says, "A feast is made for laughter, and wine makes merry; But money answers everything." Money is a result of who you are and what you do. It is a combination of the many things you do well. It is a servant; it should not be your master. It does not discriminate. Study the principles of money and practice them consistently, and you will be amazed at how blessed you are. I recommend reading *How to Save Money for Investment* by Rev. Ken Monyoncho. He offers practical principles to follow to achieve financial success. His book teaches you how to be a good manager of your money. If you know how to manage your life, time, and money well, that is greatness.

What does the Bible say about greatness? "You shall increase my greatness, And comfort me on every side" (Psalm 71:21). Every one of us was born with a measure of greatness. That measure can be increased through study, knowledge, understanding, and wisdom. Like King David, you can ask the Lord to increase your greatness and comfort you on every side.

> Yours, O Lord, *is* the *greatness* [italics mine], The power and the glory, The victory and the majesty; For all *that is* in heaven and in earth *is Yours;* Yours *is* the kingdom, O Lord, And You are exalted as head over all. (1 Chronicles 29:11)

> Then she [the queen of Sheba] said to the king: "*It was* a true report which I heard in my own land about your words and your wisdom. However I did not believe their words until I came and saw with my own eyes; and indeed the half of the *greatness* [italics mine] of your wisdom was not told me. You exceed the fame of which I heard." (2 Chronicles 9:5–6)

Solomon always delivered his services and products beyond expectations. He manifested God's greatness within himself. You, too, can deliver your services and products beyond expectations. Doing so will distinguish you from the rest of the crowd.

Ecclesiastes 1:16 says, "I communed with my heart, saying, 'Look, I have attained greatness, and have gained more wisdom than all who were before me in Jerusalem. My heart has understood great wisdom and knowledge.'"

How can greatness be obtained? By meditating on God's Word and His goodness. You may often find yourself meditating on the negativity around you. Be aware that what you constantly meditate upon in your heart and mind, you will attract.

Let's note a very important point from this reading: True greatness is demonstrated through the revelation of knowledge, understanding, and God's wisdom. You are called to declare God's greatness here on Earth. Greatness is attained and gained through God's wisdom.

> Great *is* the Lord, and greatly to be praised; And His *greatness* [italics mine] *is* unsearchable. (Psalm 145:3)

> *Men* shall speak of the might of Your awesome acts, And I will declare Your *greatness* [italics mine]. (Psalm 145:6)

> Praise Him for His mighty acts; Praise Him according to His excellent *greatness* [italics mine]! (Psalm 150:2)

From these scripture passages, we see that our God is great, and His greatness is unmatched. He is excellent in greatness. You have your Heavenly Father's DNA within your heart to be great and to do amazing things through the power of the Holy Spirit.

True greatness comes from God. He can empower you with His greatness and comfort you from every side. He can raise you from zero to being a great hero. He picked up David, the shepherd boy, and made him the second king of Israel. He took Joseph from prison and made him the prime minister of Egypt. What can't He do for you when you ask for something that is in accordance with His will? He took Esther, a maid and orphan, and made her a queen. You are next in line for God's greatness, which is all for His glory. He desires to make you great because that is His nature.

When God called Abraham, He said to him in Genesis 12:2:

> I will make you a great nation;
> I will bless you
> And make your name great;
> And you shall be a blessing.

In 2 Chronicles 1:7, God, on the night that He appeared before Solomon, said to him, "Ask! What shall I give you?" Solomon asked Him to give him wisdom and knowledge. The very wisdom that God gave him made Solomon a great king.

2 Chronicles 1:10 says, "Now give me wisdom and knowledge, that I may go out and come in before this people; for who can judge this great people of Yours?"

Our God is excellent in greatness, and you and I have His Image and likeness. His DNA is within us. It distinguishes each one of us wherever we are and wherever we go. However, with this greatness comes a great responsibility: to study God's Word in order to know the true, living God through Jesus Christ, with the help of the Holy Spirit. You have to know yourself and know that it is God's will to bless and empower you to achieve greatness. That is why you can boldly say, "I am destined for greatness, and I have what it takes to succeed."

We are spirit, we have a soul and live in a body. Within our spirits we have God's DNA.

> Love has been perfected among us in this: that we may
> have boldness in the day of judgment; because as He is,
> so are we in this world. (John 4:17)

But what does "I have what it takes to succeed" mean? It means that you have everything you need to break through, to rejoice, and to pursue your God-given dreams and visions.

First and foremost, know that good success is the will of God. This is based on Joshua 1:8, which says, "This Book of the Law shall not depart from your mouth, but you shall meditate in it day and night, that you may observe to do according to all that is written in it. For then you will make your way prosperous, and then you will have good success."

Here, God gives Joshua the master key. Good success comes through meditation on His written Word. God assures Joshua that if he constantly meditated on His Word, Joshua would prosper and have not just success, but good success.

Here are seven important points to bear in mind in your pursuit of good success:

1. Know God and make Him your total Source. He is more than enough for you.
2. Discover and make use of the resources that are at your disposal.
3. Be a faithful and diligent leader, and manage well all of the resources that have been entrusted to you.
4. Know that God is looking for leaders and managers who can effectively take care of all the resources that He deposited into and on the earth during creation.
5. As stated in scripture, God withholds the resources He gives us if we do not know how to manage them well. In other words, the resources that we do not manage well will unfortunately be taken away.
6. Family is the first place to learn sets of values that will prepare you for great and good success. We all start the day from home and finish it at home. Let home be a place of inner rest, peace, happiness, and great joy.
7. Develop and sharpen your gifts, talents, and skills. King Solomon says in Proverbs 18:16, "A man's gift makes room for him And brings him before great men."

This *is* the history of the heavens and the earth when they were created, in the day that the Lord God made the earth and the heavens, before any plant of the field was in the earth and before any herb of the field had grown. For the Lord God had not caused it to rain on the earth, and *there was* no man to till the ground; but a mist went up from the earth and watered the whole face of the ground. And the LORD God formed man *of* the dust of the ground, and breathed into his nostrils the breath of life; and man became a living being. (Genesis 2:4–7)

God formed a man, Adam, to manage His resources. In Genesis 2:19–20, Adam and God were in partnership: "Out of the ground the LORD God formed every beast of the field and every bird of the air, and brought them to Adam to see what he would call them. And whatever Adam called each living creature, that was its name." If you want to succeed, you must recognize and acknowledge God as your Senior Partner in your life, family, education, career, profession, business, ministry, and anything else you may wish to do.

Adam gave names to all the cattle, to the birds of the air, and to every beast of the field. But he found no helper comparable to him. He was an effective manager of God's resources. As a reward for his management of the garden, God blessed him with a wonderful wife:

And the LORD God caused a deep sleep to fall on Adam, and he slept; and He took one of his ribs, and closed up the flesh in its place. Then the rib which the LORD God had taken from man He made into a woman, and He brought her to the man. And Adam said: "This *is* now bone of my bones And flesh of my flesh; She shall be called Woman, Because she was taken out of Man." Therefore, a man shall leave his father and mother and be joined to his wife, and they shall become one flesh. And they were both naked, the man and his wife, and were not ashamed. (Genesis 2:21–25)

Here's a very important point: All you are looking for is within you. Where was Eve during all that time in which Adam was alone? She was within him.

You see, when you walk with, work with, and partner with God, He works on your behalf and gives you "wows" (surprises and fantastic experiences). Can you imagine Adam being presented with a very beautiful and precious wife by God, the Creator Himself? It was certainly a "wow" moment for him. "And Adam said, 'This *is* now bone of my bones And flesh of my flesh.; She shall be called Woman, Because she was taken out of Man.'"

I can only imagine how Adam felt in his heart; he was excited, overjoyed, and happy to have this wonderful, precious gift taken out of him, given life, and presented to him by his Senior Partner in business, the Lord God Almighty Himself.

Eve was the first woman on the earth. She was never a baby, and she didn't have parents or siblings. Adam did not have to ask her, "Excuse me, what is your name, madam?" He also did not have to introduce himself to her. He chose to call her Eve. He gave her this name to reflect that she was the mother of all the living, as stated in Genesis 3:20. He saw in her a family that would multiply and fill the earth.

The family is the first institution started by God. As a result of this single, special family of Adam and Eve, we have billions of families around the world that total 7.9 billion people as of August 2021, according to United Nations estimates and Worldometer.

The family was founded by divine creation, according to Genesis 1:26–28. The will of God was to bless all the families of the earth through Adam and Eve. Adam was the foundation of his family. He was the source of his family. He was to sustain and maintain that family with all the resources God had given him. He had all he needed to keep the family intact.

In Genesis 2:8–15, you can read about Adam and Eve's beautiful home. I should emphasize that when it is well with you as an individual, it will be well with your family, and when it is well with your family, it will be well with your profession, business, ministry, community, town, city, nation, and the world. The brokenness we see in today's world is the result of broken homes. Let's arise and begin to rebuild our personal lives and our homes. That is my challenge to all of us if we want to see a better and greater tomorrow. A widely quoted Saint Teresa of Calcutta saying goes like this: "If you want to bring peace to the whole world, go home and love your family." Let us go to our homes and begin to love our own people, and we will experience a great revival and amazing transformations in our world.

Family values and structure will bring forth a great community. It is very important to belong to a good community of like-minded people. In both good and challenging times, your community is a strong pillar that will hold you up, rejoice with you, and cry with you. Indeed, Romans 12:15 says, "Rejoice with those who rejoice, and weep with those who weep."

Develop your gifts, talents, and skills to usher you onto the global stage. Everyone on the planet has something to contribute to that stage. Your contribution, whether big or small, will add value to our planet and change our environment. What is it that you can bring us? Think about it, and then do something about it.

Finally, I would like to mention several more resources that will enable you to see and manifest your greatness. These are evident in Revelation 5:11–12. It says:

> Then I looked, and I heard the voice of many angels around the throne, the living creatures, and the elders; and the number of them was ten thousand times ten thousand, and thousands of thousands, saying with a loud voice: "Worthy is the Lamb who was slain To receive power and riches and wisdom, And strength and honour and glory and blessing!"

Let's briefly look at what Christ Jesus received on your behalf two thousand years ago.

Power

Power is the ability to do the work the Lord has given you here on Earth. No abilities are without responsibility. You must know that God has equipped you well for your assignment. Luke 10:19–20 says, "Behold, I give you the authority to trample on serpents and scorpions, and over all the power of the enemy, and nothing shall by any means hurt you. Nevertheless, do not rejoice in this, that the spirits are subject to you, but rather rejoice because your names are written in heaven."

Riches

The resources and supplies of heaven are available for you to use to serve God effectively without struggle. You are not lacking at all.

> The Lord is my shepherd. I shall not want. (Psalm 23:1)

> My God will supply all your need according to His riches in heaven. (Philippians 4:19)

> For the LORD your God is bringing you into a good land, a land of brooks of water, of fountains and springs, that flow out of valleys and hills; a land of wheat and barley, of vines and fig trees and pomegranates, a land of olive oil and honey; a land in which you will eat bread without scarcity, in which you will lack nothing; a land whose stones *are* iron and out of whose hills you can dig copper. The earth is full of good and great resources which needs to be well managed. (Deuteronomy 8:7–9)

> When you go, you will come to a secure people and a large land. For God has given it into your hands, a place where *there is* no lack of anything that *is* on the earth. (Judges 18:10)

What a wonderful place this is where there is no lack of anything on the earth! I can only imagine that this place where there lacks nothing is being first in Christ and being in God's kingdom. There is no lack or scarcity in the Lord and in the kingdom of God. It is from there that you can function and do all you have been assigned by the Lord, which includes your studies, career, profession, ministry, business, and anything else you could ever imagine. That means that you have to be in partnership and network with heaven through the Lord Jesus Christ and by the Holy Spirit of God. The Bible is God's great manual; it has all details that you need to study and understand the timeless principles that never fail. If you desire to begin, continue, and finish well, strong, and greater, I recommend starting with the book of Proverbs. In it, you meet King Solomon, who will give you instructions for your life. As you act on these instructions, you will see great transformation in yourself.

Matthew 6:33 says: "But seek first his kingdom and his righteousness, and all these things will be given to you as well." I especially like the phrase "all these things." These things include good health, God-given wealth, peace, love, freedom, and all the other good things you can imagine. All these things should glorify God, be a blessing to His people, and bring joy and peace into our lives. That is the kingdom of God's culture. It is a selfless culture. Jesus came down from heaven to show us how to live selflessly.

"Do not be afraid, little flock, for your Father has been pleased to give you the kingdom"

(Luke 12:32). If it is our Father's good pleasure to give us the kingdom that has all the supplies we need, then it is worth investing our time, energy, and resources into studying how it functions and discovering the timeless principles that never fail.

Any land requires you to prepare it well, plant the right seeds on it, protect those seeds, and wait for the harvest. You will have to be intentional to cultivate, tend, guard, and watch over it. You will have to work hard and smart. You will have to walk and work with the Lord. He wants you to succeed in all the things that He has called you to do. He says in Isaiah 48:17:

> Thus says the LORD, your Redeemer,
> The Holy One of Israel:
> "I *am* the LORD your God,
> Who teaches you to profit,
> Who leads you by the way you should go.

God wants you to profit and to not lose time, money, energy, or anything else. As I coach and mentor young entrepreneurs, professionals, and ministers, I observe the struggles some of them go through because they do not know how to apply kingdom principles. Some of them lack good spiritual, mental, professional, and business parenting. We need mothers and fathers in all areas of our lives to help us to succeed in our professions and the assignments in which we are involved. I share this from personal experience, as I struggled a lot in my earlier work and ministry. Later, as I began identifying fathers and mothers in my work and ministry, I saw tremendous changes. Hence, I am passionate for people like you reading this book.

Wisdom

Wisdom is the ability to solve problems and to know right from wrong. It's also the ability to make wise decisions on a daily basis and to know the consequences of the decisions that you make. It's the ability to see well, do well, and finish well.

Seek the Lord for wisdom. Read the books of Proverbs and Ecclesiastes in the Bible as many times as you can. These two books have great counsel and advice that will increase your wisdom, understanding, and knowledge, as well as protect you from all evil.

Strength

Proverbs 24:10 says, "If you faint in the day of adversity, Your strength is small."

Joel 3:10 says, "Beat your plowshares into swords And your pruning hooks into spears; Let the weak say, 'I *am* strong.'"

The Lord is the strength of your life. Learn to renew your strength in God's presence in prayer. Read His Word and practice having quiet times. Learn to be a great listener in stillness and meditative moments. I have been practicing quiet times for over thirty years, and I can assure you that they are rewarding—a great blessing. We often speak to God in prayer, but we never wait to hear what He is saying to us. If you can speak less and listen more, you will be surprised at how God will speak to you. Psalm 46:10 says, "He says, 'Be still, and know that I am God; I will be exalted among the nations. I will be exalted in the earth.'"

Honour

Honour encompasses respect, trust, and dignity. There is no shame in Christ Jesus and in your life. Millions around the world are ashamed of their past mistakes and failures that occurred due to immaturity, a lack of guidance, evil influence, or temptation. Yes, you might have done shameful things that you regret. But how long will you carry that shame? It is in the past. Repent of your sins and ask the Lord Jesus to forgive you. He is the same yesterday, today, and forever (Hebrews 13:8). He will take care of your past mistakes. He will take care of your present and future sins and failures. Receive His love and forgiveness, move on, and begin to serve Him.

Jesus said, "He who serves Me, My Father will honour him." As you serve the Lord with your gifts and talents, the Lord will honour you and your family and bless the works of your hands.

John 12:26 says, "If anyone serves Me, let him follow Me; and where I am, there My servant will be also. If anyone serves Me, him *My* Father will honor."

Glory

Glory is beauty and splendour upon us. It makes us shine wherever we go. Isaiah 60:1 says, "Arise, shine; For your light has come! And the glory of the Lord is risen upon you." In Christ, you are full of the glory of God. See the beauty of God in yourself and others.

Blessing

God's blessing empowers you to succeed and prosper in all things. The first thing God did when He created Adam and Eve was to bless them. The last thing Jesus did while he was being taken to heaven was to lift His hand and bless us. Luke 24:50–51 says, "And He led them out as far as Bethany, and He lifted up His hands and blessed them. Now it came to pass, while He blessed them, that He was parted from them and carried up into heaven."

Proverbs 10:22 says, "The blessing of the Lord makes *one* rich, And He adds no sorrow with it." Walk and work in that very blessing.

There is much I could write, but time and space do not allow me to do so. In conclusion, see and seize every God-given resource. Be a good and great steward, leader, and manager. Do you see how rich, wealthy, and resourceful you are? You are destined for greatness, and you have what it takes to succeed by the Spirit of the true living God.

Why I Wrote This Book

I've wanted to write my first book for a long time, and I was inspired, motivated, and challenged by great authors. Dr. Myles Munroe and Dr. John C. Maxwell have thoughts on the subject of how to write a book. I followed their advice, and this is the result.

"It takes a village to raise a child" is an African proverb that means that a child's entire community of people must interact with them for them to grow up in a safe and healthy environment. Indeed, it has taken a community of authors to help a young author like me to write. I have quoted some of those authors and am forever grateful for the time, energy, and resources they invested into their writing. I can boldly say, like Isaac Newton, "If I have seen further, it is by standing on the shoulders of giants." I have indeed stood on the shoulders of many authors.

Dr Maxwell says, "One is too small a number to achieve greatness. No accomplishment of real value has ever been achieved by a human being working alone." (Movemequotes.com – John Maxwell quotes on greatness)

In addition, having worked for over twenty-one years with wonderful people in both the ministry and the marketplace, I realize that most people are challenged by many of the topics I cover in this book. Some of these challenges include those related to health, relationships, and finances. Questions of identity, if not answered, lead to identity crises: Who am I? Where do I come from? What am I doing here? Where am I going? What am I worth? With much research and study, I have tried to answer some of these questions at the level of my spiritual growth.

Above all, I really want to bring hope, comfort, and encouragement to those precious and wonderful people going through tough and challenging times in their personal lives, families, ministries, careers, professions, and businesses. We need each other today like we never have before. Together, we can stand and make a difference in our world. We can make it a better place.

I have written this book from my heart, praying that you will get at least one, two, or three things out of the twenty-one chapters that will inspire you, motivate you, and challenge you to see that you are precious and valuable. I hope and trust that you conclude that, no matter your circumstances, you are destined for greatness. Happy reading, and thanks for your time and attention.

Daniel O. Ondieki

PART I

KNOW YOUR SOURCE AND THE RESOURCES AT YOUR DISPOSAL

CHAPTER 1

THE POWER OF WORDS

A father once wanted to teach his young son the effect of his angry words. He asked that every time his son lost his temper and wanted to shout at his siblings, he go into the backyard and throw stones against the wall.

The next time the boy lost his temper, he ran quickly to the backyard and threw a stone for every angry word that he had said. He did this for some time. After a while, he gained some self-control and no longer needed to throw the stones.

He proudly informed his father of the self-discipline he had gained. His father listened quietly and then took him outside to view the backyard wall, now riddled with pockmarks. His father said to him, "Yes, son, you feel much better, but look at the cost of your words. If this were someone's life, each mark would represent the damage you inflicted on that soul. This can never be revoked."

The wall served as a visual reminder of the lasting damage of the boy's angry and thoughtless words. He learnt a sobering lesson about the power of his words.

In this story, we see how powerful our words are. They frame and determine the world in which we live. If you are unhappy with your world, it is never too late to change it. You can start by changing your words.

Your world refers to your health, relationships, finances, environment, surroundings, circumstances, and situations. It also includes your bank account, ministry, business, profession, career, and expertise.

You either love your world or you hate it. It brings you either joy or pain. You are either grateful or you are regretful for your world . Either way, you have the power to change your world through your words.

How to Change Your World

There are many ways you can change your world. Here are seven important ones:

1. *Words.* Words are powerful and can affect our lives both positively and negatively. Words spoken will come back to you like the sound of an echo in the mountains. I would like you to imagine standing on the mountains and shouting in a very loud voice, "A very good morning, ladies and gentlemen!" The echo will not come back with the greeting "A very good afternoon, madam!" or "A very good evening, sir!" You will hear what you have said. Start to change your world simply by speaking good words.

2. *Thoughts.* You are exactly what you think. King Solomon said, "For as he thinketh in his heart, so is he: Eat and drink, saith he to thee; but his heart is not with thee" (Proverbs 23:7). Your thoughts direct your life. You are the sum of your thoughts.

3. *Beliefs.* Be careful what you believe. Beliefs have the power to shape your life. Many have believed untruths about themselves and allowed those untruths to shape their lives. When you believe the truth—what God says about you in His Word—this belief also shapes your thoughts and perceptions. However, this also works in the reverse. Many believe that they are not loved and cannot live beyond their circumstances. Jesus said in Matthew 8:13, "Go **you**r way; and **as you have believed**, *so* let it be done for **you**."

4. *Attitude.* Your attitude will determine how far you go in life. Your attitude is affected by your thoughts and emotions. Your attitude is your choice; it's the way you choose to respond to life. It's the first thing people notice when they meet you. There is a saying that your *attitude* will affect your *altitude*.

5. *Perception.* You can also change your world through the way you see things. We do not see life as it really is; we see it as *we* are.

2

The way you look at life determines a lot. You can change your perception by actively reading and meditating on the Word of God.

6. *Listening.* It is important to resist listening to negative words and conversations. The Apostle Paul states that we should listen to whatever things are true, whatever things *are* noble, whatever things *are* just, whatever things *are* pure, whatever things *are* lovely, and whatever things *are* of good report; if *there is* any virtue and if *there is* anything praiseworthy—meditate on these things (Philippians 4:8). The things we listen to have the power to shape our lives.

7. *Doing.* Finally, you can change your world by the way you do things. There is a miracle in doing. Every time you act on the Word of God as you hear it, you will experience God's grace and power. A wise man hears and does, but a foolish man hears but does not do. Be intentional about being a hearer and doer of God's word.

> Therefore whoever hears these sayings of Mine, and does them, I will liken him to a wise man who built his house on the rock: and the rain descended, the floods came, and the winds blew and beat on that house; and it did not fall, for it was founded on the rock. But everyone who hears these sayings of Mine, and does not do them, will be like a foolish man who built his house on the sand: and the rain descended, the floods came, and the winds blew and beat on that house; and it fell. And great was its fall. (Matthew 7:24–27)

> But be doers of the word, and not hearers only, deceiving yourselves. For if anyone is a hearer of the word and not a doer, he is like a man observing his natural face in a mirror; for he observes himself, goes away, and immediately forgets what kind of man he was. But he who looks into the perfect law of liberty and continues in it, and is not a forgetful hearer but a doer of the work, this one will be blessed in what he does. (James 2:22–25)

The Power of Your Words

There are some important things you should know about your words. The words you speak are the highest authority in the world. What you say is influenced by what you believe in your heart. In Matthew 12:34, Jesus said, "Brood of vipers! How can you, being evil, speak good things? For out of the abundance of the heart the mouth speaks."

The mind, heart, and mouth all work together to release words. What you spend time thinking about will eventually influence your heart and what you say. The tongue is a powerful force that charts the course of your life for either good or bad. Its power is not limited to your life on Earth—it also affects your life in eternity. "For with the heart one believes unto righteousness, and with the mouth confession is made unto salvation" (Romans 10:10).

Here is what the Apostle James had to say in James 3:3–12:

> Indeed, we put bits in horses' mouths that they may obey us, and we turn their whole body.
> Look also at ships: although they are so large and are driven by fierce winds, they are turned by a very small rudder wherever the pilot desires.
>
> Even so the tongue is a little member and boasts great things. And the tongue is a fire, a world of iniquity. The tongue is so set among our members that it defiles the whole body and sets on fire the course of nature; and it is set on fire by hell.
>
> For every kind of beast and bird, of reptile and creature of the sea, is tamed and has been tamed by mankind.
>
> But no man can tame the tongue. It is an unruly evil, full of deadly poison. With it we bless our God and Father, and with it we curse men, who have been made in the similitude of God.
> Out of the same mouth proceed blessing and cursing. My brethren, these things ought not to be so.

Does a spring send forth fresh water and bitter from the same opening?

Can a fig tree, my brethren, bear olives, or a grapevine bear figs? Thus no spring yields both salt water and fresh.

It is important to note the powerful nature of the tongue. No matter the situation you're going through, your tongue pilots your life. Through the tongue's influence, you can guide your life to your desired destination.

Use your tongue to:

1. Speak of God's righteousness.
2. Sing praises unto the Lord.
3. Speak God's Word, and He will watch over it and perform it.
4. Proclaim Jesus Christ as your Lord and Saviour, and you will receive eternal life.
   Every knee shall bow, and every tongue shall confess that Jesus Christ is the Lord.
5. Speak life, blessings, and every good thing in your life and in your circumstances.

Words are also seeds. As soon as they are sown in the heart and mind, they begin to grow and will produce either a good or bad harvest, depending on their nature. Your heart and mind are two good gardens given to you by God. You plant either good seeds or bad seeds. You decide to either take care of your gardens or abandon them to become overgrown with weeds.

Everyone is a sower, and the first seeds we sow in our lives are our words. What we say can either make or break us. Our words can heal us or make us sick, make us laugh or make us cry.

Through words, we can express either love or hate. The words we have spoken in the past have brought us to where we are today. What we said yesterday has become our reality today.

Words travel swiftly. Psalm 147:15 says, "He sends out His command *to the* earth;

His word runs very swiftly." We are imprisoned or set free by our choice of words. We knowingly or unknowingly bless or curse our own world.

Words begin with thoughts. These thoughts are then communicated through both words and actions. Once spoken, words can never be recalled. They can establish peace or start a war. Captains of armies have begun or ended wars through their words.

On page 112 of her book *Salem Falls*, author Jodi Picoult writes, "Words are like eggs dropped from great heights; you can no more call them back nor ignore the mess they leave when they fall."

You can mess up your life with your words. Do all you can to avoid making such a mess.

The good news is that you can rebuild your world by changing your words. Start by aligning your words with what God says in His Word. "For indeed the gospel was preached to us as well as to them; but the word which they heard did not profit them, not being mixed with faith in those who heard it" (Hebrews 4:2).

Your words, when mixed with faith, will benefit you greatly. Let's look at what the Word of God says about words:

> For by your words you will be justified, and by your words you will be condemned. (Matthew 12:37)

> It is the Spirit who gives life; the flesh profits nothing. The words that I speak to you are spirit, and *they* are life. (John 6:63)

> But Simon Peter answered Him, "Lord, to whom shall we go? You have the words of eternal life." (John 6:68)

> So all bore witness to Him, and marvelled at the gracious words which proceeded out of His mouth. And they said, "Is this not Joseph's son?" (Luke 4:22)

> You are snared by the words of your mouth; You are taken by the words of your mouth. (Proverbs 6:2)

Heaven and earth will pass away, but My words will by no means pass away. (Matthew 24:35)

I have shown you in every way, by labouring like this, that you must support the weak. And remember the words of the Lord Jesus, that He said, "It is more blessed to give than to receive." (Acts 20:35)

Blessed *is* he who reads and those who hear the words of this prophecy and keep those things which are written in it; for the time *is* near. (Revelation 1:3)

Behold, I am coming quickly! Blessed *is* he who keeps the words of the prophecy of this book. (Revelation 22:7)

How sweet are Your words to my taste, *Sweeter* than honey to my mouth. (Psalm 119:103)

The words of a man's mouth *are* deep waters; The wellspring of wisdom *is* a flowing brook. (Proverbs 18:4)

How long will you torment my soul, And break me in pieces with words? (Job 19:2)

Death and life *are* in the power of the tongue, And those who love it will eat its fruit. (Proverbs 18:21)

All the words of my mouth *are* with righteousness; Nothing crooked or perverse *is* in them. (Proverbs 8:8)

A man will be satisfied with good by the fruit of *his* mouth, And the recompense of a man's hands will be rendered to him. (Proverbs 12:14)

Let the words of my mouth and the meditation of my heart be acceptable in Your sight, O Lord, my strength and my Redeemer. (Psalm 19:14)

The words of the wise are like goads, and the words of scholars are like well-driven nails, given by one Shepherd. (Ecclesiastes 12:11)

I have intentionally chosen the entirety of Genesis 1:1–31 to show you how God turned a very bad situation into a very good one by using words. You, too, can change your very bad circumstances into very good ones. As you read through, mark every instance in the chapter where it says, "Then God said."

In the beginning, God created the heavens and the earth. The earth was without form, and void; and darkness *was* on the face of the deep. And the Spirit of God was hovering over the face of the waters.

Then God said, "Let there be light"; and there was light. And God saw the light, that *it was* good; and God divided the light from the darkness. 5 God called the light Day, and the darkness He called Night. So the evening and the morning were the first day.

Then God said, "Let there be a firmament in the midst of the waters, and let it divide the waters from the waters." Thus God made the firmament, and divided the waters which *were* under the firmament from the waters which *were* above the firmament; and it was so. And God called the firmament Heaven. So the evening and the morning were the second day.

Then God said, "Let the waters under the heavens be gathered together into one place, and let the dry *land* appear"; and it was so. And God called the dry *land* Earth, and the gathering together of the waters He called Seas. And God saw that *it was* good.

Then God said, "Let the earth bring forth grass, the herb *that* yields seed, *and* the fruit tree *that* yields fruit according to its kind, whose seed *is* in itself, on the earth"; and it was so. And the earth brought forth grass, the herb *that* yields seed according to its kind, and the tree *that* yields fruit, whose seed *is* in itself according to its kind. And God saw that *it was* good. So the evening and the morning were the third day.

Then God said, "Let there be lights in the firmament of the heavens to divide the day from the night; and let them be for signs and seasons, and for days and years; and let them be for lights in the firmament of the heavens to give light on the earth"; and it was so. Then God made two great lights: the greater light to rule the day, and the lesser light to rule the night.

He made the stars also. God set them in the firmament of the heavens to give light on the earth, [18] and to rule over the day and over the night, and to divide the light from the darkness. And God saw that *it was* good. So the evening and the morning were the fourth day.

Then God said, "Let the waters abound with an abundance of living creatures, and let birds fly above the earth across the face of the firmament of the heavens." So God created great sea creatures and every living thing that moves, with which the waters abounded, according to their kind, and every winged bird according to its kind. And God saw that *it was* good. And God blessed them, saying, "Be fruitful and multiply, and fill the waters in the seas, and let birds multiply on the earth." So the evening and the morning were the fifth day.

Then God said, "Let the earth bring forth the living creature according to its kind: cattle and creeping thing and beast of the earth, *each* according to its kind"; and it was so. And God made the beast of the earth according to its kind, cattle according to its kind, and everything that creeps on the earth according to its kind. And God saw that *it was* good.

Then God said, "Let Us make man in Our image, according to Our likeness; let them have dominion over the fish of the sea, over the birds of the air, and over the cattle, over all the earth and over every creeping thing that creeps on the earth." So God created man in His *own* image; in the image of God He created him; male and female He created them. Then God blessed them, and God said to them, "Be fruitful and multiply; fill the earth and subdue it; have dominion over the fish of the sea, over the birds of the air, and over every living thing that moves on the earth."

And God said, "See, I have given you every herb *that* yields seed which *is* on the face of all the earth, and every tree whose fruit yields seed; to you it shall be for food. Also, to every beast of the earth, to every bird of the air, and to everything that creeps on the earth, in which *there is* life, *I have given* every green herb for food"; and it was so. Then God saw everything that He had made, and indeed *it was* very good. So the evening and the morning were the sixth day.

There are some very important lessons to learn from the Creation story. I would like to briefly summarize some of the verses within it.

"In the beginning, God created the heavens and the earth." (Genesis 1:1)

- First, God created time: "In the beginning."
- Second, He created space: "the heavens."
- Third, He created matter: "the earth."

Trinity within three: Each of these three elements has three elements within it:

- "In the beginning" establishes time, which talks of the past, the present, and the future. The first and most precious gift that God gave mankind is time. Time is the currency of life. It is older than life. The first gift that God gives to all of us every midnight is time. He could say to you, "My son or My daughter, invest time wisely. Time is the first present I give you at the beginning of the day! Do not waste it."

  When someone gives you time and attention, those are precious gifts! Appreciate and treasure them greatly. Your health, wealth, relationships, finances, ministries, business, career, profession, and everything else you've ever wanted are dependent on time. Be intentional in being a good and great manager of time. Your return on investment in all that you do will be greater, stronger, and longer-lasting. Successful and prosperous people never waste time. They focus on major, not minor, matters.

- "The heavens" establishes space, meaning length, width, and depth. Heaven is the headquarters of God, the Lord Almighty. Who else is in heaven? The Son of God, the Holy Spirit, God's angels, the children, and the saints who have fought the good fight of faith and finished their journey here on the earth.

  Every good and perfect gift comes from above—from the Father of lights. Life and time come from God. All the gifts and talents that you and I have come from Him. Heaven is our eternal home. The heavens and the earth were created to work in partnership, in line with God's original plan, purpose, mission, and vision. We cannot do without the heavens. "Thus says the LORD: 'Heaven *is* My throne, And earth *is* My footstool. Where *is* the house that you will build Me? And where *is* the place of My rest?'" (Isaiah 66:1).

The earth is the dressing room for heaven. In other words, while on the earth, you have to put on the Lord Jesus Christ, who is the way, the truth, and the life. He is the way to the Father in heaven. Book your ticket to heaven now while you still have the time. It will be too late once you are out of time. Your life hangs on the time that you have been given here on Earth. The last chapter of this book will guide you in how to get to heaven using simple steps.

- "Earth" establishes matter, which consists of solids, liquids, and gases. The earth is the third thing God created, according to Genesis 1:1. It is our planet. It is our first home—the home in which we are born and raised. It was given to us to take care of. Before the fall of man, the earth was full of God's glory, blessings, grace, mercy, and riches. It was free from sickness, spiritual blindness, fear, and anxiety. It was also free from the climate change challenge that is occurring today. The fall of man was the beginning of all the challenges that we constantly face.

  If you combine all three forms of matter (solid, liquid, and gas) together, you will see that God had the economy in His heart and mind. The earth has more than enough resources for everyone. But because of the fallen nature of man, which brings poor governance, management, and leadership, we experience many challenges and scarcities in the world.

"The earth was without form, void, and full of darkness. The Spirit hovered over the face of the waters" (Genesis 1:2). God, His Son, and the Holy Spirit did not like the way the earth was.

God could have decided to go back to heaven and leave the earth the way it was. However, He confronted the void, the formlessness, and the darkness to focus on the solutions, not the problems. We should do the same in any situation that looks like what is written in Genesis 1:2.

God began to speak solutions and answers to the earth's problems through words of faith that came first from His heart and then through His mouth. Genesis says "Then God said" in verses 3, 6, 9, 11, 14, 20, 24, 26, 29, and 31.

God commanded light from the darkness. Where was the light? It was there all along in the darkness. 2 Corinthians 4:6 says, "For it is the God who commanded light to shine out of darkness, who has shone in our hearts to *give* the light of the knowledge of the glory of God in the face of Jesus Christ." This implies that solutions are hidden in problems. Like God, speak forth those solutions. It is written, "Be ye imitators of God as dear children" (Ephesians 5:1).

The phrase "And it was so" means that what God spoke came to pass. It was exactly what He saw and said. It was good. God never saw anything bad—He saw only the good. So see the good solutions in the spirit, and speak them out in your faith, actions, wisdom, understanding, and knowledge.

We read in Genesis 1:31, "Then God saw everything that He had made, and indeed *it was* very good."

You have God's approval and signature based on this verse, which states that you are God's original masterpiece. See yourself as God sees you. King David knew this secret, and that is why he said, "I will praise You, for I am fearfully and wonderfully made; Marvelous are Your works, And that my soul knows very well" (Psalm 139:14). Rejoice in and be glad of who you are! You are destined for greatness. You are loved, accepted, and highly valued in God's kingdom.

CHAPTER 2

KNOWING YOURSELF

Knowing yourself is the foundation for your life. Knowing yourself is wisdom. Knowing yourself is one of the greatest discoveries you can ever make. Knowing yourself will protect your life, family, ministry, business, time, energy, and resources. It will also protect you from the wrong company, the wrong connections, unhealthy partnerships, and destructive networks. Knowing yourself will position you to dream better and greater. It will connect you with the right people, some of whom you may have never imagined or dreamed of ever connecting with. Invest quality time, energy, and resources to know yourself better. It takes revelation knowledge to get to know the real you.

While Jesus was here on Earth, He wanted to be sure that the people knew who He was.

And even today, He still desires that each and every one may know Him.

When Jesus came into the region of Caesarea Philippi, He asked His disciples, saying, "Who do men say that I, the Son of Man, am?" So they said, "Some say John the Baptist, some Elijah, and others Jeremiah or one of the prophets." He said to them, "But who do you say that I am?" Simon Peter answered and said, "You are the Christ, the Son of the living God." Jesus answered and said to him, "Blessed are you, Simon Bar-Jonah, for flesh and blood has not revealed this to you, but My Father who is in heaven." (Matthew 16:13–17)

The Father in heaven opened Peter's eyes to see and know who Jesus was. That is what we call revelation knowledge.

The Apostle Paul prayed for the church of Ephesians to walk and work in revelation knowledge and enlightenment.

> Therefore I also, after I heard of your faith in the Lord Jesus and your love for all the saints, do not cease to give thanks for you, making mention of you in my prayers: that the God of our Lord Jesus Christ, the Father of glory, may give to you the spirit of wisdom and revelation in the knowledge of Him, the eyes of your understanding being enlightened; that you may know what is the hope of His calling, what are the riches of the glory of His inheritance in the saints, and what *is* the exceeding greatness of His power toward us who believe, according to the working of His mighty power. (Ephesians 1:15–19)

You will never know yourself without knowing your Creator, the Lord God Almighty. It is He who can reveal to you your true identity. Moses did not know who he was until he met with God, his Creator. When God appeared to him and introduced his leadership assignment of over two million people in Egypt, the first question Moses raised was "Who am I?" That is an identity question. At the age of 80, Moses did not know who he was. Old age does not mean that you know yourself. If identity questions are not answered, this leads to an identity crisis.

My goal in this chapter is to challenge you to get to know yourself better, to value yourself more, and to walk and work in a manner worthy of your calling and assignment from heaven. Jesus said, "Look at the birds of the air, for they neither sow nor reap nor gather into barns; yet your heavenly Father feeds them. Are you not of more value than they?" (Matthew 6:26).

Your true value is beyond comprehension, comparison, and competition. You are priceless—not because of what you have done, but because of what God has done for you. That is why Jesus had to lay down His life for you and me: because He loved you and me while we were still sinners. You were purchased with the precious blood of Jesus Christ (Acts 20:28). His blood and love qualify you for more value.

Know and believe in yourself. The law of the mirror, as stated in Dr

John C. Maxwell's book *The 15 Invaluable Laws of Growth*, says, "You must see value in yourself to add value to yourself." What you think about yourself determines the investments you will make in yourself. If your self-worth is low, then your investment in yourself will be low. If you see yourself as a two out of ten, then you will make a level-two investment. If you see yourself as an eight, you will make a level-eight investment. That matters because your growth return will not exceed your growth investment. Be intentional and willing to invest in yourself. By reading this book, you are investing in yourself. This citation is taken from the book *Leadershift* by John Maxwell, page 55. Believe in yourself.

Failure to know yourself can lead to painful experiences or even abuse. Wasting of time and resources is inevitable with failure.

It took me many years to discover the real me. If years ago you had asked me, "Who are you?" I would have thought of telling you my full name, where I come from, my family status, my academic achievements, my titles in the various areas in which I served, my age, and so forth. I guess I am not the only one who has had this problem; I am one of many.

Before I go deeper into this topic, let's find out what the Bible says about who you are.

> May God himself, the God who makes everything holy
> and whole, make you holy and whole, put you together—
> spirit, soul, and body—and keep you fit for the coming
> of our Master, Jesus Christ. The one who called you
> is completely dependable. If He said it, He'll do it! (1
> Thessalonians 5:24–25, MSG)

From this passage, you can see that you are a spirit, you have a soul, and you live in a body. You contact the spiritual realm with your spirit. You contact the intellectual realm with your soul. You contact the physical realm with your body. You need to develop these three areas and function effectively according to the light of God's Word.

Proverbs 20:27 says, "The spirit of a man is the lamp of the Lord, Searching all the inner depths of his heart." If God wants to speak to you, He will speak to you in your innermost being—your spirit self. You will hear the small inner voice in your spirit self or heart if you listen to Him diligently.

> But the natural man does not receive the things of the Spirit of God, for they are foolishness to him; nor can he know them, because they are spiritually discerned. But he who is spiritual judges all things, yet he himself is rightly judged by no one. For "who has known the mind of the Lord that he may instruct Him?" But we have the mind of Christ. (1 Corinthians 2:14–16)

Because you are a spiritual being, you will never know who you are until you study God's Word. You will never understand spiritual matters intellectually, for they can only be discerned spiritually.

Psalm 139:14 says, "I will praise You, for I am fearfully and wonderfully made; Marvelous are Your works, And that my soul knows very well." The psalmist who wrote this studied God's Word and discovered who God had made him to be. Then he said, "I will praise You." Why was he to praise the Lord? Because he discovered that he was fearfully and wonderfully made, and his soul knew this very well. In other words, he discovered from God's Word that he was one of a kind. He saw the marvellous and wonderful works of God in his life. He rejoiced and celebrated his uniqueness. You, too, can celebrate and rejoice in who God made you to be. You are one of a kind and God's masterpiece.

"See, I have inscribed you on the palms of My hands; Your walls are continually before Me" (Isaiah 49:16). That means that when God looks at you, He admires you and sees how beautiful or handsome you are. After all, He created you in His own image and likeness: "Then God said, 'Let Us make man in Our image, according to Our likeness.' …So God created man in His own image; in the image of God He created him; male and female He created them" (Genesis 1:26–27).

This is good and great news to think about. The highlight of it all is that when you are born again, you become a new creation, according to 2 Corinthians 5:17: "Therefore, if anyone is in Christ, he is a new creation; old things have passed away; behold, all things have become new." Taking this step of receiving Jesus Christ as your Lord and Saviour gives you a new identity in Christ Jesus. You become a brand-new person.

In my many years of counselling, coaching, and mentoring, I have noticed that when people are challenged in their lives, they ask many questions. If these questions are not answered, the individual enters into a circle of defeat. What is this circle of defeat? It is when the enemy of your soul takes advantage of your ignorance, lack of guidance, and immaturity. He uses any circumstance to make you experience stress, fear, worry, doubt, discouragement, weariness, and depression. Once you are in this circle, it's very hard to escape if you don't understand spiritual matters. Understand that the spiritual realm controls the mental and physical realms. Millions around the world find themselves in this circle of defeat; they are confused, frustrated, disappointed, and stressed out. This is why they feel unhappy, stuck, and unfulfilled but don't understand why.

Once upon a time, I was in such a situation. Thankfully, God had mercy on me and opened my eyes to see the solutions by studying His Word and learning from great spiritual leaders, coaches, and mentors. If you find yourself or know someone who is struggling in a circle of defeat, I have good news for you: It is never too late to come out of it. "Through knowledge the righteous shall be delivered" (Proverbs 11:9). In other words, if you study God's Word, you will gain knowledge, understanding, and wisdom that will enable you to escape from your circle of defeat and live a life of good success, total victory, and significance.

Just as the enemy of your soul uses lies and your ignorance and immaturity to defeat you, the Holy Spirit of the Lord uses the truth, God's Word, and revelation knowledge to empower, equip, teach, and train you to have a victorious and exceptional life. It is by the will of God that you come out of your circle of defeat and into a circle of victory. "But thanks be to God, who gives us the victory through our Lord Jesus Christ" (1 Corinthians 15:57).

How do you leave this circle of defeat?

First and foremost, acknowledge that you need help.
Second, determine whether you are confronted with stress, fear, worry,

doubt, discouragement, weariness, health problems, relationship problems, financial issues, or depression-or even several or of these.

Third, seek help from a mature spiritual leader, a spiritual counsellor, or a mental health professional, coach, or mentor you can trust. Do not let your pride or ego stop you. Most people think that only people who are challenged in life need counselling. But if you talk to successful people, most will tell you that they have counsellors, coaches, and mentors who have guided them to succeed in their personal lives, careers, professions, businesses, and ministries.

Fourth, be willing to learn from the written Word of God. Understand that God and His Word are one. God's Word has the supernatural power to destroy anything that is contrary to His will.

> "Is not My word like a fire?" says the Lord, "And like a hammer that breaks the rock in pieces?" (Jeremiah 23:29)

> For the word of God is living and powerful, and sharper than any two-edged sword, piercing even to the division of soul and spirit, and of joints and marrow, and is a discerner of the thoughts and intents of the heart. (Hebrews 4:12)

What you are looking for is in God's Word. Are you looking for joy, one of the antidotes for depression? Jeremiah 16:15 says, "Your words were found, and I ate them, And Your word was to me the joy and rejoicing of my heart; For I am called by Your name, O Lord God of hosts." If you wish to experience "joy and rejoicing" of your heart, feed more on God's Word.

Fifth, know the Holy Spirit, and develop a close relationship with Him. He is the greatest Teacher of all time. He is your Helper and the greatest Counsellor, Coach, and Mentor; you can completely depend on and work with Him. He will transform your entire life, family, profession, ministry, business, and much more.

A book I highly recommend is *The Most Important Person on Earth* by Dr Myles Munroe. In it, Dr Munroe explains the role of the Holy Spirit here on Earth.

The Holy Spirit will bring you into a place of love, joy, peace, patience, kindness, goodness, faithfulness, gentleness, and self-control. This is what we call the Fruit of the Spirit, according to Galatians 5:22–23.

Fruit comes from planted seeds. When seeds grow, they bear fruit. Fruit is outward, visible behaviour. You and I should embrace and evaluate ourselves against the following list of inner qualities:

- *Love*: Is my life motivated by love for people?
- *Joy*: Do I exhibit unspeakable joy, regardless of my circumstances?
- *Peace*: Do people see my inward peace and take courage?
- *Patience*: Do I wait patiently for results as I help people develop?
- *Kindness*: Am I caring and understanding towards everyone I meet?
- *Goodness*: Do I want the best of others and organizations?
- *Faithfulness*: Have I maintained my commitment to my vision and mission in life?
- *Gentleness*: Is my strength under control? Can I be both tough and tender?
- *Self-Control*: Am I disciplined enough to make progress towards my goals?

These leadership qualities and the Fruit of the Spirit are discussed by Dr John C. Maxwell in *The Maxwell Leadership Bible*. I highly recommend this Bible; it is the best leadership Bible I have ever read. Not only is it inspiring and motivating, but it challenges you to be a great leader.

You cannot buy the Fruit of the Spirit with money, but you can receive it through knowledge, understanding, and faith. The Holy Spirit gives you the Zoe life.

The word "life" as used in this verse is translated from the Greek word *Zoe*, and it refers to the "God" kind of life.

In John 5:26–27, Jesus says, "For as the Father has life in Himself so He has granted the Son to have life in Himself, and has given Him authority to execute judgment also, because He is the Son of Man."

The Fruit of the Spirit gives you the nature of Christ and the characteristics of God. That is why Jesus said, "The thief does not come except to steal, and to kill, and to destroy. I have come that they may have life, and that they may have it more abundantly" (John 10:10). This kind of life cannot be purchased; rather, it can be received by faith through revelation knowledge and understanding.

The Fruit of the Spirit gives you character, but the nine gifts of the Spirit make you effective and exceptional in your calling and assignment from heaven. These nine gifts are listed in 1 Corinthians 12:4–10 and can be summarized in three words: seeing, speaking, and doing. The Lord has equipped you inside and out for a victorious and exceptional life—a life that brings glory to Him, blesses His people, and brings peace and joy into your heart.

So how can you know yourself?

First, know your Creator, your Heavenly Father, and have a relationship with Him—not through religion, but through His Son, Jesus Christ, and by the help of the Holy Spirit. The previous chapter explains how you can begin a new life.

Second, discover your passion and purpose in life. Knowing these will help you determine and choose the right priorities for your purpose. Your priorities will protect your life, your time, your energy, and the resources that will help you stay focused in all areas of your life.

How do you discover your true personality?

- through awareness and revelation knowledge
- by studying, understanding, and applying God's Word
- through coaches and mentors (Jeremiah 3:15)
- by walking and working in a renewed mind
- by unlocking the potential within you
- by being intentional in developing your personality
- by being hungry and thirsty for personal growth
- by first seeking God's righteousness and His kingdom, and all these things shall be added unto you (Matthew 6:33)

Become More to Do More

"Become more to do more" is a statement that challenges you to break the status quo and to set new, higher standards for your life and all you are called to do and accomplish. You become more aware and conscience of who you are, and you make more intentional actions of working more in the inside of you. If you conscientiously shift from a fixed mindset to a growth mindset, you begin to see tremendous changes in your life. Break down those limiting beliefs that have held you captive for ages. When you choose to add value to yourself by becoming more, you increase your valuableness in your generation and the generations to come. Jesus said, "Do not fear therefore; you are of more value than many sparrows" (Matthew 10:31). Do not let fear hold you back from becoming more.

How do you become more to do more?

King Solomon, the wisest man who has ever lived, said, "I communed with my heart, saying, 'Look, I have attained greatness, and have gained **more** wisdom than all who were before me in Jerusalem. My heart has understood great wisdom and knowledge'" (Ecclesiastes 1:16).

By meditating on God's Word and communing with your heart, you will become more aware and conscious of who you really are and know why you were created by your Creator. God's wisdom, understanding, and knowledge will enable you to know your valuableness and your true meaning here on the earth. In doing so, you will protect your time, energy, resources, and focus on your top priorities in life. Not doing these things can lead to painful and regretful experiences.

King Solomon goes on to say, "So I became great and excelled **more** than all who were before me in Jerusalem. Also, my wisdom remained with me" (Ecclesiastes 2:9).

God's wisdom—not human wisdom—will enable you to become more and great in your life's purpose. (Knowing your WHY is key if you want to become more to do more.)

It is important to know that you come from the God of "more." You must have a relationship and partnership to connect with the more that is in Him (the Lord God Almighty).

The original Hebrew word for Almighty is **El Shaddai**, which means "the all-sufficient One," or the God of plenty. In other words, our God has more than enough for every one of us.

A good example of more than enough that God has given us is the air we breathe in. We never compete for it. It is more than enough for everyone. "From abundance, we take abundance and abundance is left". (Bob proctor)

That is why we should avoid air pollution. Some of the ways to avoid air pollution are as follows:

- Using public transport
- Turning off the lights when they're not in use
- Recycling and reusing
- Saying no to plastic bags
- Teleconferencing and teleworking

Think of other ways you can avoid polluting the air. That is one way of becoming more to do more.

Let us all take full responsibility to care for our earth that God has given to us. Psalms 115:16 says, "The heaven, *even* the heavens, *are* the Lord's; But the earth He has given to the children of men." This is a climate change topic written to us over six thousand years ago. The Bible is a great book that provides us with sustainable solutions for topics related to climate change. If we take the time to read it and become doers of the Word, we will see a great transformation. "Hearing and doing God's word is true greatness and transformational leadership" (Daniel O. Ondieki).

King David said, "You *are* **more** glorious and excellent *Than* the mountains of prey" (Psalm 74:6).

We see king David knowing and seeing the God of more than enough. He knew Him as an excellent God than the mountains of prey.

The mountains of prey refers of those rulers of injustice systems that oppress the poor and the innocent lives. We see those mountains of prey in our times. That is why as believers of Christ need to pray and intercede for all those in authority that we may lead a peaceful and quiet lives. We should pray for wisdom, understanding and godly knowledge and above all for the fear of the Lord be upon us all. The fear of the Lord is to hate evil and to depart from it.

1 Timothy 2:1-4 says, "I urge, then, first of all, that petitions, prayers, intercession and thanksgiving be made for all people—for kings and all those in authority, that we may live peaceful and quiet lives in all godliness

and holiness. This is good, and pleases God our Savior, who wants all people to be saved and to come to a knowledge of the truth."

You become more through the Lord Jesus Christ.

He has made you more than you can imagine, as it is written, "Yet in all these things we are more than conquerors through Him who loved us" (Romans 8:37). Notwithstanding all that you go through in life, you are more than a conqueror.

Becoming more to do more gives you clarity of purpose. Know where you are. Know where you are going. Know why and how you are going to get there. Choose your dream team carefully, for this, too, will determine your results.

Work more on your way of thinking. The quality of your thinking will determine the quality of your life, profession, business, ministry, and work.

You must be intentional to work on your way of thinking, for as a man thinks in his heart, so is he (Proverbs 23:7a). High-quality thinking happens in both the heart and the mind.

A business, ministry, career, or profession can never outgrow the quality of thinking the owner brings to it. In other words, you will never deliver beyond your personal growth and thinking level. Good success, health, and wealth begin with the wise decisions that you make and the intentional actions that you take.

We believe in and become the things we think about and meditate on constantly.

Our belief systems are the architects of our results. Our beliefs sponsor habitual ways of thinking and drive our behaviour. Everything starts with you and the quality of your thinking.

Nothing will change for the better until the quality of your thinking improves.

Inside-out transformation takes a lot of work. If you want to see outside changes, work more on the inside of yourself. Invest more quality time, energy, and resources to know yourself and God, the Creator of the heavens and the earth, who will reveal to you your true identity and purpose in life. Additionally, seek good coaches and mentors who can help you unlock the great potential that is within you.

When the inside and the outside come together, you will be more fulfilled and able to make a difference in not only your generation, but to many more generations to come.

It is no wonder that Jesus invested about thirty years into planning and preparing Himself for a three-and-a-half-year ministry. Becoming more to do more was His secret. Two thousand years later, His Kingdom business, His church, and His ministry continue. He has put His signature concerning His church on Matthew 16:18, which says, "And I also say to you that you are Peter, and on this rock I will build My church, and the gates of Hades shall not prevail against it. And I will give you the keys of the kingdom of heaven, and whatever you bind on earth will be bound in heaven, and whatever you loose on earth will be loosed in heaven."

He has a very large following. Some of His followers are already in heaven, and some are here on Earth waiting for His second coming, although no one except His Father in heaven knows when He will return.

You attract who you are. Who would you like to attract? Become more like Jesus and be that salt and light to attract more souls into the kingdom of our God. In other words, be an agent of change here on Earth. Stay thirsty and hungry for God's presence, kingdom, and righteousness. Matthew 5:6 says, "Blessed are those who hunger and thirst for righteousness, For they shall be filled." May you always minister from the overflow, and may your cup continue overflowing.

Know your God-given calling in life. Know your vision and mission. Be fully focused, and deliver your services and products with integrity, excellence, and diligence. Exceed both your own expectations and those of whom you serve. Continually develop your talents, gifts, and skills.

Be not only goal-oriented but growth-oriented. Make growth your top priority. The truth is that you will never deliver beyond your growth level and the quality of your thinking.

John the Baptist had to grow and become strong in spirit (Luke 1:80). Likewise, Jesus had to grow and became strong in spirit (Luke 1:40). These two men had great assignments from heaven. Their top priorities were to grow from the inside out. It's no wonder they were used mightily by God, with signs, wonders, and miracles following them. Romans 12:2 says, "And do not be conformed to this world, but be transformed by the renewing of your mind, that you may prove what *is* that good and acceptable and perfect will of God."

I can confidently say that true and great transformational leadership begins from the inside out. Find the place for your gifts and talents, and serve the Lord passionately. Continually walk and work in a renewed mind. Never forget that "the quality of your thinking will determine the quality of your life" (A. R. Bernard).

As coach John Wooden, who made a difference to so many people, said, "Be true to yourself, help others, make each day your masterpiece, make friendship a fine art, drink deeply from good books, especially the Bible, build a shelter against a rainy day, give thanks for your blessings and pray for guidance every day. Your life is your canvas, and you are the masterpiece" (90+ John Wooden Quotes, Quoteish).

Psalm 92:13 says, "Those who are planted in the house of the Lord shall flourish in the courts of our God."

Philemon 1:6 says that sharing your faith is made more effective by acknowledging every good thing that is in you in Christ Jesus. Take the challenge, and begin to acknowledge every good thing that is in you in Christ Jesus. Then watch the Lord bless you and use you for His glory.

Remember this: Your personality will affect how and where you use your spiritual gifts, heart, mind, and abilities. Whenever God gives you an assignment, He equips you with what you need to accomplish it. Your God-given vision gives you direction, provision, and protection.

Never give up. You are destined for greatness, and you have what it takes to succeed. I close this chapter with the following words from Isaiah 28:29: "This also comes from the Lord of hosts, who is wonderful in counsel and excellent in guidance."

Ask the Lord for wisdom and guidance in all areas of your life.

‹⁂›

CHAPTER 3

THE HOLY SPIRIT, YOUR MENTOR

The Holy Spirit is the greatest person on Earth. Knowing Him will enable you to become a transformational, good, and great leader. It took me a long time to get to know Him, and He has enabled me to become the person I am today. I speak with Him all the time. He helps and encourages me to pursue my purpose in life. I love Him so much. Who is He?

The Holy Spirit is the third person of the Trinity. In Luke 3:21–23, we read, "When all the people were baptized, it came to pass that Jesus also was baptized; and while He prayed, the heaven was opened. And the Holy Spirit descended in bodily form like a dove upon Him, and a voice came from heaven which said, 'You are My Beloved Son; in You I am well pleased.'"

From this passage, we see that God the Father, God the Son, and God the Holy Spirit work together.

The Holy Spirit is a person—not a fire, a wind, or a dove, as some people think. "And I will pray the Father, and He will give you another Helper, that He may abide with you forever" (John 14:16).

The Holy Spirit created you and me. "The Spirit of God has made me, And the breath of the Almighty gives me life" (Job 33:4). The Holy Spirit knew you before you were formed in your mother's womb. He knows all your details inside out. Learn to speak to Him and ask Him questions concerning your life. He has all the answers for you. Know His voice. "He who has an ear, let him hear what the Spirit says to the churches" (Revelation 2:29).

The Holy Spirit is the Author and inspiration for all scripture. "All Scripture is given by inspiration of God, and is profitable for doctrine, for reproof, for correction, for instruction in righteousness" (2 Timothy 3:16).

In God's plan of salvation, the Holy Spirit worked in and through the authors of the Bible to reveal God's design and purpose for us. Paul describes the Spirit's work as "God-breathed." Just as the Holy Spirit breathed into Adam's nostrils, giving him life (see Genesis 2:7 And the Lord God formed man of the dust of the ground, and breathed into his nostrils the breath of life; and man became a living being.), so the Holy Spirit breathed into the work of the Bible's human authors, giving the Scriptures divine life and ultimate authority for questions about faith and life.

A devotion shared in 2016 by Kurt Selles-

the director of Back to God Ministries International.

The Holy Spirit speaks through men. It is written; for prophecy never came by the will of man, but holy men of God spoke as they were moved by the Holy Spirit. (2 Peter 1:21)

The Holy Spirit confirms that you are a child of God and that Jesus Christ is within you.

> The Spirit Himself bears witness with our spirit that we are children of God. (Romans 8:16)

> By this we know that we abide in Him, and He in us, because He has given us of His Spirit. (1 John 4:14)

The Holy Spirit gives us life—the Zoe life of God and the abundant life Jesus talked about.

> Who also made us sufficient as ministers of the new covenant, not of the letter but of the Spirit; for the letter kills, but the Spirit gives life. (2 Corinthians 3:6)

> The thief does not come except to steal, and to kill, and to destroy. I have come that they may have life, and that they may have *it* more abundantly. (John 10:10)

The Holy Spirit imparts a personal prayer language that can dramatically increase your strength and improve your faith.

> But you, beloved, building yourselves up on your most holy faith, praying in the Holy Spirit. (Jude 20)

> For if you have the ability to speak in tongues, you will be talking only to God, since people won't be able to understand. You will be speaking by the power of the Spirit, but it will all be mysterious. (1 Corinthians 14:2)

The Holy Spirit reveals the truth that you need to live a victorious life. "However, when He, the Spirit of truth, has come, He will guide you into all truth; for He will not speak on His own *authority,* but whatever He hears He will speak; and He will tell you things to come" (John 16:13).

The Holy Spirit speaks to us. We need to know and hear His voice. "He who has an ear, let him hear what the Spirit says to the churches. To him who overcomes I will give to eat from the tree of life, which is in the midst of the Paradise of God" (Revelation 2:7).

The Holy Spirit is the source of the anointing. This anointing is God's supernatural ability that enables us to complete the assignment we have from heaven. "The Spirit of the LORD *is* upon Me, Because He has anointed Me To preach the gospel to *the* poor; He has sent Me to heal the broken-hearted, to proclaim liberty to *the* captives And recovery of sight to *the* blind, *To* set at liberty those who are oppressed" (Luke 4:18).

The Holy Spirit helps us to begin, continue, and finish the work God has assigned us to do here on Earth. "Jesus said to [His disciples], 'My food is to do the will of Him who sent Me, and to finish His work'" (John 4:34).

Many people begin projects but never finish them. Thus, there are numerous incomplete projects in the world. If you ever have a project that you begin but have trouble finishing, ask the Holy Spirit to help you finish it, and finish it well. He is your Helper.

John 19:30 says, "So when Jesus had received the sour wine, He said, 'It is finished!' And bowing His head, He gave up His spirit." The Holy Spirit helped Jesus begin His assignment, continue it, and finish well, despite the painful experience He went through.

The Holy Spirit is your greatest intercessor here on the earth. "Likewise, the Spirit also helps in our weaknesses. For we do not know what we should pray for as we ought, but the Spirit Himself makes intercession for us with groanings which cannot be uttered. Now He who searches the hearts knows what the mind of the Spirit is, because He makes intercession for the saints according to the will of God" (Romans 8:26–27).

Christ Jesus also lives to make intercession for us. "Therefore He is also able to save to the uttermost those who come to God through Him, since He always lives to make intercession for them" (Hebrews 7:25). As a child of God, you have two great intercessors who intercede for you: one in heaven, Jesus, and one on the earth, the Holy Spirit. What a privilege!

The Holy Spirit is the source of your joy. "You will show me the path of life; In Your presence is fullness of joy; At Your right hand are pleasures forevermore" (Psalm 16:11).

The Holy Spirit removes all the fear that comes from the enemy. "For God has not given us a spirit of fear, but of power and of love and of a sound mind" (2 Timothy 1:7).

The Holy Spirit shows you a picture of your future:

> But he, being full of the Holy Spirit, gazed into heaven and saw the glory of God, and Jesus standing at the right hand of God. (Acts 7:55)

> When the Spirit of truth comes, He will guide you into all truth. He will not speak on his own but will tell you what he has heard. He will tell you about the future. (John 16:13)

The Holy Spirit decides what kind of work or ministry you can do. "As they ministered to the Lord and fasted, the Holy Spirit said, 'Now separate to Me Barnabas and Saul for the work to which I have called them.' Then, having fasted and prayed, and laid hands on them, they sent them away" (Acts 13:2–4).

The Holy Spirit will send you warnings to protect you from the wrong people and places. "Now when they had gone through Phrygia and the region of Galatia, they were forbidden by the Holy Spirit to preach the word in Asia. After they had come to Mysia, they tried to go into Bithynia, but the Spirit did not permit them" (Acts 16:6–7).

The Holy Spirit is saddened by bad conduct. "And do not grieve the Holy Spirit of God, by whom you were sealed for the day of redemption. Let all bitterness, wrath, anger, clamor, and evil speaking be put away from you, with all malice. And be kind to one another, tender-hearted, forgiving one another, even as God in Christ forgave you" (Ephesians 4:30–32).

The Holy Spirit withdraws when offended. "I will return again to My place till they acknowledge their offense. Then they will seek My face; In their affliction, they will earnestly seek Me" (Hosea 5:15).

The Holy Spirit raised Jesus from the dead, and He will raise the dead when the Lord returns. He can also raise dead projects or situations. "But if the Spirit of Him who raised Jesus from the dead dwells in you, He who raised Christ from the dead will also give life to your mortal bodies through His Spirit who dwells in you" (Romans 8:11).

The Holy Spirit leads the sons and daughters of God. "For as many as are led by the Spirit of God, these are sons of God" (Romans 8:14).

The Holy Spirit searches our hearts and examines our minds. He knows everything that goes on within us. His desire is to help us to do God's will, and He will reward us according to the fruit that our actions produce. "I, the LORD, search the heart, test the mind, Even to give every man according to his ways, According to the fruit of his doings" (Jeremiah 17:10).

The Holy Spirit knows who you have been assigned to by God. I always remind myself, "Daniel, know that you are not assigned to everybody," as I used to think I was assigned to the whole world. Pray for the people you are assigned to. God will direct you to them or bring them to you. Love and care for them, and help them to grow up. Help them to find their purpose and mission in life. Help them to unlock their potential. "Then the Spirit said to Philip, 'Go near and overtake this chariot'" (Acts 8:29). The Holy Spirit knows who you can connect and communicate with.

The Holy Spirit knows the gifts, talents, and skills that are within us.

> There are diversities of gifts, but the same Spirit. There are differences of ministries, but the same Lord. And there are diversities of activities, but it is the same God who works

all in all. But the manifestation of the Spirit is given to each one for the profit of all: for to one is given the word of wisdom through the Spirit, to another the word of knowledge through the same Spirit, to another faith by the same Spirit, to another gifts of healings by the same Spirit, to another the working of miracles, to another prophecy, to another discerning of spirits, to another different kinds of tongues, to another the interpretation of tongues. But one and the same Spirit works all these things, distributing to each one individually as He wills. (1 Corinthians 12:4–12)

The Holy Spirit is your Helper. He will help you when you are going through trials and temptations. "Then Jesus, being filled with the Holy Spirit, returned from the Jordan and was led by the Spirit into the wilderness, being tempted for forty days by the devil. And in those days, He ate nothing, and afterward, when they had ended, He was hungry" (Luke 4:1–2).

The Holy Spirit fills our hearts with God's love. "Now hope does not disappoint, because the love of God has been poured out in our hearts by the Holy Spirit who was given to us" (Romans 5:5).

The Holy Spirit invites us all to God. "And the Spirit and the bride say, 'Come'! And let him who hears say, 'Come!' And let him who thirsts come. Whoever desires, let him take the water of life freely" (Revelation 22:17).

The Holy Spirit transforms our lives into the image of Christ. We are a spirit, we have a soul, and we live in the body. When we give our lives to the Lord and welcome the Holy Spirit of God to work through our spirits, and as we read, hear, study, memorize, and meditate on God's word, transformation takes place from the inside out.

The Apostle Paul wrote in 2 Corinthians 3:17–18, "Now the Lord is the Spirit; and where the Spirit of the Lord *is*, there *is* liberty. But we all, with unveiled faces, beholding as in a mirror the glory of the Lord, are being transformed into the same image from glory to glory, just as by the Spirit of the Lord."

Good and great transformational leadership begins from within us. This is where the Holy Spirit plays a major role in helping you go through spiritual, personal, economic, and community development. Any person who wants to see lasting changes must develop in these areas.

The Holy Spirit enables you to enter the kingdom of God. "Jesus answered, 'Most assuredly, I say to you, unless one is born of water and the Spirit, he cannot enter the kingdom of God. That which is born of the flesh is flesh, and that which is born of the Spirit is spirit'" (John 3:5–6).

The Holy Spirit is here on the earth bringing people to Christ. He was sent from heaven shortly after Jesus ascended to heaven. He has the nature of both God and Jesus Christ. They are all One: God the Father, God the Son, and God the Holy Spirit. They work together. They walk in unity. They agree. There is no disunity or misunderstanding among them. They are always in harmony. We should be one in harmony with them.

Spend quality time with the Holy Spirit to get to know Him better. He longs to see you grow up, mature, and take full responsibility for the Father's kingdom business.

To know Him, you have to love God's Word. The Word is His sword. Recognizing His voice will unlock God's favour and many blessings to you. Let the Holy Spirit be your Senior Partner in all your affairs. He knows what is good for you. Appreciate Him all day long. He longs to connect you to people you have never imagined you would be connected to in your life. He turns bitter situations into better ones (2 Kings 4:1–7).

Our God is awesome and a miracle worker. He lives forever and ever!

❧

CHAPTER 4

TRUE RICHES

The New Testament is rife with the true riches that can be found only in Christ Jesus. They do not come from Earth but are found in the Lord, and we have access to them as we are seated with the Lord in heavenly places. They flow into our hearts through our union with God. The Apostle James said, "Every good gift and every perfect gift is from above, and comes down from the Father of lights, with whom there is no variation or shadow of turning" (James 1:17).

God never gives bad things to us, as people often say. He is a good and great Father. He desires the best for His sons and daughters, as they walk uprightly and blamelessly.

Matthew 7:11–12 says, "If you then, being evil, know how to give good gifts to your children, how much more will your Father who is in heaven give good things to those who ask Him! Therefore, whatever you want men to do to you, do also to them, for this is the Law and the Prophets."

> For the LORD God *is* a sun and shield;
> The LORD will give grace and glory;
> No good *thing* will He withhold
> From those who walk uprightly. (Psalm 84:11)

It is also important to understand that while God's love is unconditional to all of us, His blessings and favour to us are conditional. You must fulfil God's conditions if you want to experience His blessings, favour, and eternal life. That challenges us to seek His will in His written Word in the Bible.

Here are what scriptures says about true riches:

> If then you were raised with Christ, seek those things which are above, where Christ is, sitting at the right hand of God. Set your mind on things above, not on things on the earth. For you died, and your life is hidden with Christ in God. When Christ who is our life appears, then you also will appear with Him in glory. (Colossians 3:1–4)

True riches are committed to those who have been faithful with little things, unrighteous mammon, and things you've been given charge over.

> He who *is* faithful in *what is* least is faithful also in much; and he who is unjust in *what is* least is unjust also in much. Therefore if you have not been faithful in the unrighteous mammon, who will commit to your trust the true *riches?* And if you have not been faithful in what is another man's, who will give you what is your own? (Luke 16:10–12)

True riches are not temporary, but eternal. They are not physical, but spiritual.

> While we do not look at the things which are seen, but at the things which are not seen. For the things which are seen are temporary, but the things which are not seen are eternal. (2 Corinthians 4:18)

We can conclude that true riches come from knowledge, understanding, wisdom, the ability to access the resources of heaven on earth, and the use of those resources righteously and according to God's will.

Let's look at what else the Bible says about true riches.

Riches of Grace

> "In Him we have redemption through His blood, the forgiveness of sins, according to the riches of His grace" (Ephesians 1:7).

Riches of the Glory and Inheritance of the Saints

> "The eyes of your understanding being enlightened; that you may know what is the hope of His calling, what are the riches of the glory of His inheritance in the saints" (Ephesians 1:18).

Unsearchable Riches of Christ

> "To me, who am less than the least of all the saints, this grace was given, that I should preach among the Gentiles the unsearchable [hidden] riches of Christ" (Ephesians 3:8).

Riches of His Goodness

> "Or do you despise the riches of His goodness, forbearance, and longsuffering, not knowing that the goodness of God leads you to repentance?" (Romans 2:4)

Riches of His Glory

> "For this reason I bow my knees to the Father of our Lord Jesus Christ, from whom the whole family in heaven and earth is named, that He would grant you, according to the riches of His glory, to be strengthened with might through His Spirit in the inner man" (Ephesians 3:14–16).

Riches of Knowledge, Understanding, and Wisdom

> "For as you were once disobedient to God, yet have now obtained mercy through their disobedience, even so these also have now been disobedient, that through the mercy shown you they also may obtain mercy. For God has committed them all to disobedience, that He might have mercy on all. Oh, the depth of the riches both of the wisdom and knowledge of God! How unsearchable are

His judgments and His ways past finding out!" (Romans 11:30–33)

Riches in Glory

"And my God shall supply all your need according to His riches in glory by Christ Jesus" (Philippians 4:19).

Christ in You, the Hope of Glory

"To them God willed to make known what are the riches of the glory of this mystery among the Gentiles: which is Christ in you, the hope of glory" (Colossians 1:27).

The Reproach of Christ Is Greater Riches than the Treasures in Egypt

"By faith Moses, when he became of age, refused to be called the son of Pharaoh's daughter, choosing rather to suffer affliction with the people of God than to enjoy the passing pleasures of sin, esteeming the reproach of Christ greater riches than the treasures in Egypt; for he looked to the reward" (Hebrews 11:24–26).

These gifts are treasures given to us from God as His children; they are our inheritance as saints. They are endless, accessible, and inexhaustible heavenly resources. God expects us to use them righteously as the need arises. As we use them, we are filled with unspeakable joy, and God receives all the glory and honour. The Holy Spirit gives us the ability to see, know, and use these gifts. Everyone who is born of God has access to them through the Lord Jesus Christ.

When we do not recognize these gifts, we fail to live the more abundant life Jesus promised us. As a result, we continue to struggle, ultimately living an unfulfilled life. We must become aware of these gifts, learn how to access them, and use them to live the exceptional life Jesus promised us. John 10:10 says, "The thief does not come except to steal, and to kill, and to destroy. I have come that they may have life, and that they may have *it* more abundantly."

Jesus came to show us how to access the resources of heaven. Seek those things which are above, where Christ is, sitting at the right hand of God. Set your mind on the things above, not on the things on the earth.

The secret to accessing these resources is found in Matthew 6:33, which says, "But seek first the kingdom of God and His righteousness, and all these things shall be added to you."

You are truly blessed and destined for greatness. You have what it takes to succeed in life! All these true riches will make you a transformational leader.

CHAPTER 5

YOU ARE GIFTED

A gift is something good given to someone without payment. God's gifts to us should be well received and utilized accordingly.

There are two different types of gifts: spiritual and natural. Let us look at each of them in more detail.

The Spiritual Gifts

Jesus Christ

The most precious gift given to humanity was the unspeakable, indescribable, and incomparable gift of the Lord Jesus Christ. "Thanks be to God for His indescribable gift!" (2 Corinthians 9:15).

The Holy Spirit

God the Father has blessed us with another precious gift: the Holy Spirit. "Behold, I send the Promise of My Father upon you; but tarry in the city of Jerusalem until you are endued with power from on high" (Luke 24:49).

Gifts from Jesus to the Church

According to Ephesians 4:11–16, Jesus Christ blessed His church with the fivefold ministry gifts. "And He Himself gave some *to be* apostles, some prophets, some evangelists, and some pastors and teachers, for the equipping of the saints for the work of ministry, for the edifying of the body of Christ, till we all come to the unity of the faith and of the knowledge of the Son of God, to a perfect man, to the measure of the stature of the fullness of Christ; that we should no longer be children, tossed to and fro and carried about with every wind of doctrine, by the trickery of men, in the cunning craftiness of deceitful plotting, but, speaking the truth in love, may grow up in all things into Him who is the head—Christ— from whom the whole body, joined and knit together by what every joint supplies, according to the effective working by which every part does its share, causes growth of the body for the edifying of itself in love."

The fivefold ministry is not limited to the church; it also applies to the marketplace, business, sports, music, politics, social media, and all other areas.

These gifts were given to perfect His body, the church on Earth.

The gifts of the Holy Spirit enable us to minister effectively.

The Holy Spirit has blessed us with nine powerful gifts as we do His work in the ministry. They help us to see, speak, and do. They equip us to serve effectively and supernaturally, using the Holy Spirit's anointing power.

> There are diversities of gifts, but the same Spirit. There are differences of ministries, but the same Lord. And there are diversities of activities, but it is the same God who works all in all. But the manifestation of the Spirit is given to each one for the profit of all: for to one is given the word of wisdom through the Spirit, to another the word of knowledge through the same Spirit, to another faith by the same Spirit, to another gift of healings by the same Spirit, to another the working of miracles, to another prophecy, to another discerning of spirits, to another different kinds of tongues, to another the interpretation of tongues. But one and the same Spirit works all these things, distributing to each one individually as He wills. (1 Corinthians 12:4–11)

Natural Gifts

These gifts, which are also called talents or natural abilities, are gifts we were born with and find easy to do. They are not taught; rather, they are inherent in us. Many are passed down as blessings through generations. Examples of such gifts include the natural ability to sing, draw, teach, dance, or write.

What Does the Bible Say About These Gifts?

> A man's gift makes room for him, And brings him before great men. (Proverbs 18:16)

> Every good gift and every perfect gift is from above, and comes down from the Father of lights, with whom there is no variation or shadow of turning. (James 1:17)

> Having then gifts differing according to the grace that is given to us, let us use them: if prophecy, let us prophesy in proportion to our faith; or ministry, let us use it in our ministering; he who teaches, in teaching; he who exhorts, in exhortation; he who gives, with liberality; he who leads, with diligence; he who shows mercy, with cheerfulness. (Romans 12:6–8)

Important Things to Know about Gifts

Each of us receives gifts from the Lord which are good and perfect. Your gift will always make room for you, open doors for you, and create opportunities for you. You will find yourself becoming connected to people you never knew because they sought your gift.

In Matthew 7:11, Jesus recognizes that God gives us wonderful gifts and talents: "If you then, being evil, know how to give good gifts to your children, how much more will your Father who is in heaven give good things to those who ask Him!"

In 1 Corinthians 12:4, the Apostle Paul acknowledges that the Holy Spirit gives us all the gifts we have: "There are diversities of gifts, but the same Spirit."

The purpose of your gifts is to solve problems and serve the people around you. "Do not withhold good from those to whom it is due, when it is in the power of your hand to do so" (Proverbs 3:27).

God rewards us financially when we use our gifts and talents well. What the Lord has given to us should bring Him glory. We can do this by being a blessing to others. This will also bring joy to our own hearts.

How to Discover Your Gifts

You can discover your gifts and talents by desiring to do something. God may reveal your gifts and talents to you through dreams and visions, like He did for Joseph. One way to discover a gift is to ask yourself, "What would I do if there was nothing to limit me?"

You can discover your gifts and talents through your parents, teachers, spiritual leaders, friends, or circumstances. Even your enemies can be used to reveal your hidden gifts. For instance, regarding the story of David and Goliath, David had not realized that he had the power to kill a giant.

Your gift will require that you acquire specific knowledge, skills, and experience. This can be achieved through mentors and coaches in the field of your gift. The more attention you give to your gift, the more it will grow. Two major gifts that you should not fail to recognize are the gift of life and the gift of time here on Earth.

God-given gifts will transform your life. Earnestly desire the best gifts, both spiritual and natural. Learn, study, grow, and become aware of the gifts God has given you. Invest your time, energy, and finances into developing them. You will need to identify good mentors and coaches to help you do this. Whatever the cost, it is always worth it.

It is important to realize that each of us will give an account to God as to how we have used our gifts to bless humanity. God is an excellent investor; He wants a good return on His investment.

Always remember this: Your gift can take you to the highest floor in the world, but the thing that will keep you at the top is your character. Your character is the foundation of your life and gift. It is your asset. Treasure it at all times. Keep becoming more to do more, from the inside out. You are destined for greatness. You are that transformational leader the world is seeking and waiting for to manifest God's glory and power. It is written in Isaiah 60:1, which says,

Arise, shine;
For your light has come!
And the glory of the LORD is risen upon you.

Lastly, never allow any kind of fear to prevent you from using your gifts, talents, skills, and experience. You are destined for greatness, and you are a transformational leader. There is greatness in you.

CHAPTER 6

THE BLESSINGS OF THE FEAR OF THE LORD

What does it mean to have the fear of the Lord?

When the Bible refers to the "fear of the Lord," it means having deep respect, reverence, and awe for God's majestic power and authority. Rather than causing one to be afraid of God, a proper fear of the Lord leads one to love Him—to hunger and thirst for His presence, His righteousness, and His kingdom. There are many untold blessings in fearing the Lord.

In my study of God's Word, I have found that the fear of the Lord is a treasure. In understanding what it is, you will surely be destined for greatness. It is more than silver and gold. Life, honour, and riches, which most people pursue hard and passionately, are all in the fear of the Lord!

Let us carefully examine what the Word of God says about the fear of the Lord.

> Therefore, since we are receiving a kingdom which cannot be shaken, let us have grace, by which we may serve God acceptably with reverence and godly fear. For our God *is* a consuming fire. (Hebrews 12:28–29)

> Come, you children, listen to me; I will teach you the fear of the Lord. (Psalm 34:11)

> Wisdom and knowledge will be the stability of your times,
> And the strength of salvation; The fear of the LORD is His
> treasure. (Isaiah 33:6)

Instability can be painful to anyone who experiences it. In this last verse, we find the cure for it. God's wisdom and knowledge gives one stability, especially in the days we are living in.

What the fear of the Lord is not:

- natural fear
- evil fear
- human fear

Instead, the fear of the Lord means to:

- respect Him
- love Him
- obey Him
- submit to His discipline
- worship Him in reverence

The fear of the Lord is the act of holding God in reverence in such a way that it influences the way we live our lives. To fear the Lord means to respect Him, obey Him, submit to His discipline, and worship Him in awe and love.

This topic used to make me feel afraid of God instead of loving Him. Many think that God is waiting for them to make a mistake, and that He is ready to punish them when they do wrong or fall into sin.

The fear of the Lord means recognizing and acknowledging:

- *God's majesty.* "Who would not fear You, O King of the nations? For this is Your rightful due. For among all the wise *men* of the nations, and in all their kingdoms, *there is* none like You" (Jeremiah 10:7).
- *God's holiness.* "Who shall not fear You, O Lord, and glorify Your name? For *You* alone *are* holy. For all nations shall come and

worship before You, For Your judgments have been manifested" (Revelation 15:4).

- *God's forgiveness.* "But *there is* forgiveness with You, That You may be feared" (Psalm 130:4).
- *God's power.* "For the Lord your God dried up the waters of the Jordan before you until you had crossed over, as the Lord your God did to the Red Sea, which He dried up before us until we had crossed over, that all the peoples of the earth may know the hand of the Lord, that it *is* mighty, that you may fear the Lord your God forever" (Joshua 4:23–24).
- *God's goodness.* "Only fear the Lord, and serve Him in truth with all your heart; for consider what great things He has done for you" (1 Samuel 12:24).
- *God's judgement.* "Then I saw another angel flying during heaven, having the everlasting gospel to preach to those who dwell on the earth—to every nation, tribe, tongue, and people—saying with a loud voice, 'Fear God and give glory to Him, for the hour of His judgment has come; and worship Him who made heaven and earth, the sea and springs of water'" (Revelation 14:6–7).

The fear of the Lord brings many blessings:

- *It brings knowledge.* "The fear of the Lord *is* the beginning of knowledge, *but* fools despise wisdom and instruction" (Proverbs 1:7).
- *It brings wisdom.* "Give instruction to a wise man, and he will be still wiser; Teach a just man, and he will increase in learning. The fear of the Lord *is* the beginning of wisdom, And the knowledge of the Holy One *is* understanding" (Proverbs 9:9–10).
- *It helps us to hate evil.* "The fear of the Lord *is* to hate evil; Pride and arrogance and the evil way and the perverse mouth I hate" (Proverbs 8:13).
- *It helps us to depart from evil.* "Do not be wise in your own eyes; Fear the Lord and depart from evil" (Proverbs 3:7). "In mercy and truth, Atonement is provided for iniquity; And by the fear of the Lord *one* departs from evil" (Proverbs 16:6).

- *It is a fountain of life.* "The fear of the Lord *is* a fountain of life, to turn *one* away from the snares of death" (Proverbs 14:27).
- *It prolongs your days here on Earth.* "The fear of the Lord prolongs days, But the years of the wicked will be shortened" (Proverbs 10:27).
- *It gives confidence.* "In the fear of the Lord *there is* strong confidence, And His children will have a place of refuge. It produces or gives us satisfaction in life" (Proverbs 14:26). Do you sometimes feel that you lack confidence in your life? That you are not confident or good enough to accomplish your tasks? Your solution to that problem can be found right in this passage.
- *It is the instruction of wisdom.* "The fear of the Lord *is* the instruction of wisdom, and before honour *is* humility" (Proverbs 15:33).
- *It gives riches, honour, and life.* "By humility *and* the fear of the Lord *Are* riches and honour and life" (Proverbs 22:4). The riches, honour, and life both temporally and eternally are found in humility and in fearing God. Ask the Holy Spirit to help you understand the fear of the Lord.
- *It brings blessings to God's people.* "Though a sinner does evil a hundred *times,* and his *days* are prolonged, yet I surely know that it will be well with those who fear God, who fear before Him" (Ecclesiastes 8:12).
- *It produces satisfaction in our lives.* "Better is a little with the fear of the Lord Than great treasure with trouble" (Proverbs 15:16).

In all these scripture passages are hidden treasures of life. If the simple instructions that are given are followed, many lives will be transformed, protected, and provided for.

King Solomon uses three key words, but most people are unclear on their meaning and hence mix them up. These words are *knowledge,* *understanding,* and *wisdom.* I would like to explain them individually.

- *Knowledge*: Gathered information which, if well meditated upon, will bring revelation knowledge. Operating in revelation knowledge will give you major breakthroughs in all your operations. God, by His Holy Spirit, gives you revelation knowledge.

- *Understanding*: Comprehension, or the ability to grasp something in your heart and see all the relevant details at a given time.
- *Wisdom*: Application of what you know and understand. In other words, knowledge and understanding without any application will not give you the desired results.

> The Lord by wisdom founded the earth; By understanding He established the heavens; By His knowledge the depths were broken up, And clouds drop down the dew. (Proverbs 3:19–20)

We see God using these three powerful principles and turning the very bad into the very good. You, too, can do this. If you seek the Lord diligently for those principles, He will be willing to give them to you. As Matthew 7:7–8 says, "Ask, and it will be given to you; seek, and you will find; knock, and it will be opened to you. For everyone who asks receives, and he who seeks finds, and to him who knocks it will be opened."

- *It determines one's destiny*. "Then they will call on me, but I will not answer; they will seek me diligently, but they will not find me. Because they hated knowledge and did not choose the fear of the Lord" (Proverbs 1:28–29).

> While you have the opportunity, love and seek God's knowledge. Seek Him diligently and serve Him passionately. Choose the fear of the Lord. Later may be too late, according to King Solomon, who said, "They hated knowledge and did not choose the fear of the Lord."

Is there anything that will stop you from loving God and seeking for His knowledge?

Remember that the number one killer in the world, which is also very costly, is ignorance. It has killed millions and millions of lives globally.

What is ignorance? It is a lack of knowledge and information. It is being clueless, innocent and inexperienced. It is unawareness or unconsciousness. It can be very costly, regretful and painful. The fruits of ignorance, which include poverty and spiritual blindness, are very bitter. Many a times most people are dealing with the fruit problems and not the real root causes of the issues of life.

Ignorance can be confronted through awareness, education and with revelation knowledge. Be aware of it, detest it and become more hungry and thirsty for God's knowledge, understanding and wisdom. Become more diligent and intelligent in all that you do and you will begin to see greatness and transformation in your life.

Do not allow laziness or excuses in your life hinder you. Work wisely and diligently.

King Solomon says in Proverbs 12:27: "The lazy man does not roast what he took in hunting, But diligence is man's precious possession."

Someone once said if you think knowledge is expensive, try ignorance. It is extremely expensive. It is a destroyer of lives and destinies.

> My people are destroyed for lack of knowledge.
> Because you have rejected knowledge,
> I also will reject you from being priest for Me;
> Because you have forgotten the law of your God,
> I also will forget your children. (Hosea 4:6)

> Therefore my people have gone into captivity, Because they have no knowledge; Their honorable men are famished, And their multitude dried up with thirst. Therefore Sheol has enlarged itself And opened its mouth beyond measure; Their glory and their multitude and their pomp, And he who is jubilant, shall descend into it. (Isaiah 5:13–14)

It is a serious matter to reject God's knowledge. The consequences are painful and regretful. Now is the time to seek the Lord diligently. The rewards of finding Him and knowing Him are beyond measure.

Biblical Examples of People Who Had Godly Fear

Due to their internal godly fear, the following people responded wisely, differently than those who do not have the fear of the Lord. They obeyed God in the circumstances they found themselves in:

Noah

> "By faith Noah, being divinely warned of things not yet seen, moved with godly fear, prepared an ark for the saving of his household, by which he condemned the world and became heir of the righteousness which is according to faith" (Hebrews 11:7).

Abraham

> "And He said, 'Do not lay your hand on the lad, or do anything to him; for now, I know that you fear God, since you have not withheld your son, your only *son,* from Me'" (Genesis 22:12).

Jacob

> "Then Jacob awoke from his sleep and said, 'Surely the LORD is in this place, and I did not know *it.*' And he was afraid and said, 'How awesome *is* this place! This *is* none other than the house of God, and this *is* the gate of heaven!'" (Genesis 28:16–17).

Then Jacob made a vow, saying, "If God will be with me, and keep me in this way that I am going, and give me bread to eat and clothing to put on, so that I come back to my father's house in peace, then the LORD shall be my God" (Genesis 28:20–21).

"And this stone which I have set as a pillar shall be God's house, and of all that You give me I will surely give a tenth to You" (Genesis 28:22). With the fear of the Lord, Jacob made this vow to the Lord, and we see how God richly blessed Jacob.

Joseph

> "Then Joseph said to them the third day, 'Do this and live, *for* I fear God'" (Genesis 42:18).

David

> "But as for me, I will come into Your house in the multitude of Your mercy; In fear of You, I will worship toward Your holy temple" (Psalm 5:7).

Obadiah

"Now as Obadiah was on his way, suddenly Elijah met him; and he recognized him, and fell on his face, and said, '*Is* that you, my lord Elijah? ... And it shall come to pass, *as soon as* I am gone from you, that the Spirit of the Lord will carry you to a place I do not know; so, when I go and tell Ahab, and he cannot find you, he will kill me. But I your servant have feared the Lord from my youth'" (1 Kings 18:7, 12).

Job

"Then the Lord said to Satan, 'Have you considered My Servant Job, that *there is* none like him on the earth, a blameless and upright man, one who fears God and shuns evil?'" (Job 1:8).

Nehemiah

"But the former governors who *were* before me laid burdens on the people, and took from them bread and wine, besides forty shekels of silver. Yes, even their servants bore rule over the people, but I did not do so, because of the fear of God" (Nehemiah 5:15).

Jonah

"So he said to them, 'I *am* a Hebrew; and I fear the Lord, the God of heaven, who made the sea and the dry *land*'" (Jonah 1:9).

The Early Church

The early church also understood the secret of walking in the fear of the Lord. Acts 9:31 says, "Then the churches throughout all Judea, Galilee, and Samaria had peace and were edified. And walking in the fear of the Lord and in the comfort of the Holy Spirit, they were multiplied."

Peace, edification, and the comfort of the Holy Spirit are received by the fear of the Lord.

Learning, studying, growing, and walking in the fear of the Lord will bring great transformational dividends to all areas of your operation. Learning is the beginning of earning. Learning will also determine your earning.

Earning speaks of the fruits or the results of your investments of time, energy, and money. Take stock of your operations, and see where you rate yourself on a scale of one to ten (ten being "excellent") when it comes to learning new things. If your rating is low, then do something about it to upgrade and improve yourself.

In Jeremiah 4:22, the Bible says:

> For My people are foolish,
> They have not known Me.
> They are silly children,
> And they have no understanding.
> They are wise to do evil,
> But to do good they have no knowledge.

What a very sharp rebuke from the Lord Himself in this reading!

Fearing the Lord means loving God and giving Him all that He deserves. This will always keep you on top of all that He has called you to do. You shall be the head and not the tail. You shall be above and not beneath. The greatness of God will be within your reach.

Fearing the Lord will reward you beyond measure. It will protect you, your family, and all that He has entrusted you with. You will know how to conduct yourself in every area of your life. You will overcome the fear of man and all the other kinds of fears that may try to appear. The Holy Spirit and God's Word will both help you understand how to fear the Lord.

The Lord invites you according to Psalm 34:11, which says, "Come, you children, listen to me; I will teach you the fear of the Lord." Accept that invitation, and you will be forever grateful.

Here is a great prayer from the Apostle Paul. In it, Paul prays for knowledge, understanding, and wisdom. You, too, should pray this prayer often. It has no negative side effects; instead, it has great rewards.

> Therefore I also, after I heard of your faith in the Lord
> Jesus and your love for all the saints, do not cease to give

thanks for you, making mention of you in my prayers: that the God of our Lord Jesus Christ, the Father of glory, may give to you the spirit of wisdom and revelation in the knowledge of Him, the eyes of your understanding being enlightened; that you may know what is the hope of His calling, what are the riches of the glory of His inheritance in the saints, and what is the exceeding greatness of His power toward us who believe, according to the working of His mighty power which He worked in Christ when He raised Him from the dead and seated Him at His right hand in the heavenly places, far above all principality and power and might and dominion, and every name that is named, not only in this age but also in that which is to come. And He put all things under His feet, and gave Him to be head over all things to the church, which is His body, the fullness of Him who fills all in all. (Ephesians 1:15–22)

CHAPTER 7

THE WHOLE ARMOUR OF GOD

According to the *Collins English Dictionary*, armour is a protective covering that prevents damage from being inflicted upon an object, individual, or vehicle by direct contact, weapons, or projectiles, usually during combat, or from damage caused by a potentially dangerous environment or action.

There are different types of armour mentioned in the Bible. These include:

- *Christ Jesus.* "But put on the Lord Jesus Christ, and make no provision for the flesh, to fulfil its lusts" (Romans 13:14).
- *The whole armour of God for battle.* "Finally, my brethren, be strong in the Lord and in the power of His might. Put on the whole armor of God, that you may be able to stand against the wiles of the devil" (Ephesians 6:10).
- *The armour of the enemy.* "But when a stronger than he comes upon him and overcomes him, he takes from him all his armor in which he trusted and divides his spoils" (Luke 11:22).
- *The armour of light.* "The night is far spent; the day is at hand. Therefore, let us cast off the works of darkness, and let us put on the armor of light" (Romans 13:12).
- *The armour of righteousness.* "By the word of truth, by the power of God, by the armor of righteousness on the right hand and on the left" (2 Corinthians 6:7).

- *The physical armour of man.* "Harness the horses, and mount up, you horsemen! Stand forth with *your* helmets, Polish the spears, Put on the armor!" (Jeremiah 46:4).
- *The armour of kings.* "Thus says the Lord to His anointed, To Cyrus, whose right hand I have held—To subdue nations before him and loose the armour of kings, to open before him the double doors, so that the gates will not be shut" (Isaiah 45:1).
- *Protective and offensive armour.* Ephesians 6:10–18 says:

> Finally, my brethren, be strong in the Lord and in the power of His might. Put on the whole armor of God, that you may be able to stand against the wiles of the devil. For we do not wrestle against flesh and blood, but against principalities, against powers, against the rulers of the darkness of this age, against spiritual *hosts* of wickedness in the heavenly *places.* Therefore take up the whole armour of God, that you may be able to withstand in the evil day, and having done all, to stand. Stand therefore, having girded your waist with truth, having put on the breastplate of righteousness, and having shod your feet with the preparation of the gospel of peace; above all, taking the shield of faith with which you will be able to quench all the fiery darts of the wicked one. And take the helmet of salvation, and the sword of the Spirit, which is the word of God; praying always with all prayer and supplication in the Spirit, being watchful to this end with all perseverance and supplication for all the saints.

As a soldier in the army of the Lord, you are required to wear the armour of God.

- *The armour is God's strength and His power.* When you wait upon the Lord in prayer, fasting, and meditation, you receive strength and power (Isaiah 40:31). God has not called us to confront the enemy in our own strength, but in His power, which flows from the Holy Spirit through us.

- *The armour is the truth.* The truth flows from the Holy Spirit to your spirit. As you meditate on the Word of God, the Holy Spirit will quicken His truth to your heart. As you yield to it, it serves as protection, keeping you from the deception that is in the world and showing you the way in which you should live.

Put on the breastplate of righteousness. We put on Jesus Christ, who is our righteousness. We have no righteousness of our own. The Bible says in Isaiah 64:6, "But we are all like an unclean *thing,* And all our righteousness's *are* like filthy rags; We all fade as a leaf, And our iniquities, like the wind, Have taken us away."

Jesus died and took upon Himself our unrighteousness, nailing it to the cross. In exchange, He gave us His righteousness. *Righteousness* means right standing with God. We stand upright before God, and this serves as a defence before the enemy of our souls. Righteousness is God's gift to us. It is a gift we receive, not a reward we achieve.

Shod your feet with the preparation of the gospel of peace. Always be prepared with a word of encouragement, a testimony, or a message to share with someone about your transformational stories and faith whenever you have the opportunity. You are an ambassador to the Prince of Peace. Blessed are the peacemakers, for they will be called children of God (Matthew 5:9).

Faith. Your faith serves as a shield. Through your faith, you quench all the enemy's fiery darts, lies, and accusations. Faith is strengthened by hearing the Word, meditating on it, and doing what it says. Romans 10:17 says, "So then faith *comes* by hearing, and hearing by the word of God." Faith is a spiritual currency in transacting with heaven.

Hebrews 11:6 also says, "But without faith *it is* impossible to please *Him,* for he who comes to God must believe that He is, and *that* He is a rewarder of those who diligently seek Him." Take quality time in prayer, in meditation and in studying God's word for this will help you develop your faith in God. It rewards to walk and work in faith. To increase your faith you must constantly listen, hear, understand and be the doer of God's word.

God is a rewarder of those who diligently seek Him.

- *The helmet of salvation.* The helmet protects the mind against mental attacks, such as depression, despondency, and discouragement. The helmet gives us hope and the love and assurance of God's salvation (1 Thessalonians 5:8).
- *The sword of the Spirit.* The sword of the Spirit is the personal word the Holy Spirit gives you in a season when the enemy comes against you. It is a word that is revealed and that, when applied, swiftly defuses the lies of the enemy.
- *Pray in the Spirit.* Speak in the heavenly language the Holy Spirit gives. We often do not know how to pray as we should. Praying in tongues helps us to pray powerfully and accurately.
- *WATCH*: The acronym WATCH speaks of being aware, alert, sober, and vigilant. Things to watch out for include your words, actions, thoughts, character, company, heart, and home.
- *Words.* By your words, you are both justified and condemned. No word is irrelevant. We will be judged by every word we speak. Our words drive our actions.
- *Actions.* There is a space between provocation and response. In this space is our power to choose whether to respond positively or negatively. Our choice of action determines whether we experience the natural or the supernatural. Learn to respond and not react to the things around you.
- *Thoughts.* As a man thinks in his heart, so is he. You cannot live beyond the way you think. The Apostle Paul wrote to the Philippian church, saying, "Finally, brethren, whatever things are true, whatever things are noble, whatever things are just, whatever things are pure, whatever things are lovely, whatever things are of good report, if there is any virtue and if there is anything praiseworthy—meditate on these things" (Philippians 4:8). If you do this, you will experience the peace of God. Refuse the negative, and meditate on things that build your faith and confidence.
- *Character.* The *Merriam-Webster Dictionary* defines *character* as "the mental and moral qualities distinctive to an individual." Develop your character by surrounding yourself with people who have good moral standards. Talent and gifts may grant you opportunities and get you promoted, but character sustains you and helps you

retain good relationships. By their fruits, you shall know them. Character is who you really are and determines whether you will qualify to fulfil your destiny. Guard your character by keeping good company.

- *Company.* The sayings "Birds of a feather flock together" and "Show me your friends, and I'll show you who you are" are both true. By the friends you keep, others can determine your true character.
- *Heart.* It is written in Proverbs 4:23,

"Keep your heart with all diligence, for out of it *spring* the issues of life."

The state of your heart determines many things: your health, relationships, finances, attitude, and choices. Constantly bring your heart to the Lord in prayer, and God's word will search you, convict and correct you of wrongdoing, refresh you, and bless you.

- *Home.* God intended the home to be a place of love, learning, discipline, and rest. In such an environment, children grow up mentally and emotionally strong. As the first place of training, the home is also where children learn culture and receive spiritual training. This helps them establish their true identity. A good home produces children who not only know who they are but can also overcome the challenges they face in life. They learn home culture before they step into the world. The love and understanding generated in the home make it a unit of harmony and support. Its members can mutually unwind and rejuvenate. This prepares them to face life with all its challenges. Thus, the home is powerful armour against the enemy who comes to steal, kill, and destroy innocent lives.

As a soldier, be vigilant with whatever God has called you to do. In 2 Timothy 2:3–5, the Apostle Paul makes the following command to Timothy:

You therefore must endure hardship as a good soldier of Jesus Christ. No one engaged in warfare entangles himself with the affairs of this life, that he may please him who enlisted him as a soldier. And also, if anyone competes in athletics, he is not crowned unless he competes according to the rules.

In 1 Corinthians 9:25–27, he says:

And everyone who competes for the prize is temperate in all things. Now they do it to obtain a perishable crown, but we for an imperishable crown. Therefore I run thus: not with uncertainty. Thus, I fight: not as one who beats the air. But I discipline my body and bring it into subjection, lest, when I have preached to others, I myself should become disqualified.

As a soldier, it is important to constantly renew your mind.

I beseech you therefore, brethren, by the mercies of God, that you present your bodies a living sacrifice, holy, acceptable to God, *which is* your reasonable service. And do not be conformed to this world, but be transformed by the renewing of your mind, that you may prove what *is* that good and acceptable and perfect will of God. (Romans 12:1–2)

In conclusion, the armour of God will keep you strong against any attack of the enemy and allow you to walk confidently and victoriously in Christ.

If you have been wounded by the challenges life brings, come before the Lord, and renew your strength. In His presence, there is fullness of joy. Take time to magnify the Lord more than your wounds and circumstances. May you experience the overcoming power in Christ, and know that you are more than a conqueror through Christ Jesus.

You are a good ambassador of God's kingdom as you use His weaponry against the enemy of your soul.

Using the whole armour of God will allow you to live a supernatural life, which is deepened and maintained by renewing your mind through God's word.

Know that the challenges of life become opportunities to experience more of God and His supernatural power.

The fruit of the Spirit becomes more evident in your life and makes you more effective in your assignment.

The armour of God will lead you to see, say, and do what you have been assigned to do by the Lord Jesus Christ, your Master and King.

PART II

KNOW YOUR PURPOSE AND THE PRIORITIES OF YOUR LIFE

CHAPTER 8

Understanding Your Assignment

An assignment is a task that has been given to you to carry out according to specific instructions. It is a job that you are responsible for. It can be a career, profession, business, or ministry. An assignment requires skill, knowledge, understanding, wisdom, and experience.

> Therefore, brethren, be even more diligent to make your call and election sure, for if you do these things, you will never stumble. (2 Peter 1:10)

> Whatever your hand finds to do, do it with your might; for there is no work or device or knowledge or wisdom in the grave where you are going. (Ecclesiastes 9:10)

Important Things to Know about Your Assignment

Everything God created was made to solve a problem, and this includes you. Your problem is your assignment. An assignment comes with passion, purpose, priorities, power, and authority. People are remembered for either solving problems or creating them. Therefore, make up your mind to be a problem-solver.

Jesus came to solve specific problems; these include sin, which separated man from God, health issues, ignorance, poverty, spiritual blindness and the many other challenges that we experience. He brought us grace and truth, His righteousness and the kingdom of heaven, salvation, healing and the total restoration of all things.

Acts 10:38 says, "how God anointed Jesus of Nazareth with the Holy Spirit and with power, who went about doing good and healing all who were oppressed by the devil, for God was with Him". In the same way, you have been sent here on the earth to solve a specific problem.

Your assignment can be discovered through your painful or gainful experiences. It can also be discovered through your passion and compassion for what you love to do. You do not decide to become someone, but you may discover that you are good at something. In the Old Testament, Joseph discovered that he was good at interpreting dreams. He was also a good economist, planner, and a great and wonderful leader. He saw economic solutions in times of crisis and came up with sustainable solutions.

What you hate is an indication of something you are assigned to correct. What do you hate? Is it poverty? Injustice? Sickness? Disease? What are you doing about it? Study the root causes of the problem to come up with specific solutions. If you don't address the problem, chances are that no one else will, and if someone does try, chances are that they will not include your distinct flair and skills.

What grieves you is a clue to something you are assigned to heal. What you love is a clue to your gifts, skills, and wisdom. Your assignment is geographical; this means there is a specific location for you to work from.

God told Abram to leave his kindred and go to a land He would show him. "Now the LORD had said to Abram: 'Get out of your country, from your family and from your father's house, to a land that I will show you'" (Genesis 12:1).

God promises to be with us and bless us where He sends us on our assignments. "I will make you a great nation; I will bless you and make your name great; And you shall be a blessing. I will bless those who bless you, And I will curse him who curses you; And in you all the families of the earth shall be blessed" (Genesis 12:2–3).

Our assignments require total obedience and not convenience. Many people prefer convenience instead of obedience. Being at the right place with the right people at the right time and doing the right things in the right way bring God's direction, providence, provision, and protection to us and to our given assignments.

Your assignment will take you to where you are celebrated and not tolerated. What does that mean? When you are at the right place, with the right people who recognize your anointing, the gifts and talents, they celebrate you. With those same gifts and talents, people just see you as one of them—they tolerate you but do not celebrate you. People did that for Jesus while He was here on the earth.

> Now He could do no mighty work there, except that He laid His hands on a few sick people and healed them. And He marvelled because of their unbelief. Then He went about the villages in a circuit, teaching. (Mark 6:5–6)

From this reading, we see that even our Lord Jesus was not recognized well, especially in His hometown. One of the main reasons a prophet is not accepted in his own hometown is familiarity. Those who knew Jesus well rejected Him. Those people included His own family. The people in Nazareth could not find any fault in His preaching, but because He had lived among them for 30 years, He was familiar to them. Maybe you, too, are not accepted or honoured in your own town. Seek guidance from God as Jesus did, and He will lead you to the right place and the right people.

> However, he went out and began to proclaim it freely, and to spread the matter, so that Jesus could no longer openly enter the city, but was outside in deserted places; and they came to Him from every direction. (Mark 1:45)

The location and timing of your assignment are very important. While Jesus was not accepted in His hometown, He went to where He was celebrated.

Your assignment distinguishes you from others. You must become so good in your assignment that you are irreplaceable. Excellence, diligence, and integrity make you shine. Jesus said you are the light of the world and the salt of the earth.

If you rebel or walk in disobedience against your assignment, God may cause you to endure painful circumstances in order to correct you. Jonah experienced this. He preferred convenience over obedience. However, because God loved him, He tossed him into the belly of a whale, after which Jonah vowed to obey God if He delivered him to safety (Jonah 2:1–3).

> If you endure chastening, God deals with you as with sons; for what son is there whom a father does not chasten? But if you are without chastening, of which all have become partakers, then you are illegitimate and not sons. (Hebrews 12:8)

> As many as I love, I rebuke and chasten. Therefore, be zealous and repent. (Revelation 3:19)

To *repent* means to change your ways of thinking, speaking, seeing, believing, and doing things. Your assignment will require seasons of preparation. Good preparation brings good results. God prepared the earth before He created anything on it. He prepared Eden, which means "delight" or "pleasant," before He created Adam and Eve. He created the water before He created the creatures of the sea. He created the air before He created the birds of the air. He prepared mansions for the saints before He created the foundation of the earth. When the time of these saints and their work is over, they check out from the earth and go to heaven to live with God forever and ever in their mansions. Jesus has given us words of comfort and hope not to be afraid or let our hearts be troubled. He is asking us to believe in God and also in Him.

> Let not your heart be troubled; you believe in God, believe also in Me. In My Father's house are many mansions; if *it were* not *so,* I would have told you. I go to prepare a place for you. And if I go and prepare a place for you, I will come again and receive you to Myself; that where I am, *there* you may be also. (John 14:1–3)

God is the Master Planner. Let us learn from our Heavenly Father as His dear children. Your planning and preparation will determine your performance. Jesus prepared Himself for thirty years for a ministry that would last just three-and-a-half years. How prepared are you for your assignment? Proper preparation significantly impacts the success of your assignment.

> If the axe is dull, and one does not sharpen the edge, then he must use more strength; But wisdom brings success. (Ecclesiastes 10:10)

> Give me six hours to chop down a tree and I will spend the first four sharpening the axe. (President Abraham Lincoln)

> By failing to prepare, you are preparing to fail. (Benjamin Franklin)

> We should live our lives as though Christ were coming this afternoon. (President Jimmy Carter)

> The best preparation for tomorrow is doing your best today. (H. Jackson Brown Jr.)

> The best time to plant a tree was twenty years ago. The second-best time is now. (Chinese Proverb)

If you want success and growth in the future, the best time to act is now.

I conclude with a tool called the "Eight Ps." These Eight Ps are prayer, power, purpose, passion, planning, preparation, performance, and potential.

1. Prayer

Prayer helps you to connect with God and know His will. It gives you clarity and direction as you seek Him diligently. "Then you will call upon Me and go and pray to Me, and I will listen to you. And you will seek Me and find Me, when you search for Me with all your heart" (Jeremiah 29:12–13).

Be intentional, and pray without ceasing. Never underestimate the power of prayer. Jesus began His ministry with prayer, He continued it with prayer, and He finished it with prayer. At the cross, He said, "It is finished."

"After this, Jesus, knowing that all things were now accomplished, that the Scripture might be fulfilled, said, 'I thirst!' Now a vessel full of sour wine was sitting there; and they filled a sponge with sour wine, put *it* on hyssop, and put *it* to His mouth. So when Jesus had received the sour wine, He said, 'It is finished!' And bowing His head, He gave up His spirit. (John 19:28–30)

He now lives to make intercession for His church in heaven (see Hebrews 7:25).

Prayer is the master key for your assignment and all other areas of your life. It opens closed doors.

2. Power

Power speaks of the abilities and responsibilities you have in your assignment.

3. Purpose

Purpose reminds you of your big "why": Why are you doing what you are doing? Be focused first on your why, and your how, what, when, who, where, and which questions will follow. I call these the seven most important questions you need to ask yourself in your decision making. If you carefully and prayerfully seek the Lord for the answers, you will receive clarity and direction.

4. Passion

Passion is the fuel and the driving force to your purpose. Don't lose it. Whatever you do, do it passionately.

5. Planning

Planning is the process of thinking about the activities required to achieve a desired goal. In failing to plan, you are planning to fail.

6. Preparation

Preparation is making ready for a future event as a goal and an acceptable, accomplished final outcome. The quality of one's preparation will determine the quality of their performance.

7. Performance.

Time and again, check your progress and the results that you are getting in your assignment. Performance talks of your harvest. As my wife Edith says, "If you do not like your harvest, change your seeds." Your seeds determine the roots and fruits.

8. Potential

Potential will always challenge you to not settle for your last success. Keep unlocking your potential.

> Potential is God's gift to us, and what we do with it is our gift to God!
>
> —Dr John Maxwell

CHAPTER 9

MENTORING AND COACHING

Mentoring and coaching are two developmental relationships that can lead to profound changes in your life. Mentors and coaches work to encourage, guide, and improve your performance. Although often used interchangeably, the terms are distinct. These relationships are crucial to helping you live out your full potential.

Mentorship

Mentorship is a personal developmental relationship in which someone who is more experienced or knowledgeable guides someone who is still developing and learning. The mentor may be older or younger, but they have a certain area of expertise. It is a caring and growth-related partnership between someone with vast experience and someone who wants to learn. A person who receives mentorship is known as a mentee.

Mentoring is a process for the informal transmission of knowledge and the psychosocial support perceived by the recipient as relevant to work, career, or professional development. It entails informal communication, usually face-to-face or virtually and over a sustained period, between the mentor and the mentee.

Coaching

Coaching is training in which the coach supports a learner in achieving a specific personal or professional goal. The learner is sometimes called a coachee. Coaching sometimes refers to an informal relationship between two people, one with more experience and expertise than the other. Coaching differs from mentoring by focusing on competence specifics as opposed to general overall development (from Wikipedia, the free encyclopedia).

Coaching and mentoring can be done between individuals or within a group. With modern technology, they can occur face-to-face or through live web conferences, Skype, Zoom, telephone, or other apps.

Mentors

Mentors are teachers of wisdom, knowledge, and understanding. Various mentors will come into and leave your life. The Holy Spirit is the most important Mentor of all time (John 16:13). Through mentors, not only will you receive specific wisdom, knowledge, and understanding, but you will also discover God's purpose, plan, and will for your life. You will learn how to protect your time, energy, and resources.

You were born for a great purpose. Your ultimate purpose is to turn others away from the power of Satan to the true, living God. "For I have appeared to you for this purpose, to make you a minister and a witness, to open their eyes and to turn them from darkness to light and from the power of Satan to God" (Acts 26:14–18).

Darkness talks of ignorance, all kinds of evil, poverty, injustice, and every negative thing you can think of. Light talks of development, revelation knowledge, justice, love, peace, joy, and all the blessings of the Lord.

Your purpose in life is exceptional. "The greatest tragedy in life is not death, but a life without a purpose" (featured in Myles Munroe quotes).

Through mentors, you will mutually discover and recover the talents and gifts that God gave you even before He created the heavens and the earth. "Before I formed you in the womb, I knew you; before you were born, I sanctified you and ordained you a prophet to the nations" (Jeremiah 1:5).

Mentors can make the difference between poverty and prosperity, decrease and increase, loss and gain, pain and pleasure, deterioration and restoration, defeat and victory. They do this through learning and study, which gives them understanding, faith, and freedom from darkness.

Mentorship is lacking in many people's lives. There is a loud cry from someone out there, saying, "Who can hold my hand and guide me in the right direction to a good and great prosperous life?" Do you know someone who needs this kind of support and guidance? Or perhaps you could be the one I am referring to. Stop crying and seek the right guidance, coaching and mentorship. Begin to invest in yourself. You were born to win. You have a purpose in life. Position yourself strategically to accept God's wisdom and blessings. Have clear goals of who you wish to become. Know where you are and where you desire to be. Design a five to ten-year personal development plan for your life, family and all that you wish to accomplish. Assemble an accountability team that will assist you in making progress. Get serious with life. Don't waste the most precious resources – time, gifts and talents – that God has given you. Life will always give you back what you give it. Give it good seeds and you will be grateful for the good and great harvest it will bring back to you.

As you act on these simple instructions, your life will begin to change, and you will become a transformational leader. There is greatness in you, and know that you are destined for greatness. It is never too late.

This book is the result of many good and great mentors I have had in my life, and I am still being coached and mentored on a weekly basis. You have to be intentional when it comes to personal growth. There is no substitute for it, unfortunately. Be growth and goal oriented.

You never graduate from the school of coaching and mentorship. You will only graduate when you check out of the earth and, when the time comes, relocate to heaven.

However, I have to remind you that, while you make all your investments here on the earth, it is important to never forget the view of heaven. That is your eternal home prepared for you by your heavenly Father. This is good and great news to all of us. You are destined for a glorious future. Be aware of it, know it, and set your mind on the things above.

The Apostle Paul challenges us to be single-minded while we are here on the earth. Colossians 3:1–3 says, "If then you were raised with Christ, seek those things which are above, where Christ is, sitting at the right hand of God. Set your mind on things above, not on things on the earth. For you died, and your life is hidden with Christ in God."

There is no doubt that God will richly bless you as you prioritize Him in your life. However, as that happens, never be distracted by the blessings of material wealth, as these are temporary. Instead, set your mind on eternal things.

Types of Mentorship

There are different kinds of mentorship, including spiritual, social, mental, economic, political, and professional. We need mentorship in all these fields. We need good, great, and mature mentors and coaches in all areas of our lives.

Five Facts about Mentors

- A great mentor is key to the success of a mentee.
- Mentors transfer their experiences, skills, and wisdom through relationships and partnership. "He that walks with the wise men shall be wise: but a companion of fools shall be destroyed" (Proverbs 13:20). Joshua, the servant of Moses, knew this: "And Joshua the son of Nun was full of the spirit of wisdom; for Moses had laid his hands upon him" (Deuteronomy 34:9).
- Great mentors will lead influential people to listen to you. "And the children of Israel hearkened to Joshua" (Deuteronomy 34:9).
- Great mentors are not interested in where you are right now, but where you are going. Jesus saw where His disciples were going and not where they had been before the Holy Spirit came upon them. He saw them in the Spirit, reaching out to the ends of the earth

(Acts 1:8). Great mentors see your great future and begin to guide you to that place.

- Great mentors focus not on your weaknesses, but on your inherent strengths. They also show you how to deal with your weaknesses.

Invest in Mentorship

From my personal experience, while it is costly to be coached and mentored, it is more costly not to be coached and mentored. Choose the former, if you can. While working on your monthly budget, plan to budget for your personal GROWTH in all areas of your life in terms of valuable time, energy, and resources to glean from the wisdom and experience of good and great mentors. God has chosen specific people to sow into your life. The mentees of Christ Jesus seized their moments and learnt much from their Master; later, they turned the world upside down. "These who have turned the world upside down have come here too" (Acts 17:6).

People in the Bible Who Were Mentored

- Moses mentored Joshua, and Joshua mentored the children of Israel.
- Elijah mentored Elisha, and Elisha mentored Gehazi and the sons of the prophets.
- Elia the priest mentored the young Samuel, who would turn out to be a great prophet of God.
- Samuel mentored King Saul and King David, and King David mentored the four hundred men who were in distress and pain (1 Samuel 22:1–2).
- Mordecai mentored Esther, and Esther mentored her maids.
- Naomi mentored Ruth, who later became the great-grandmother of King David. Our Lord and Saviour, Jesus Christ, came from David's lineage.

In the same way, Jesus Christ was mentored by His earthly parents, and at the age of 12, He likewise sought mentorship from the teachers of the law.

Luke 2:43–49 says, "When they had finished the days, as they returned, the Boy Jesus lingered behind in Jerusalem. And Joseph and His mother did not know *it;* but supposing Him to have been in the company, they went a day's journey, and sought Him among *their* relatives and acquaintances. So when they did not find Him, they returned to Jerusalem, seeking Him. Now so it was *that* after three days they found Him in the temple, sitting in the midst of the teachers, both listening to them and asking them questions. And all who heard Him were astonished at His understanding and answers. So when they saw Him, they were amazed; and His mother said to Him, 'Son, why have You done this to us? Look, Your father and I have sought You anxiously.' And He said to them, 'Why did you seek Me? Did you not know that I must be about My Father's business?'"

- What a challenge that at the age of 12, Jesus knew the power of coaching and mentorship.
- Jesus knew His purpose in life and pursued it wisely with great preparation.
- Never think you are too young or too old to seek coaching or mentorship! Transformational leaders have great mentors and coaches who empower them.
- Jesus also mentored the twelve apostles, and the twelve apostles mentored the early church after they received the Holy Spirit.
- Barnabas mentored the Apostle Paul for a short time, and the Apostle Paul mentored his spiritual son Timothy as well as many others.

And the list goes on. Mentorship is God's will for His people. However, it is our personal responsibility to seek the right mentors. Unfortunately, there are many who go through life without realizing that their good success is linked to a mentor. Someone once said, "If you think knowledge is expensive, try ignorance." Ignorance is very costly. The cure for it is specialized knowledge, understanding, and wisdom, obtained under the guidance of good and great mentors.

Who is your mentor, and who do you mentor?

To flourish, prosper, and fulfil the call of God upon our lives, God has designed us for relationships. We not only need to be mentored, but we also need to mentor others.

Sometimes God chooses who your mentors will be. For example, you did not choose your parents; God chose them for you. Parents are the first and primary mentors we have in our lives. Unfortunately, some parents did not have a good chance to be well and carefully mentored themselves and therefore do not know how to mentor their own children. This leads to love deficit, inner pain, and ultimately, rejection.

Think of the fathers who went to the war for weeks, months, or years, leaving their little children behind. As a result, the child/children missed out on having that father figure during that time. Another example is parents who are very busy with their careers, professions, businesses, or ministries. Over sixteen years of having my counselling practice, I have witnessed a lot of tears from those I have counselled crying out, "I missed having my mother or father's love and care." When children miss out on receiving love, quality time, attention, guidance, and discipline, they experience a love deficit, which leads to inner pain and rejection as they grow up. Parents, be there for your children. While it is costly in terms of the time and attention required, being away from your beloved child/children is even more costly. It can affect the rest of your children's lives.

However, in some cases, those who suffered from the pain of poor parenting have turned out to be great parents. You can turn your pain into gain. My dear father lost his father when he was only eight years old. Someone had mercy on him, taking him by his hand and fathering him so well that, in return, he became a good and wonderful father.

I recommend Dr Myles Munroe's book, *The Fatherhood Principle.* It is an amazing book that will challenge you to be a father or mother to not only your own children, but also those children who are fatherless and motherless.

Today, we have a fatherless and motherless generation. God wants to restore fatherhood and motherhood to these individuals. We read in Malachi 4:6, "And he will turn the hearts of fathers to their children, and the hearts of the children to their fathers, lest I come and strike the earth with a curse" (Malachi 4:6).

If you have good and great mentors, thank God for them. Do all you can to learn from them. If you do not have a good mentor, it is not too late to find someone. Ask God to show you who your mentor should be. In return, have it in your heart to mentor someone or as many others as the Lord leads you to. Always remember to appreciate your mentors: respect, honour, and pray for them. I am forever grateful to the Lord for all my mentors and coaches.

Below are some words of wisdom from our mentor, Dr. John C. Maxwell. I have had the great privilege to be mentored by both him and his team, the John Maxwell Team (JMT).

Dr. Maxwell says that mentors do the following three things for you:

1. They know the way; thus, they have insights and wisdom born out of experience.
2. They show the way by generously applying their insight and wisdom to your specific situation.
3. They go the way by walking with you through your own journey and helping you learn from your experiences.

There is no greater accomplishment for mentors to see the people they develop, do better than them.

The John Maxwell team offers great mentorship programmes that have transformed millions around the world. I am part of these programmes, and I have been truly blessed as a result. Now I am passing on these blessings to others.

Jesus said to his mentees in John 14:12, "Most assuredly, I say to you, he who believes in Me, the works that I do he will do also; and greater *works* than these he will do, because I go to My Father." Jesus wanted them to do more and greater works because He was going to pass the baton to them. Make sure you pass on the baton that you receive from your mentors.

I would like to leave you with these two questions: 1) Who is mentoring you? 2) Who are you mentoring?

Take some time to answer these two questions, and know that mentorship is God's will.

"Return, O backsliding children," says the Lord; "for I am married to you. I will take you, one from a city and two from a family, and I will bring you to Zion. And I will give you shepherds according to My heart, who will feed you with knowledge and understanding." (Jeremiah 3:14–15)

Good and great mentors come from God and will feed you with knowledge and understanding. Through mentorship, you will gain the wisdom to apply what you have learnt to your life.

CHAPTER 10

THE SINGLE AND DOUBLE
CALLING OF GOD

I would like to begin this topic with the scripture readings focusing on various books in the Bible that talk about the calling of God for different people.

> And Jesus, walking by the Sea of Galilee, saw two brothers, Simon called Peter, and Andrew his brother, casting a net into the sea; for they were fishermen. Then He said to them, "Follow Me, and I will make you fishers of men" (Matthew 4:18–19).

> As Jesus passed on from there, He saw a man named Matthew sitting at the tax office. And He said to him, "Follow Me." So he arose and followed Him (Matthew 9:9).

> Then Jesus spoke to them again, saying, "I am the light of the world. He who follows Me shall not walk in darkness, but have the light of life" (John 8:12).

There are two callings in our lives and that is a single and a double calling. This means that God calls people in different ways and times. For example, the prophet Samuel was called at earlier age. For Jeremiah, he was called when he was a teenager. For Abraham, Aaron and Moses, they were called at old age. He called all these people with specific instructions and different responsibilities. There are those who are called with less responsibility and those called with more, but they are both performing important tasks. When we understand this, we see each other's unique value, and there is no need for competition. Instead, we complement and complete each other.

Let's look at the people God called twice, as well as the one who cried out twice:

- *Abraham.* "But the Angel of the Lord called to him from heaven and said, 'Abraham, Abraham!' So he said, 'Here I am'" (Genesis 22:11).
- *Jacob.* "Then God spoke to Israel in the visions of the night, and said, 'Jacob, Jacob!' And he said, 'Here I am'" (Genesis 46:2).
- *Moses.* "So when the Lord saw that he turned aside to look, God called to him from the midst of the bush and said, 'Moses, Moses!' And he said, 'Here I am'" (Exodus 3:4).
- *Samuel.* "Now the Lord came and stood and called as at other times, 'Samuel! Samuel!' And Samuel answered, 'Speak, for Your servant hears'" (1 Samuel 3:10).
- *Martha.* "And Jesus answered and said to her, 'Martha, Martha, you are worried and troubled about many things'" (Luke 10:41).
- *Simon.* "And the Lord said, 'Simon, Simon! Indeed, Satan has asked for you, that he may sift *you* as wheat'" (Luke 22:31–32).
- *Saul.* "And when we all had fallen to the ground, I heard a voice speaking to me and saying in the Hebrew language, 'Saul, Saul, why are you persecuting Me? *It is* hard for you to kick against the goads'" (Acts 9:4).
- *Jerusalem.* "Jerusalem, Jerusalem, you who kill the prophets and stone those sent to you, how often I have longed to gather your children together, as a hen gathers her chicks under her wings, and you were not willing" (Luke 13:34).
- *Jesus Christ.* Jesus had a double cry. "About three in the afternoon Jesus cried out in a loud voice, 'Eli, Eli, lema sabachthani?' ['My God, my God, why have you forsaken me?']" (Matthew 27:46). And again, "And at the ninth hour Jesus cried out with a loud

voice, saying, 'Eloi, Eloi, lama sabachthani?' ['My God, My God, why have You forsaken Me?'] (Mark 15:34).

Important Lessons

When God calls you twice, it comes with greater responsibility and greater sacrifice. This implies that there is always a higher price to pay with a double calling. God, who made us, knows what we are good at and calls us accordingly.

This suggests that He will not give us what we cannot handle. When He calls us, He prepares and equips us in every way. With His call, He gives us clarity and informs us of the vision, mission, provision, direction, providence, and protection that He has in mind. He promises to always be with us in both the good times and when we are going through challenges.

God has also given us the Holy Spirit to help and mentor us in our calling and all other areas. We will also encounter many doors to go through at different stages of the call. Prayer and God's Word are the master keys that will open all these doors.

For those called by God twice, He either came down Himself and spoke to them directly like Moses and Abraham. The others were called by Jesus. God calls us in many ways to fulfil His assignment. Our positive response of obedience is our gift to Him, which also brings Him honour.

Notably, God does not call lazy people. Those He called twice in the Bible were busy doing something. They had an occupation and a good work ethic. Jesus said His Father was busy, and He was also busy doing His Father's business. There is no room for laziness in His kingdom. Jesus also said in John 9:4, "I must work the works of Him who sent Me while it is day; *the* night is coming when no one can work." But Jesus answered them, "My Father has been working until now, and I have been working" (John 5:17).

The call of God upon your life will always take you out of your comfort zone and into something new. Abraham is a classic example of this— leaving his father's land and all that he knew was a big sacrifice.

Jacob had to step out of the comfort of his sojourn in a foreign land and make his way back home. He had to trust that God had already gone ahead of him and that all would be well with his brother, Esau.

Moses had to remove his shoes to step into his new assignment and walk with God. This symbolized a walk of the supernatural. It involved being led by God, who is holy. It symbolized no longer being limited by Moses's weaknesses. It signified a new season and a new assignment of supernatural encounters, provisions, directions, and protection.

Samuel's new life led him to service in the sanctuary. It involved ministry to God and His people and would later lead him to the unique role in which he would serve his nation as both prophet and judge.

Martha's new life required her to reset her priorities. She was troubled and worried about many things; thus, she forgot her most important role: to seek God, His kingdom, and His righteousness. Her sister Mary had known the secret of God's top priorities. This is what the Lord wants for all of us.

Simon had to learn to trust in God's protection and receive strength from the Master to remain stable and steadfast.

Saul was successfully pursuing the wrong course for his life. That all changed after his salvation, when he received the right assignment and began to walk faithfully in it. His life completely changed course after his encounter with Jesus. If you are succeeding in the wrong assignment, you can turn around, too. It is never too late.

Although Jesus Christ was the Son of God, He also had to respond to His Father's call on His life. Before He could become the Lord of all, He had to reconcile us back to God, as He took upon himself the sins of the entire human race. He not only sacrificed His life, but he also went through a place of great discomfort, being disconnected from His Father. That is why He cried, "My God, My God why have You forsaken Me?"

What about you? Have you discovered your single or double calling? May the Lord show you and lead you along the way. "Then you will call upon Me and go and pray to Me, and I will listen to you. And you will seek Me and find Me, when you search for Me with all your heart" (Jeremiah 29:12–13).

CHAPTER 11

A GOOD MENTOR: ELIJAH

Elijah was a prophet who established himself as a mighty man of God. At the peak of his ministry, God asked him to mentor a young farmer called Elisha. Their relationship portrays the uniqueness of mentorship. It reveals the positive influence a mentor can have on the life of a mentee. The relationship is so unique that it is possible you may not realize that the person you are serving is your mentor. Let's take a closer look at what qualified Elijah to be a mentor.

The name Elijah means "my God is Jehovah" or "Yahweh is God."

The Bible does not talk about Elijah's family. He had a unique anointing on his ministry. There is a prophecy concerning his Second Coming: "Behold, I will send you Elijah the prophet Before the coming of the great and dreadful day of the LORD. And he will turn the hearts of the fathers to the children, and the hearts of the children to their fathers, lest I come and strike the earth with a curse" (Malachi 4:5–6).

He appeared with Jesus at the Mount of Transfiguration:

> Now after six days Jesus took Peter, James, and John his brother, led them up on a high mountain by themselves; and He was transfigured before them. His face shone like the sun, and His clothes became as white as the light. And behold, Moses and Elijah appeared to them, talking with Him. Then Peter answered and said to Jesus, "Lord, it is good for us to be here; if You wish, let us make here

three tabernacles: one for You, one for Moses, and one for Elijah." (Matthew 17:1–4)

Elijah was like John the Baptist and preceded the coming of the Lord. "He will also go before Him in the spirit and power of Elijah, to turn the hearts of the fathers to the children, and the disobedient to the wisdom of the just, to make ready a people prepared for the Lord" (Luke 1:17).

Elijah received the ability to hear, know, and understand the voice of God because he was willing and obedient. His anointing and power to perform miracles came to him through God's backing. Many of the miracles he performed were recorded in the books of Kings.

In 1 Kings 17:1, he caused the rain to cease for three-and-a-half years: "And Elijah the Tishbite, of the inhabitants of Gilead, said to Ahab, 'As the LORD God of Israel lives, before whom I stand, there shall not be dew nor rain these years, except at my word.'"

In 1 Kings 17:4, he was fed by ravens: "And it will be that you shall drink from the brook, and I have commanded the ravens to feed you there."

In 1 Kings 17:14, he blessed the barrel of meal and the jar of oil: "For thus says the LORD God of Israel: 'The bin of flour shall not be used up, nor shall the jar of oil run dry, until the day the LORD sends rain on the earth.'"

In 1 Kings 17:22, he resurrected the widow's son: "Then the LORD heard the voice of Elijah; and the soul of the child came back to him, and he revived."

In 1 Kings 18:38, he called down fire from heaven onto the altar: "Then the fire of the LORD fell and consumed the burnt sacrifice, and the wood and the stones and the dust, and it licked up the water that was in the trench."

In 1 Kings 18:45, he caused it to rain: "Now it happened in the meantime that the sky became black with clouds and wind, and there was a heavy rain. So Ahab rode away and went to Jezreel."

In 1 Kings 18:46, supernatural power came upon him to run faster than the horses: "Then the hand of the LORD came upon Elijah; and he girded up his loins and ran ahead of Ahab to the entrance of Jezreel."

In 1 Kings 21:22, he prophesied that Ahab's sons would all be destroyed: "I will make your house like the house of Jeroboam the son of Nebat, and like the house of Baasha the son of Ahijah, because of the provocation with which you have provoked Me to anger, and made Israel sin."

In 1 Kings 21:23, he prophesied that Jezebel would be eaten by dogs: "And concerning Jezebel the LORD also spoke, saying, 'The dogs shall eat Jezebel by the wall of Jezreel.'"

In 2 Kings 1:4, he prophesied that Ahaziah would die of his illness: "Now therefore, thus says the LORD: 'You shall not come down from the bed to which you have gone up, but you shall surely die.' So Alijah departed."

In 2 Kings 1:10, he called fire from heaven upon the first fifty soldiers: "So Elijah answered and said to the captain of fifty, 'If I am a man of God, then let fire come down from heaven and consume you and your fifty men.' And fire came down from heaven and consumed him and his fifty."

In 2 Kings 1:12, he called fire from heaven upon the second fifty soldiers: "So, Elijah answered and said to them, 'If I am a man of God, let fire come down from heaven and consume you and your fifty men.' And the fire of God came down from heaven and consumed him and his fifty."

In 2 Kings 2:8, he parted the Jordan: "Now Elijah took his mantle, rolled it up, and struck the water; and it was divided this way and that, so that the two of them crossed over on dry ground."

In 2 Kings 2:9, a double portion of the spirit of Elijah came upon Elisha: "And so it was, when they had crossed over, that Elijah said to Elisha, "Ask! What may I do for you, before I am taken away from you?" Elisha said, "Please let a double portion of your spirit be upon me."

In 2 Kings 2:10, he prophesied that Elisha would have a double portion of his spirit: So he said, "You have asked a hard thing. *Nevertheless,* if you see me *when I am* taken from you, it shall be so for you; but if not, it shall not be *so.*"

As I read these miracles of the prophet Elijah, I see God's greatness and marvel at how God can use us for the very purposes He created us for. He is seeking for people who are faithful, available, teachable and who are willing to walk and work with Him.

My takeaways from the prophet Elijah are as follows:

- He loved God and was fully sold out for Him.
- He was very obedient to God's call and had burned all the bridges behind him.

- He walked and worked with God and was very sensitive to His voice.
- He performed many miracles through the power and the anointing of the Holy Spirit of God.
- He challenged the false prophets by proving to them that he served the true living God who answered by fire.
- There was a time when he was afraid and prayed and wished to die because he felt that he was not better than his fathers. God did not answer his prayers.
- He prayed out of frustration and disappointment. He was a man like us.
- In our lowest moments, God still listens to us, and answers our prayers.
- He had a very good succession plan. He trained and raised his successor who performed double the miracles, as he had blessed him with the double portion of anointing.
- He did not experience death. Elijah and Enoch were the only people who did not see and go through death.

These two scriptures below explains of Elijah and Enoch who did not die. They were taken to heaven without experiencing death. There is no account in the Bible that talks of other persons who did not die except these two gentlemen.

In 2 Kings 2:11, he was caught in a whirlwind and went up to heaven: "Then it happened, as they continued and talked, that suddenly a chariot of fire appeared with horses of fire, and separated the two of them; and Elijah went up by a whirlwind into heaven."

In Genesis 5:21-24 says, "Enoch lived sixty-five years, and begot Methuselah. After he begot Methuselah, Enoch walked with God three hundred years, and had sons and daughters. So all the days of Enoch were three hundred and sixty-five years. And Enoch walked with God; and he *was* not, for God took him."

Before Jesus went to heaven, He gave us a double portion of His anointing: "Most assuredly, I say to you, he who believes in Me, the works that I do he will do also; and greater *works* than these he will do, because I go to My Father" (John 14:12).

He has given us the power and the authority to help us to work in His kingdom. He has promised to be with us and work with us. He has given us the Holy Spirit to help us to do great and greater works as it is written in the scripture. What did Jesus mean by saying, the works that I do he will do also; and greater *works* than these he will do, because I go to My Father? He saw the Holy Spirit coming to take over His ministry, working with all believers around the world. He told His disciples "But you shall receive power when the Holy Spirit has come upon you; and you shall be witnesses to Me in Jerusalem, and in all Judea and Samaria, and to the end of the earth." (Acts 1:8). We are called to be witnesses for Christ by the power of the Holy Spirit. We are so blessed to have the Holy Spirit in the land. He is everywhere bringing many people to Christ constantly. By the way of the internet we can even have greater impact more than ever. It was not so for the early church and yet thousands and millions of souls were won into the kingdom of God. Let us take the advantage of the modern technology to spread the good news of the kingdom of God.

Hunger and thirst to know and understand the anointing of God are the key to your success.

Spend quality time with the Word of God. Learn to listen to and understand what the Holy Spirit is saying to you, and do it. "So then, after the Lord had spoken to them, He was received up into heaven, and sat down at the right hand of God. And they went out and preached everywhere, the Lord working with them and confirming the word through the accompanying signs" (Mark 16:19–20).

CHAPTER 12

A GOOD MENTEE: ELISHA

Elisha was a young man, working hard and taking care of his father's business, when Elijah approached him. Little did he know that this encounter would forever change his life. From the moment he set eyes on the prophet, he loved him, and he would serve him until his master was taken up to heaven by the chariot of fire.

Elisha began his ministry as Elijah's student and personal attendant. This is where he first proved himself faithful in doing small things, such as through the humble duty of pouring water on the prophet's hands. "But Jehoshaphat said, '*Is there* no prophet of the LORD here, that we may inquire of the LORD by him?' So one of the servants of the king of Israel answered and said, 'Elisha the son of Shaphat *is* here, who poured water on the hands of Elijah'" (2 Kings 3:11).

Elisha's training under Elijah gradually prepared the former for work that he would one day take up alone.

Elisha was not seeking worldly honour or a high place among men; what he desired instead was a double measure of the anointing that God had so freely placed upon the Prophet Elijah. He knew that He needed God's Holy Spirit to equip him for the responsibilities that lay ahead. He patiently served Elijah until the very end.

Elisha performed many miracles with the double portion of anointing.

In 2 Kings 2:14, Elisha took up Elijah's mantle: "Then he took the mantle of Elijah that had fallen from him, and struck the water, and said,

'Where is the LORD God of Elijah?' And when he also had struck the water, it was divided this way and that; and Elisha crossed over."

In 2 Kings 2:21, he healed the bitter waters: "Then he went out to the source of the water, and cast in the salt there, and said, 'Thus says the LORD: "I have healed this water; from it there shall be no more death or barrenness."'"

In 2 Kings 2:24, he cursed a group of youths, and they met an untimely end: "So he turned around and looked at them, and pronounced a curse on them in the name of the LORD. And two female bears came out of the woods and mauled forty-two of the youths."

In 2 Kings 3:17, he filled the valley with water: "For thus says the LORD: 'You shall not see wind, nor shall you see rain; yet that valley shall be filled with water, so that you, your cattle, and your animals may drink.'"

In 2 Kings 3:22, he deceived the Moabites with the valley of blood: "Then they rose up early in the morning, and the sun was shining on the water; and the Moabites saw the water on the other side as red as blood."

In 2 Kings 4:1–7, he performed the miracle with the vessels of oil:

A certain woman of the wives of the sons of the prophets cried out to Elisha, saying, "Your servant my husband is dead, and you know that your servant feared the LORD. And the creditor is coming to take my two sons to be his slaves." So Elisha said to her, "What shall I do for you? Tell me, what do you have in the house?" And she said, "Your maidservant has nothing in the house but a jar of oil." Then he said, "Go, borrow vessels from everywhere, from all your neighbors—empty vessels; do not gather just a few. And when you have come in, you shall shut the door behind you and your sons; then pour it into all those vessels, and set aside the full ones." So she went from him and shut the door behind her and her sons, who brought *the vessels* to her; and she poured *it* out. Now it came to pass, when the vessels were full, that she said to her son, "Bring me another vessel." And he said to her, "*There is* not another vessel." So he oil ceased. Then she came and told the man of God. And he said, "Go, sell the oil and pay your debt; and you *and* your sons live on the rest."

In 2 Kings 4:16, he prophesied that the Shunammite woman would have a son: "Then he said, 'About this time next year you shall embrace a son.' And she said, 'No, my lord. Man of God, do not lie to your maidservant!'"

In 2 Kings 4:34, he resurrected the Shunammite woman's son: "And he went up and lay on the child, and put his mouth on his mouth, his eyes on his eyes, and his hands on his hands; and he stretched himself out on the child, and the flesh of the child became warm."

In 2 Kings 4:41, he healed the gourds: "So he said, 'Then bring some flour.' And he put *it* into the pot, and said, 'Serve *it* to the people, that they may eat.' And there was nothing harmful in the pot."

In 2 Kings 4:43, he performed the miracle with the bread: "But his servant said, 'What? Shall I set this before one hundred men?' He said again, 'Give it to the people, that they may eat; for thus says the LORD: "They shall eat and have *some* left over.""

In 2 Kings 5:14, he healed Naaman: "So he went down and dipped seven times in the Jordan, according to the saying of the man of God; and his flesh was restored like the flesh of a little child, and he was clean."

In 2 Kings 5:26, he perceived Gehazi's transgression: "Then he said to him, 'Did not my heart go with you when the man turned back from his chariot to meet you? Is it time to receive money and to receive clothing, olive groves and vineyards, sheep and oxen, male and female servants?'"

In 2 Kings 5:27, he cursed Gehazi with leprosy: "'Therefore, the leprosy of Naaman shall cling to you and your descendants forever.' And he went out from his presence leprous, as white as snow."

In 2 Kings 6:8–12, he revealed the intelligence of the Syrian king:

> Now the king of Syria was making war against Israel; and he consulted with his servants, saying, "My camp *will be* in such and such a place." And the man of God sent to the king of Israel, saying, "Beware that you do not pass this place, for the Syrians are coming down there." Then the king of Israel sent *someone* to the place of which the man

of God had told him. Thus he warned him, and he was watchful there, not just once or twice. Therefore the heart of the king of Syria was greatly troubled by this thing; and he called his servants and said to them, "Will you not show me which of us *is* for the king of Israel?" And one of his servants said, "None, my lord, O king; but Elisha, the prophet who *is* in Israel, tells the king of Israel the words that you speak in your bedroom."

Elisha was the intelligence advisor to the king of Israel. The Lord is able to open your eyes to see when your enemy is coming to attack as well as give you strategies to defeat him. There is a great lesson to learn here. Political leaders should walk and work closely with men and women of God who are spiritual for the common good of the citizens of every nation.

In 2 Kings 6:13–17, he prayed for the eyes of his servant to be opened:

So he said, "Go and see where he *is,* that I may send and get him."

And it was told him, saying, "Surely *he is* in Dothan."

Therefore he sent horses and chariots and a great army there, and they came by night and surrounded the city. And when the servant of the man of God arose early and went out, there was an army, surrounding the city with horses and chariots. And his servant said to him, "Alas, my master! What shall we do?" S.E

So he answered, "Do not fear, for those who *are* with us *are* more than those who *are* with them." And Elisha prayed, and said, "LORD, I pray, open his eyes that he may see." Then the LORD opened the eyes of the young man, and he saw. And behold, the mountain *was* full of horses and chariots of fire all around Elisha.

In 2 Kings 6:32–33, he was already aware of the king's actions and knew that he would try to kill him:

> Elisha was sitting in his house with the elders of Israel when the king sent a messenger to summon him. But before the messenger arrived, Elisha said to the elders, "A murderer has sent a man to cut off my head. When he arrives, shut the door and keep him out. We will soon hear his master's steps following him." While Elisha was still saying this, the messenger arrived. And the king said, "All this misery is from the Lord! Why should I wait for the Lord any longer?"

In 2 Kings 6:9, he prophesied and revealed the Syrian battle plans: "And the man of God sent to the king of Israel, saying, 'Beware that you do not pass this place, for the Syrians are coming down there.'"

In 2 Kings 6:17, he saw the vision of the chariots: "And Elisha prayed, and said, 'Lord, I pray, open his eyes that he may see.' Then the Lord opened the eyes of the young man, and he saw. And behold, the mountain was full of horses and chariots of fire all around Elisha."

In 2 Kings 6:18, he smote the Syrian army with blindness: "So when the Syrians came down to him, Elisha prayed to the Lord, and said, 'Strike this people, I pray, with blindness.' And He struck them with blindness according to the word of Elisha."

In 2 Kings 6:20, he restored the sight of the Syrian army: "So it was, when they had come to Samaria, that Elisha said, 'Lord, open the eyes of these men, that they may see.' And the Lord opened their eyes, and they saw; and there they were, inside Samaria!"

In 2 Kings 7:1, he prophesied of the end of the great famine: "Then Elisha said, 'Hear the word of the Lord. Thus, says the Lord: "Tomorrow, about this time a seah of fine flour shall be sold for a shekel, and two seahs of barley for a shekel, at the gate of Samaria."'"

In 2 Kings 7:2, he prophesied that the scoffing nobleman would see but not partake in the abundance: "So an officer on whose hand the king leaned answered the man of God and said, 'Look, if the Lord would make windows in heaven, could this thing be?' And he said, 'In fact, you shall see it with your eyes, but you shall not eat of it.'"

In 2 Kings 7:6, the Syrians were deceived by the sound of chariots: "For the Lord had caused the army of the Syrians to hear the noise of chariots and the noise of horses—the noise of a great army; so they said to one another, 'Look, the king of Israel has hired against us the kings of the Hittites and the kings of the Egyptians to attack us!'"

In 2 Kings 8:1, he prophesied the seven-year famine: "Then Elisha spoke to the woman whose son he had restored to life, saying, 'Arise and go, you and your household, and stay wherever you can; for the LORD has called for a famine, and furthermore, it will come upon the land for seven years.'"

In 2 Kings 8:10, he prophesied of Benhadad's untimely death: "And Elisha said to him, 'Go, say to him, "You shall certainly recover." However, the LORD has shown me that he will really die.'"

In 2 Kings 8:12, he prophesied Hazael's cruelty to Israel: "And Hazael said, 'Why is my lord weeping?' He answered, 'Because I know the evil that you will do to the children of Israel: Their strongholds you will set on fire, and their young men you will kill with the sword; and you will dash their children, and rip open their women with child.'"

In 2 Kings 9:7, he prophesied that Jehu would smite the house of Ahab: "You shall strike down the house of Ahab your master, that I may avenge the blood of My servants the prophets, and the blood of all the servants of the LORD, at the hand of Jezebel."

In 2 Kings 13:17, he prophesied that Joash would smite the Syrians at Aphek: "And he said, 'Open the east window'; and he opened it. Then Elisha said, 'Shoot'; and he shot. And he said, 'The arrow of the LORD's deliverance and the arrow of deliverance from Syria; for you must strike the Syrians at Aphek till you have destroyed them.'"

In 2 Kings 13:19, he prophesied that Joash would smite Syria thrice but not consume it: "And the man of God was angry with him, and said, 'You should have struck five or six times; then you would have struck Syria till you had destroyed it! But now you will strike Syria only three times.'"

In 2 Kings 13:20–21, his dead bones brought a dead man to life: "Then Elisha died, and they buried him. And the raiding bands from Moab invaded the land in the spring of the year. So it was, as they were burying a man, that suddenly they spied a band of raiders; and they put the man in the tomb of Elisha; and when the man was let down and touched the bones of Elisha, he revived and stood on his feet."

In 2 Kings 6:1–6, he caused an axe head to float:

And the sons of the prophets said to Elisha, "See now, the place where we dwell with you is too small for us. Please, let us go to the Jordan, and let every man take a beam from there, and let us make there a place where we may dwell." So he answered, "Go." Then one said, "Please consent to go with your servants." And he answered, "I will go." So he went with them. And when they came to the Jordan, they cut down trees. But as one was cutting down a tree, the iron ax head fell into the water; and he cried out and said, "Alas, master! For it was borrowed." So, the man of God said, "Where did it fall?" And he showed him the place. So he cut off a stick, and threw it in there; and he made the iron float.

Therefore he said, "Pick it up for yourself." So he reached out his hand and took it.

The sons of the prophets were serious people. They worked hard and achieved their goals by the anointing of God and with the help of their coach and mentor prophet Elisha.

As time went by, these young prophets had a challenge: their accommodation was too small as their numbers had increased. Before they moved, they consulted with their mentor and requested if he could go with them. He agreed to go with them. They knew the blessing of having a father figure with them.

Elisha had been well brought up by his mentor Elijah and hence he wanted to do the same.

As they arrived, they began to work but unfortunately, the iron axe head fell into the water.

The axe head had been borrowed. It had been given by someone for the furtherance of the work, just as are spiritual gifts. It is the responsibility of us all to ensure that these gifts are kept "sharp" and available for service. Should we fail in this, we may still be engaged busily, but without results.

What is the answer to such a problem? The workman turned to Elisha. He had the answer. No other could restore the axe head. It is, therefore, to the Lord that we turn to restore the power, the "cutting edge" of our service.

But Elisha asked, "Where did it fall?" We have to search our hearts and identify where the problem took place, what caused us to lose our power or passion. This involves confession on our part, with the acknowledgment that restoration is God's work.

But Elisha, having made the axe head available again, calls on the man to say: "Pick it up for yourself." Elisha performed the miracle, but the young prophet had to play his part and take the axe head up by himself. It is always this way in recovery. The work of the cross, pictured in the stick that was cast into the river, is the basis of the recovery of the servant, but he had to reach out and take it by himself what had been made available for him.

All good and perfect gifts have been made available including salvation and eternal life. The price has been fully paid for you. Reach out and receive the indescribable and incomparable Gift of God, Jesus Christ.

We can learn many lessons from this great prophet Elijah. First, he knew his Creator personally. He walked in a double portion of Elijah's anointing. He had an intimate relationship with God Himself. He walked and worked with God daily. That is the secret to winning in life and being an example of a transformational leader.

Second, he was firmly engaged in his profession as a farmer until God called him to the prophetic ministry. He worked hard, diligently and intelligently. He was not idle. It was with this same zeal that he served the Lord.

Third, the Lord sent him a good mentor and coach, from whom he learned everything about his ministry. When you are faithful with a little, you will be faithful with much. When you are faithful with that which belongs to someone else, God will set you before greater men.

Fourth, he remained humble and faithful to his calling until he died. He was faithful until God took him home.

Fifth, the anointing that Elisha carried was still at work even after he was dead. His dead bones brought a dead man to life!

Borrowed things can also enslave. Avoid borrowing things, as they can make you a servant especially if you are unable to pay or return them back. If Elisha was not able to perform a miracle for the sons of the prophets, they could have been in trouble to pay for the axe. If you have to borrow, do it wisely and diligently with a wise consultant double checking everything.

Also do all you can to get out of debt. Trust God to help you, empower, enrich and bless you to be financially independent.

It is written: "The rich rules over the poor, And the borrower *is* servant to the lender" (Proverbs 22:7).

Gehazi: The Mentee Who Failed to Fulfil His Destiny

The magnitude of what is lost when mentorship is not received or acknowledged well can be seen in the life of Gehazi.

But Gehazi, the servant of Elisha the man of God, said, "Look, my master has spared Naaman this Syrian, while not receiving from his hands what he brought; but *as* the LORD lives, I will run after him and take something from him." So Gehazi pursued Naaman. When Naaman saw *him* running after him, he got down from the chariot to meet him, and said, "*Is* all well?"

And he said, "All *is* well. My master has sent me, saying, 'Indeed, just now two young men of the sons of the prophets have come to me from the mountains of Ephraim. Please give them a talent of silver and two changes of garments.'"

So Naaman said, "Please, take two talents." And he urged him, and bound two talents of silver in two bags, with two changes of garments, and handed *them* to two of his servants; and they carried *them* on ahead of him. When he came to the citadel, he took *them* from their hand, and stored *them* away in the house; then he let the men go, and they departed. Now he went in and stood before his master. Elisha said to him, "Where *did you go*, Gehazi?"

And he said, "Your servant did not go anywhere."

Then he said to him, "Did not my heart go *with you* when the man turned back from his chariot to meet you? *Is it* time to receive money and to receive clothing, olive groves and vineyards, sheep and oxen, male and female servants? Therefore the leprosy of Naaman shall cling to you and your descendants forever." And he went out from his presence leprous, *as white* as snow.

Sadly, Gehazi's heart disqualified him for ministry, and he was cut off. He neither understood nor trusted the provisions of the Lord. God had provided him with an excellent mentor, a man who had received a double portion of Elijah's anointing. Elisha could not pass it on to Gehazi nor to the next generation; hence, he went to the grave with it.

Gehazi's life shows that you can have an excellent mentor yet still fail to receive all that God has in store for you.

Gehazi missed his destiny because of the condition of his heart.

His heart became distracted by vanity. He failed to see that the mantle (a covering) upon his mentor was of far greater worth than the trendy garments of a once-leprous soldier.

It is important to keep your focus on what God has promised you, especially in times of crisis. When all hope seems gone, the temptations of this world often appear more enticing. However, if you remain focused, you will receive and fulfil your eternal mandate, just like Elisha did. He poured water on the hands of Elijah until the very end. You, too, will overcome and live out your purpose.

Judas was another mentee destined for greatness; his mentor was Jesus Christ in the flesh. He missed his purpose for thirty pieces of silver. Be careful what you receive as an alternative to mentorship. Judas received blood money, which he ended up giving back. There is truly no comparison between spiritual and carnal blessings.

Peter was another disciple who the enemy tried to use to thwart the purposes of God for his life. However, his life was preserved, and he was given a second chance. Guard your heart, and make sure you keep it free from vanities. Present it to the Lord frequently to receive spiritual cleansing and refreshing.

We can find a great prayer from King David: "Search me, O God, and know my heart; Try me, and know my anxieties; And see if there is any wicked way in me, And lead me in the way everlasting" (Psalm 139: 23–24).

CHAPTER 13

SEASONS OF LIFE

We live our lives in seasons. Seasons help us to manage our time better. In the book of Genesis, we read that God established seasons. "While the earth remains, Seedtime and harvest, cold and heat, winter and summer, And day and night Shall not cease" (Genesis 8:22).

In the book of Daniel, we see again that seasons determine who is removed from and placed in power, as well as who receives wisdom and understanding. "And He changes the times and the seasons; He removes kings and raises up kings; He gives wisdom to the wise and knowledge to those who have understanding" (Daniel 2:21).

There are four seasons of the year: spring, summer, autumn, and winter. Just as there are natural seasons, there are four seasons to our lives, and these seasons follow the same pattern.

Spring

Spring is a time of nature's rebirth – of new beginnings and opportunities. It is a season of good things and the revival of things once dead. In this season, dreams and visions come alive or are launched to whole new levels. Spring is a season when people receive their healing, gain good health, and are restored. It is a time of expectation, as new seeds are planted and watered.

My beloved spoke, and said to me: "Rise up, my love, my fair one, And come away. For lo, the winter is past, The rain is over and gone. The flowers appear on the earth; The time of singing has come, And the voice of the turtledove Is heard in our land. The fig tree puts forth her green figs, And the vines with the tender grapes Give a good smell. Rise up, my love, my fair one, And come away! O my dove, in the clefts of the rock, In the secret places of the cliff, Let me see your face, Let me hear your voice; For your voice is sweet, And your face is lovely." (Song of Solomon 2:10–14)

Summer

In summer, seeds that have been planted are protected from garden invaders. It is a time that we go out to meet new people and tell them of the great things that have happened in our lives and families. It is a time to celebrate your success and progress in life. Nature teaches us that summer is a good time to gather.

Go to the ant, you sluggard! Consider her ways and be wise, Which, having no captain, Overseer or ruler, Provides her supplies in the summer, and gathers her food in the harvest. How long will you slumber, O sluggard? When will you rise from your sleep? A little sleep, a little slumber, A little folding of the hands to sleep—So shall your poverty come on you like a prowler, And your need like an armed man. (Proverbs 3:6–8)

Summer is a time to reflect upon your previous works and discover ways to do things differently. It's a time to become more responsible and discern how to manage your time, energy, and resources properly. It is a season to become more industrious and become totally dependent on the Lord for His guidance, knowledge, understanding, and wisdom.

Summer is a time to enjoy your harvest and be grateful. Gather a network of friends who can help you in your harvest. Summer is also a season to get a personal mentor or a coach to help you improve and progress towards your goals.

Autumn

Like all other seasons, Autumn is a season that brings both good and bad; it is ever-changing. It is therefore a season to focus on the God, who never changes and remains steadfast. "LORD, You have been our dwelling place in all generations. Before the mountains were brought forth, or ever You had formed the earth and the world, even from everlasting to everlasting, You are God" (Psalm 90:1–2).

Autumn is also harvest time. Deuteronomy 11:14, James 5:7–8, and Jeremiah 5:24 talks of the harvest of grapes and other foods.

Autumn rains are very important for farmers to prepare the earth for the seeds that will be planted in the spring.

Some of the saddest words in the Bible are in Jeremiah 8:20: "The harvest is past, the summer is ended, and we are not saved." If you have never made a commitment to Jesus Christ, do it now while there is still time.

Autumn is a time of shedding, letting go, and releasing things that have been a burden to carry. It is a good time to focus on your commitment to God. It is a time to reflect and make changes in our lives, families, jobs, professions, and ministries. We shake off old ways, often turning from negative attitudes to positive ones to experience the glory and splendour of God and to welcome new seasons.

Autumn reminds us that it is time to prepare for winter again. Even as we do so, we know that spring is not far off.

Winter

The winter of life represents hard times—in one's personal life, at the workplace, in business, or in ministry. With winter often comes the feeling of being forsaken and forgotten. This season reflects periods of opposition, obstacles, and oppression. You may face personal or corporate leadership challenges. You may feel alone, disconnected, or secluded.

The flowers appear on the earth; The time of singing has come, And the voice of the turtledove is heard in our land. The fig tree puts forth her green figs, And the vines with the tender grapes Give a good smell. Rise up, my love, my fair one, and come away! (Song of Solomon 2:12–13)

Lessons on the Seasons of Life

During our lives, we all experience both good and challenging times. Fortunately, through God's grace and the help of the Holy Spirit, we can enjoy the good times and overcome the bad ones. Regardless of the season, it is important to remain calm to achieve peace. The fruit of the Holy Spirit will protect and preserve you during these times. Remind yourself that in spite of the season, you will fulfil God's plans and purposes for you.

Remain as steadfast as a tree, which stands rooted in place throughout the seasons. Remain rooted in your Source: God. Let your mind and heart stay focused on God through all the seasons. For it is God who changes the times and seasons.

Some seasons come to test our faith. However, it is important to remain strong and courageous in the Lord. Everyone experiences the four seasons of life. We may not be able to change the seasons overnight, but we can change our attitudes and the direction of our lives. One way to do this is to build up an inner circle of friends you can connect with in both good and challenging times. Jesus had twelve disciples, and his inner circle among them consisted of three: Peter, John, and James. When Jesus was faced with death, He called these men to stand with Him in prayer.

Know that each season will require daily discipline and steady practice. Depending on your choices, you will experience either the pain of discipline or the pain of regret. Both come into the seasons of life and time. Irrespective of the season, God has promised never to leave or abandon us. Instead, He has promised to bless and provide for us.

CHAPTER 14

TIMES OF REFRESHING

We all need to set aside time to be refreshed so that we can continue to grow spiritually and improve our productivity. To *refresh* means to restore, renew, revive, replenish, reinvigorate, breathe a new life into something, kickstart, repair, or become fresh again.

> They longed for me to speak as people long for rain. They drank my words like a refreshing spring rain. (Job 29:23, NLT)

> It *is* a sign between Me and the children of Israel forever; for *in* six days the Lord made the heavens and the earth, and on the seventh day He rested and was refreshed. (Exodus 31:19)

This is an amazing passage. If God can work for six days and on the seventh day rest and be refreshed, how often should we have times of rest and refreshment? God is a great and excellent planner.

Even the Lord Jesus and His disciples took some time to rest. "And He said to them, 'Come aside by yourselves to a deserted place and rest a while.' For there were many coming and going, and they did not even have time to eat" (Mark 6:31).

Resting is as important as working. Working + resting = Great innovation and creativity (Daniel O. Ondieki).

Now it's time to change your ways! Turn to face God so he can wipe away your sins, pour out showers of blessing to refresh you, and send you the Messiah he prepared for you, namely, Jesus. (Acts 3:19, MSG)

Refreshing involves cooling, bracing, strengthening, supporting, reviving, thirst-quenching, or going back to the original.

The following passages show that we need to be refreshed "in every way," "in all things," and "in all ways."

> Abraham was now an old man. GOD had blessed Abraham in *every way*.... The LORD has *greatly blessed* my master, and he has become great (wealthy, powerful); He has given him flocks and herds, and silver and gold, and servants and maids, and camels and donkeys. (Genesis 24:1, 35, MSG).

> Beloved, I pray that you may prosper *in all things* and be in health, just as your soul prospers.
>
> (3 John 1:2)

> The Father loves the Son, and has given *all things* into His hand. (John 3:35)

> Jesus, knowing that the Father had given *all things* into His hands, and that He had come from God and was going to God, rose from supper and laid aside His garments, took a towel and girded Himself. After that, He poured water into a basin and began to wash the disciples' feet, and to wipe them with the towel with which He was girded. (John 13:3)

> Therefore let no one boast in men. For *all things* are yours. (1 Corinthians 3:21)

> And David behaved wisely in *all his ways*, and the Lord *was* with him. (1 Samuel 18:14)

> Every moving thing that lives shall be food for you. I have given you *all things*, even as the green herbs. (Genesis 9:3)

Who does the refreshing? The answer is; God and His Word, by His Holy Spirit, through His Son, Jesus Christ. "Jesus answered and said to them, 'Indeed, Elijah is coming first and will restore all things.'" (Matthew 17:11). God longs to refresh and restore you in all things, in all areas, and in all ways. That is His will for us all.

God refreshed His Son as He began His public ministry:

> When all the people were baptized, it came to pass that Jesus also was baptized; and while He prayed, the heaven was opened. And the Holy Spirit descended in bodily form like a dove upon Him, and a voice came from heaven which said, "You are My beloved Son; in You I am well pleased." (Luke 3:21–22)

The greatest times of refreshing are when you can hear the voice of God and know what He wants you to do. During His water baptism, while Jesus was praying, the heavens were opened for Him. The Holy Spirit of the Lord descended upon Him. God spoke from heaven and assured Him that He was pleased with Him! That was quite refreshing. Jesus received clarity, confirmation, and direction for His ministry.

God refreshed His Son and the disciples:

> Now after six days Jesus took Peter, James, and John his brother, led them up on a high mountain by themselves; and He was transfigured before them. His face shone like the sun, and His clothes became as white as the light. And behold, Moses and Elijah appeared to them, talking with Him. Then Peter answered and said to Jesus, "Lord, it is good for us to be here; if You wish, let us make here three tabernacles: one for You, one for Moses, and one for Elijah."

> While he was still speaking, behold, a bright cloud overshadowed them; and suddenly a voice came out of the cloud, saying, "This is My beloved Son, in whom I am well pleased. Hear Him!" And when the disciples

heard it, they fell on their faces and were greatly afraid. (Matthew 17:1–6)

This was a great visitation from heaven. Moses and Elijah were sent by God to refresh Jesus and His three disciples. Peter did not feel like going down to the valley to join the nine other disciples. Peter said to Jesus, "Lord, it is good for us to be here; if You wish, let us make here three tabernacles: one for You, one for Moses, and one for Elijah." While Peter was speaking, God assured Jesus and His three disciples that He was with them, and He was pleased with His Son asking them to hear Him. This was quite refreshing.

God rejoices over you with gladness and wishes to refresh you. "The LORD your God in your midst, The Mighty One, will save; He will rejoice over you with gladness, He will quiet you with His love, He will rejoice over you with singing" (Zephaniah 3:17).

These passages show how God loves you and rejoices over you. He is for you, not against you. Shake off your sin consciousness, your guilt, your feelings of condemnation, and the accusations of the enemies of your soul. Instead, begin to confidently magnify the Lord, His greatness, and His goodness.

God's children often think that God is against them. Be assured, though, that He is on your side as you acknowledge Him as your Father through the Lord Jesus Christ! Receive His love, forgiveness, peace, and joy in your heart. He fully paid for your total victory, freedom, good health, and wealth. On the cross, Jesus said, "It is finished."

Romans 8:31–32 says, "What then shall we say to these things? If God is for us, who can be against us? He who did not spare His own Son, but delivered Him up for us all, how shall He not with Him also freely give us all things?"

We overcome by taking the right actions. God's Word is a refresher of our hearts and all areas of our lives.

> Your words were found, and I ate them, And Your word was to me the joy and rejoicing of my heart; For I am called by Your name, O Lord God of hosts. (Jeremiah 15:16)

The statutes of the Lord *are* right, rejoicing the heart; The commandment of the Lord *is* pure, enlightening the eyes. (Psalm 19:8)

Your testimonies I have taken as a heritage forever, for they *are* the rejoicing of my heart. (Psalm 119:16)

In God's presence, we can be greatly refreshed.

You will show me the path of life; In Your presence is fullness of joy; At Your right hand are pleasures forevermore. (Psalm 16:11)

You have made known to me the ways of life; You will make me full of joy in Your presence. (Acts 2:28)

The mountains melt like wax at the presence of the Lord, at the presence of the Lord of the whole earth. (Psalm 97:5)

The mountains quake before Him, the hills melt, And the earth heaves at His presence, Yes, the world and all who dwell in it. (Nahum 1:5)

Other Refreshers

Good and healthy foods and drinks can refresh your physical body. Your health is your wealth.

Time and again, it is important to go for full check-ups.

Also, keep all your medical and dental appointments. Do all you can to keep from getting sick. If you're sick, you won't be able to do what your loved ones need. Ask for help when you need it to get away, and take care of your health. Get enough sleep. A good night's rest can refresh and restore your body.

Take care of your business, ministry, career, and profession. Make sure your bills are paid on time. Any delays can give you penalties. Manage your time well, and track it at all times.

Get out once in a while – go somewhere enjoyable to have healthy and good fun.

Attend a class or an event that inspires, motivates, and challenges you to become more to do more.

Think and foster a positive attitude all the time. Take time every day to renew and refresh your mind.

Good seminars and conferences with good speakers and programmes can be refreshing.

Bodily exercise is also important. Take care of your body. It is the only house you have for your spirit and soul to live in.

Good mentors, shepherds, and teachers can inspire, motivate, and refresh you. Good friends and brethren in the Lord can also refresh you.

"Come to Me, all who are weary and heavily burdened [by religious rituals that provide no peace], and I will give you rest [refreshing your souls with salvation]" (Matthew 11:28, AMP). Always hunger and thirst for more of God's righteousness and presence. He has promised to fill your cup until it overflows.

Being in God's presence is crucial. Learn to fellowship and commune with Him. His Word has more than you could ever desire for your life. Meditate on it constantly. God is always ready to refresh you, but you have to be willing to receive it. "For with stammering lips and another tongue He will speak to this people, To whom He said, 'This is the rest with which You may cause the weary to rest,' And, 'This is the refreshing'; Yet they would not hear" (Isaiah 28:11–12). Learn to listen to God's simple instructions in His Word. If you speak in tongues (if you know what that means), speak more and take more time to listen to God and hear what He is saying or showing to you. For more about speaking in tongues, you can read (1 Corinthians 14:1-25).

Jesus speaking with His disciples before He was taken to heaven said,… those who believe will speak with new tongues. (Mark 16:17)

I recommend a little book by Rev. Kenneth Hagan. Why Tongues. The benefits of being filled with the Holy Spirit and speaking with other tongues are discussed in this important mini book.

Let your mind stay on the Lord and not on your circumstances. In doing so, you will experience God's perfect peace.

Isaiah 26:3 says,

> You will keep *him* in perfect peace,
> *Whose* mind *is* stayed *on You,*
> Because he trusts in You.

God will keep you in perfect peace as your mind will stay on Him and not on your circumstances.

Be ready to experience personal times of refreshment every day as you focus your heart and mind on the Lord.

PART III

How to Face Real-Life Challenges

CHAPTER 15

HOW TO END SUFFERING

In the Bible, there is a story of a woman who had a bleeding issue for twelve years. She was determined to bring her suffering to an end—and she did.

> Now a certain woman had a flow of blood for twelve years, and had suffered many things from many physicians. She had spent all that she had and was no better, but rather grew worse. When she heard about Jesus, she came behind *Him* in the crowd and touched His garment. For she said, "If only I may touch His clothes, I shall be made well."
>
> Immediately the fountain of her blood was dried up, and she felt in *her* body that she was healed of the affliction. And Jesus, immediately knowing in Himself that power had gone out of Him, turned around in the crowd and said, 'Who touched My clothes?'
>
> But His disciples said to Him, "You see the multitude thronging You, and You say, 'Who touched Me?'"
>
> And He looked around to see her who had done this thing. But the woman, fearing and trembling, knowing what had happened to her, came and fell down before Him and told Him the whole truth. And He said to her,

"Daughter, your faith has made you well. Go in peace, and be healed of your affliction." (Mark 5:25–34)

Let's take a closer look and see the steps this woman took to get her results.

She said it.

She was determined to deal with the specific bodily issue she was facing. Determination is firmness of purpose. It involves making up your mind and sticking to your decision, regardless of the circumstances.

The woman made up her mind to do whatever was necessary to receive healing. In her desperation to change her painful condition, she said, "Enough is enough." She had tried all human remedies, but none had given her what she needed. She had spent all that she had on doctors and medication. She must have been rich to afford the medical bills. She had heard of Dr. Jesus Christ, the Doctor of doctors, and came to one of His meetings, and this became the turning point of her life. In this meeting, she was determined to touch Jesus with "the touch of faith," unlike many others who were touching Him with a natural touch. You can liken a natural touch to greeting someone with a handshake and feeling good and great.

She did it.

She was strategic about how she was going to touch Jesus. She carefully planned and diligently carried out the touch, even among the thousands of people around Him. She was not casual about it, nor did she make any excuses. She even proposed what she would do when the crowds got in her way.

She received it.

She carefully worked out how she was going to apply her faith, and then she acted. This simple act, mixed with faith, drew healing power from Jesus. As a result, she immediately received her healing. Jesus felt the power flowing out of His body and asked, "Who touched My clothes?" The woman knew she had been healed, as her flow of blood instantly stopped.

She told it.

She told others of her healing. She informed them of everything she had done and how she had been healed. Jesus congratulated her. Why did He openly congratulate her? Because she had keyed into the secret of healing. And He said to her, "Daughter, your faith has made you well. Go in peace, and be healed of your affliction."

We can see how faith and determination played a major role in ending this woman's twelve years of suffering. Her faith was not an emotional decision, which depended on how she felt. It was backed up by patience. She had searched expectantly for twelve years, determined to find a cure. You can bring any negative situation in your life to an end if you dare to apply the same steps and principles. Have faith and be patient. Failure is never an option. Never give up, no matter how long your issue takes to be resolved. Delay does not mean denial. God is never too late. He is never in a hurry. He is always on time. Keep trusting Him, regardless of what you may be going through. That is the determination this woman showed.

> I love what Malachi 3:6–7 (MSG) says: "'I am GOD—yes, I AM. I haven't changed. And because I haven't changed, you, the descendants of Jacob, haven't been destroyed. You have a long history of ignoring my commands. You haven't done a thing I've told you. Return to me so I can return to you,' says GOD-of-the-Angel-Armies."

God is calling you to return to Him, and He will return to you.

According to Hebrews 13:8, Jesus Christ *is* the same yesterday, today, and forever. He is waiting for you.

Notice the four powerful kingdom keys or principles the woman with the bleeding issue applied to receive her breakthrough: She said it, she did it, she received it, and she told it. These fours keys will always work for anyone in any situation, whether positive or negative.

Before he became king, young David used these same principles to kill Goliath. Likewise, the four lepers used these principles to receive provisions for themselves and their entire city during a bad famine (1 Samuel 17:20–51; 2 Kings 7:3–9). In Mark 11:23, Jesus says, "For assuredly, I say to you, whoever says to this mountain, 'Be removed and be cast into the sea,' and does not doubt in his heart, but believes that those things he says will be done, he will have whatever he says."

What we think and say will determine what we do, what we receive, and what we tell others. Your tongue has the power to direct the course of your life. "Death and life are in the power of the tongue, and those who love it will eat its fruit" (Proverbs 18:21).

For healing to take place in your life, you need to carefully guard and watch your words, actions, thoughts, company, heart, and home. These are the gates to your protection or your destruction. Great leadership transformation begins from the inside out.

Whenever you work to renew your mind and act on new decisions, you will experience peace and joy from the Lord. Use your imagination. It is a great gift and asset God has given you. If you can conceive a good idea in your heart and mind, bring it before God and ask Him to bless it. Ask him for wisdom and guidance. You were created to be innovative and creative for the glory and honour of God.

Genesis 11:5–6 says, "But the LORD came down to see the city and the tower which the sons of men had built. And the LORD said, 'Indeed the people *are* one and they all have one language, and this is what they begin to do; now nothing that they propose to do will be withheld from them.'"

The Babylonians wished to build a tower that would touch the heavens. Nothing was going to stop them. They had a clear vision, mission, provision, one language and were united to make it happen. It was only God who could stop them because the tower was not being built according to God's will. A big lesson to learn is that whatever is born of God and of love will last, and whatever is born of lust will not last. In all that you plan to do, seek the Lord's will, wisdom, and guidance.

Some Thoughts to Consider

What issue are you dealing with? How long has it been there? Are you desperate enough for the supernatural power of God's intervention?

If you answered "yes" to the third question, then, like the woman with the bleeding issue, you can bring it to an end as you allow God to lead you and let the Holy Spirit help you.

Remember, if you make up your mind to never give up, you will attract the answer to your prayers.

☸

CHAPTER 16

HOW TO GO THROUGH CRISES WITH GOD

This chapter will discuss a man who chose to invite God to help him during a time of crisis. In this chapter, you will discover not only how to go through a crisis, but also how your response to that crisis will change your life for the better.

Jehoshaphat, whose name means "Yahweh has judged," was the fourth king of Judah under the divided monarchy. We are first introduced to him in 1 Kings 15:24, which says, "So Asa rested with his fathers, and was buried with his fathers in the City of David his father. Then Jehoshaphat his son reigned in his place."

According to 1 Kings 22:42, "Jehoshaphat *was* thirty-five years old when he became king, and he reigned twenty-five years in Jerusalem. His mother's name *was* Azubah the daughter of Shilhi."

Spiritually

Jehoshaphat began his reign well. This is confirmed in 2 Chronicles 17:3–6:

> The Lord was with Jehoshaphat because he followed the ways of his father David before him. He did not consult the Baals but sought the God of his father and followed his commands rather than the practices of Israel. The

Lord established the kingdom under his control; and all Judah brought gifts to Jehoshaphat, so that he had great wealth and honour. His heart was devoted to the ways of the Lord; furthermore, he removed the high places and the Asherah poles from Judah.

Jehoshaphat was a great spiritual and economical transformational leader, and he worked hard with his leadership team.

Economically

His kingdom was prospering, and his citizens were blessed by the Lord. King Jehoshaphat brought the awareness of God and His commandments to his citizens. He taught them knowledge and faith in God.

2 Chronicles 17:9 says, "So they taught in Judah, and *had* the Book of the Law of the LORD with them; they went throughout all the cities of Judah and taught the people."

One way that a nation can rise up economically is by teaching the Word of God, bringing the knowledge and awareness of God into people's everyday lives. Once God is sincerely acknowledged, worshipped, and sought after, His blessings begin to flow in a nation. The best way to grow an economy is to grow its people in every way.

Militarily

Jehoshaphat fortified his defences, primarily against the northern kingdom of Israel, as seen in 2 Chronicles 17:1–3 which says, "Then Jehoshaphat his son reigned in his place, and strengthened himself against Israel. And he placed troops in all the fortified cities of Judah, and set garrisons in the land of Judah and in the cities of Ephraim which Asa his father had taken. Now the LORD was with Jehoshaphat, because he walked in the former ways of his father David; he did not seek the Baals..."

The surrounding nations feared Judah and brought tribute to its king (2 Chronicles 17:10–19).

However, as time went by, King Jehoshaphat and his citizens came under heavy attack by three invading armies: the people of Ammon, Moab, and Mount Seir. This account is given in 2 Chronicles 20:1–30.

I have intentionally chosen this text to help us see how King Jehoshaphat totally depended on the One who was stronger than him, and He indeed helped him through this crisis.

It happened after this *that* the people of Moab with the people of Ammon, and *others* with them besides the Ammonites came to battle against Jehoshaphat. Then some came and told Jehoshaphat, saying, "A great multitude is coming against you from beyond the sea, from Syria; and they are in Hazazon Tamar" (which *is* En Gedi). And Jehoshaphat feared, and set himself to seek the LORD, and proclaimed a fast throughout all Judah. So Judah gathered together to ask *help* from the LORD; and from all the cities of Judah they came to seek the LORD.

> Then Jehoshaphat stood in the assembly of Judah and Jerusalem, in the house of the LORD, before the new court, and said: "O LORD God of our fathers, *are* You not God in heaven, and do You *not* rule over all the kingdoms of the nations, and in Your hand *is there not* power and might, so that no one is able to withstand You? *Are* You not our God, *who* drove out the inhabitants of this land before Your people Israel, and gave it to the descendants of Abraham Your friend forever? And they dwell in it, and have built You a sanctuary in it for Your name, saying, 'If disaster comes upon us—sword, judgment, pestilence, or famine—we will stand before this temple and in Your presence (for Your name *is* in this temple), and cry out to You in our affliction, and You will hear and save.' And now, here are the people of Ammon, Moab, and Mount Seir—whom You would not let Israel invade when they came out of the land of Egypt, but they turned from them and did not destroy them—here they are, rewarding us by coming to throw us out of Your possession which You have given us to inherit. O our God, will You not judge them? For we have no power against this great multitude that is coming against us; nor do we know what to do, but our eyes *are* upon You."

Now all Judah, with their little ones, their wives, and their children, stood before the LORD.

Then the Spirit of the LORD came upon Jahaziel the son of Zechariah, the son of Benaiah, the son of Jeiel, the son of Mattaniah, a Levite of the sons of Asaph, in the midst of the assembly. And he said, "Listen, all you of Judah and you inhabitants of Jerusalem, and you, King Jehoshaphat! Thus says the LORD to you: 'Do not be afraid nor dismayed because of this great multitude, for the battle *is* not yours, but God's. Tomorrow go down against them. They will surely come up by the Ascent of Ziz, and you will find them at the end of the brook before the Wilderness of Jeruel. You will not *need* to fight in this *battle*. Position yourselves, stand still and see the salvation of the LORD, who is with you, O Judah and Jerusalem!' Do not fear or be dismayed; tomorrow go out against them, for the LORD *is* with you."

And Jehoshaphat bowed his head with *his* face to the ground, and all Judah and the inhabitants of Jerusalem bowed before the LORD, worshiping the LORD. Then the Levites of the children of the Kohathites and of the children of the Korahites stood up to praise the LORD God of Israel with voices loud and high.

So they rose early in the morning and went out into the Wilderness of Tekoa; and as they went out, Jehoshaphat stood and said, "Hear me, O Judah and you inhabitants of Jerusalem: Believe in the LORD your God, and you shall be established; believe His prophets, and you shall prosper." And when he had consulted with the people, he appointed those who should sing to the LORD, and who should praise the beauty of holiness, as they went out before the army and were saying:

"Praise the LORD,

For His mercy *endures* forever."

Now when they began to sing and to praise, the LORD set ambushes against the people of Ammon, Moab, and Mount Seir, who had come against Judah; and they were defeated. For the people of Ammon and Moab stood up against the inhabitants of Mount Seir to utterly kill and destroy *them*. And when they had made an end of the inhabitants of Seir, they helped to destroy one another.

So when Judah came to a place overlooking the wilderness, they looked toward the multitude; and there *were* their dead bodies, fallen on the earth. No one had escaped.

When Jehoshaphat and his people came to take away their spoil, they found among them an abundance of valuables on the dead bodies, and precious jewelry, which they stripped off for themselves, more than they could carry away; and they were three days gathering the spoil because there was so much. And on the fourth day they assembled in the Valley of Berachah, for there they blessed the LORD; therefore the name of that place was called The Valley of Berachah until this day. Then they returned, every man of Judah and Jerusalem, with Jehoshaphat in front of them, to go back to Jerusalem with joy, for the LORD had made them rejoice over their enemies. So they came to Jerusalem, with stringed instruments and harps and trumpets, to the house of the LORD. And the fear of God was on all the kingdoms of *those* countries when they heard that the LORD had fought against the enemies of Israel. Then the realm of Jehoshaphat was quiet, for his God gave him rest all around.

This is a classic example of a true testimony in the Old Testament. I never get tired of reading it. I am amazed at King Jehoshaphat's leadership during this time. Let's see how he navigated this crisis and emerged victoriously.

First Reaction

His first reaction to the news was fear. This was a natural reaction, considering the circumstances. However, he did not hide his fears; instead, he went straight to God and told Him exactly how he felt. Fear in its various forms can be overwhelming, as it comes with torment and stops you from doing what you should. King Jehoshaphat feared not only for his own life, but also for the lives of his family and his subjects. Nevertheless, he stayed calm and was able to take the right steps, which eventually paid off.

People naturally panic in a crisis; they make the wrong decisions and end up with results they never wanted. But if we take our fears to God in prayer, we will receive peace and triumph in the end.

I love what is written in Psalm 46:1–4.

It says: God *is* our refuge and strength,

A very present help in trouble.

Therefore we will not fear,

Even though the earth be removed,

And though the mountains be carried into the midst of the sea;

Though its waters roar *and* be troubled,

Though the mountains shake with its swelling. *Selah.*

The word Selah means: "praise, pause"

There is a river whose streams shall make glad the city of God,

The holy *place* of the tabernacle of the Most High.

King Jehoshaphat made his God his refuge and strength in a time of trouble.

Response

King Jehoshaphat fought off his fears and did not allow them to paralyse him. He took authority over the spirit of fear the moment he turned his eyes from his circumstances to God.

He ran to God as his refuge and strength. He knew that he and God were a majority. He leaned on the Lord's side and knew that God never loses battles. He chose to go through this crisis not alone, but with God.

Total and complete dependence on God. That is the secret of winning any crisis in life.

Knowing the right choices to make in times of crisis are key to winning those crises.

King Jehoshaphat chose to magnify the greatness and goodness of the Almighty God. He remembered that his God is a man of war and never loses battles. Exodus 15:3 says, "The LORD *is* a man of war; The LORD *is* His name."

He Reminded God of His Promises

Jehoshaphat knew he served a covenant-keeping God. He chose to trust Him as he prayed God's Word back to Him. This is what he said:

> You are the God of our fathers. You are the God of heaven, and you rule over all the kingdoms of the nations. You have power and might, and there is no one who is able to withstand you. You are our God who drove the inhabitants of Israel and gave it to the descendants of Abraham your friend forever. And they dwell in it and have built You a sanctuary in it for Your name, saying, "If disaster comes upon us—sword, judgment, pestilence, or famine—we will stand before this temple and in Your presence (for Your name *is* in this temple), and cry out to You in our affliction, and You will hear and save." And now, here are the people of Ammon, Moab, and Mount Seir—whom You would not let Israel invade when they came out of the land of Egypt, but they turned from them and did not destroy them—here they are, rewarding us by coming to throw us out of Your possession which You have given us to inherit. O our God, will You not judge them? For we have no power against this great multitude that is coming against us; nor do we know what to do, but our eyes *are* upon You.

I admire the way King Jehoshaphat prayed. He prayed the Word back to God, reminding Him of His promises. Jehoshaphat acknowledged God's might, power, and salvation. He declared that there was no one who could withstand Him. He reminded the Lord that he and his citizens had a covenant with Him because they were descendants of Abraham, God's friend forever. Jehoshaphat confessed to the Lord that both he and his citizens were powerless against the great multitudes that were coming against them. Indeed, without God, they were helpless. Here we see Jehoshaphat's great humility and unity with God and His word. Although he was a king, he showed total dependence on the Lord God Almighty. Humility touches the heart of God.

What results do we see from what Jehoshaphat and the citizen do?

> Now when they began to sing and to praise, the LORD set ambushes against the people of Ammon, Moab, and Mount Seir, who had come against Judah; and they were defeated. For the people of Ammon and Moab stood up against the inhabitants of Mount Seir to utterly kill and destroy *them*. And when they had made an end of the inhabitants of Seir, they helped to destroy one another. So when Judah came to a place overlooking the wilderness, they looked toward the multitude; and there were their dead bodies, fallen on the earth.

> No one had escaped. When Jehoshaphat and his people came to take away their spoil, they found among them an abundance of valuables on the dead bodies, and precious jewellery, which they stripped off for themselves, more than they could carry away; and they were three days gathering the spoil because there was so much. And on the fourth day they assembled in the Valley of Berachah, for there they blessed the Lord; therefore the name of that place was called The Valley of Berachah until this day. Then they returned, every man of Judah and Jerusalem, with Jehoshaphat in front of them, to go back to Jerusalem with joy, for the Lord had made them rejoice over their enemies. So they came to Jerusalem, with stringed

instruments and harps and trumpets, to the house of the Lord. And the fear of God was on all the kingdoms of those countries when they heard that the Lord had fought against the enemies of Israel.

Verse 31 says, "Then the realm of Jehoshaphat was quiet, for his God gave him rest all around."

Here we see the effects of thanksgiving, praise, and worship as spiritual weapons to use to defeat the enemy. Notice that when the praises went up, God came down in His glory and ambushed Jehoshaphat's enemies. Instead of the enemies attacking King Jehoshaphat and his citizens, they began to attack each other, and they continued doing so until the last man killed himself. God had said that He was going to fight for them. He gave them these instructions: "You will not *need* to fight in this *battle*. Position yourselves, stand still and see the salvation of the LORD, who is with you, O Judah and Jerusalem! Do not fear or be dismayed; tomorrow go out against them, for the LORD *is* with you." (2 Chronicles 20:17)

Jehoshaphat teaches us that when we find ourselves in a crisis, we should position ourselves, believe in God, and trust the Word from His prophets. Positioning oneself means to be focused on the priorities of the crisis. Do what needs to be done first, and trust God to establish you. This brings tremendous inner peace, and you can rest as God stills your heart and mind right in the middle of the storm.

Second, believe in God's prophets, for this brings prosperity. God will always send you the right person to help you during a crisis or crises. That person could be a man or a woman, and it will be someone who has God's heart to guide and help you in both good and difficult times.

Jeremiah 3:15 says, "And I will give you shepherds according to My heart, who will feed you with knowledge and understanding." If you have a shepherd or a spiritual leader, be grateful and pray for them. Give them your support, honour, and respect. Most importantly, you have the greatest Helper, the Holy Spirit, who will guide you into all truth and victory. Learn to develop a closer relationship with Him.

What We Learn from This Account

A crisis can come at any time. If you are not spiritually equipped, you will not be strong enough to overcome it. Try to understand what your priority is, and face it prayerfully. Whatever instructions you receive after praying, obey them fully, no matter how simple or complex they may seem. They will bring you both protection and great rewards. Identify the crisis, and discover its cause. Remember, your crisis is first spiritual. You will need to fight the good fight of faith by courageously confronting all your fears. Be responsible, and take each step as it comes. Always remember that you are not alone.

Always focus on Christ, your Deliverer, and not the crisis. The crisis comes to test your leadership foundation and the structure of what you have built. In a time of crisis, your mind can function at its best, producing innovation and creativity. A crisis can serve as a game-changer and present you with great opportunities. Time can be your greatest friend or your greatest enemy during this period. Manage it well, do what you need to do when you need to do it, and don't get distracted. Your life is valuable, so treasure it. One day, it will expire. Plan ahead, and begin to carry out the necessary steps today. Every crisis comes with lessons to be learnt. How we respond to crises will determine whether we come out with great gains, like Jehoshaphat, or with great losses, like Jehoshaphat's enemies. The choice is yours. Choose your steps carefully, wisely, and timely.

The Second Crisis: How to Go through a Crisis and Recover All

In this crisis, we see King David, his family, and his army and their families attacked by the enemy and taken captive. Returning from the war, they find their city burned—totally destroyed. How did they go through this crisis?

> Now it happened, when David and his men came to Ziklag, on the third day, that the Amalekites had invaded the South and Ziklag, attacked Ziklag and burned it with fire, and had taken captive the women and those who were there, from small to great; they did not kill anyone,

but carried them away and went their way. So David and his men came to the city, and there it was, burned with fire; and their wives, their sons, and their daughters had been taken captive. Then David and the people who were with him lifted up their voices and wept, until they had no more power to weep. And David's two wives, Ahinoam the Jezreelitess, and Abigail the widow of Nabal the Carmelite, had been taken captive. Now David was greatly distressed, for the people spoke of stoning him, because the soul of all the people was grieved, every man for his sons and his daughters. But David strengthened himself in the LORD his God. Then David said to Abiathar the priest, Ahimelech's son, "Please bring the ephod here to me." And Abiathar brought the ephod to David. So David inquired of the LORD, saying, "Shall I pursue this troop? Shall I overtake them?" And He answered him, "Pursue, for you shall surely overtake them and without fail recover all."

So David went, he and the six hundred men who were with him, and came to the Brook Besor, where those stayed who were left behind. But David pursued, he and four hundred men; for two hundred stayed behind, who were so weary that they could not cross the Brook Besor.

Then they found an Egyptian in the field and brought him to David; and they gave him bread and he ate, and they let him drink water. And they gave him a piece of a cake of figs and two clusters of raisins. So when he had eaten, his strength came back to him; for he had eaten no bread nor drunk water for three days and three nights. Then David said to him, "To whom do you belong, and where are you from?"

And he said, "I am a young man from Egypt, servant of an Amalekite; and my master left me behind, because three days ago I fell sick. We made an invasion of the southern area of the Cherethites, in the territory which belongs to Judah, and of the southern area of Caleb; and we burned Ziklag with fire."

And David said to him, "Can you take me down to this troop?"

So he said, "Swear to me by God that you will neither kill me nor deliver me into the hands of my master, and I will take you down to this troop."

And when he had brought him down, there they were, spread out over all the land, eating and drinking and dancing, because of all the great spoil which they had taken from the land of the Philistines and from the land of Judah. Then David attacked them from twilight until the evening of the next day. Not a man of them escaped, except four hundred young men who rode on camels and fled. So David recovered all that the Amalekites had carried away, and David rescued his two wives. And nothing of theirs was lacking, either small or great, sons or daughters, spoil or anything which they had taken from them; David recovered all. (1 Samuel 30:1–19)

Let us see what King David and the team of six hundred men did, and let us learn from them.

- David strengthened himself in the Lord his God.
- He inquired of the Lord, saying, "Shall I pursue this troop? Shall I overtake them?"
- He asked the right questions. It is also important to ask the right person. For David, he chose to ask God the right questions. God gave him the right answers, showing him what to do and how to do it: "Pursue, for you shall surely overtake them and without fail recover all."

How will you go through your own crisis?

- Weep or cry out if you have to until you cannot cry anymore.
- It is good to cry out sometimes to release your emotions, but do so with self-control if you can. I remember an occasion many years ago when I cried without self-control. When I looked at myself in the mirror, my eyes were swollen, and by the end, I had a headache.

On one occasion, I sought the Lord with all my heart and with many tears but also a lot of self-control. The result was amazing, refreshing, and unspeakable joy. As I sought the Lord with hunger, thirst, and tears, He heard my cry and answered me. Those memories are as fresh as if they were yesterday. It was my turning point and the start of my spiritual walk and work with the Lord. Our journey with the Lord can be inspiring, motivating, and strengthening even when we feel weak and tired sometimes. He is the strength of our lives. He always assures us of His constant abiding presence, which give us unspeakable gladness. His presence is His present to us. "You have made known to me the paths of life; you will fill me with joy in your presence" (Acts 2:28).

Here are some health benefits of crying:

- Dulls pain
- Detoxifies the body
- Improves mood
- Rallies support
- Helps you recover from grief
- Restores emotional balance
- Helps babies breathe

Medically reviewed by Timothy J. Legg, PhD CRNP – Written by Ashley Marcin and updated on 14 April 2017.

Psalm 77:1 says, "I cried out to God with my voice—
To God with my voice; And He gave ear to me."

Romans 8:15 says, "For you did not receive the spirit of bondage again to fear, but you received the Spirit of adoption by whom we **cry out**, 'Abba, Father.'" Do not hesitate to cry out to your Heavenly Father whenever you are caught up in situations which you have no solutions to. He will hear your cry. There are times I cry out to God, and in the end, I really feel refreshed and blessed in His presence.

Here are some spiritual benefits of crying out:

> And the LORD said: "I have surely seen the oppression of My people who *are* in Egypt, and have heard their cry because of their taskmasters, for I know their sorrows. So I have come down to deliver them out of the hand of the Egyptians, and to bring them up from that land to a good and large land, to a land flowing with milk and honey, to the place of the Canaanites and the Hittites and the Amorites and the Perizzites and the Hivites and the Jebusites. Now therefore, behold, the cry of the children of Israel has come to Me, and I have also seen the oppression with which the Egyptians oppress them. Come now, therefore, and I will send you to Pharaoh that you may bring My people, the children of Israel, out of Egypt."
>
> (Exodus 3:7–9)

The spiritual benefits:

- You get attention from God. I have heard the cry of my people because of their task masters.
- Tears bring God down to our level to help us in our helplessness and hopelessness.
- Freedom from the house of bondage. I have seen the afflictions and sorrows of my people.
- Freedom from all our fears, worries, and discouragements.
- God gets to know our sorrows and afflictions and does something about it.
- Through our tears, God sends the right people to help us. He sent Moses and Aaron to the children of Israel to deliver them from the house of their task masters.

Ask God to send you the right people to help you in your crises.
- God can bring us to good land flowing with milk and honey through our tears. He brings us into the centre of His will and his original plans and purposes.

For His anger *is but for* a moment, His favor *is for* life; weeping may endure for a night, but joy *comes* in the morning. He can restore us to have great joy.

However, I have to say that it is not enough to cry out to God while you do nothing on your end. Your tears should be accompanied with the right decisions and actions.

What else can you do in your crises?

- Wipe your tears away, take enough time to rest, and encourage yourself in the Lord your God! David encouraged himself in the Lord, made the right decisions, took the right actions, and recovered all that he had lost.
- Drink enough water after you have shed many tears. Eat healthy foods for physical restoration and strength.
- Seek out someone spiritually mature or a professional person for support and the wisdom to offer advice.

David connected with a high priest by the name of Abiathar, who was able to support him in his time of crisis. Jesus made a reference of this connection in Mark 2:25–26:

> But He said to them, "Have you never read what David did when he was in need and hungry, he and those with him: how he went into the house of God in the days of Abiathar the high priest, and ate the showbread, which is not lawful to eat except for the priests, and also gave some to those who were with him?"

Surround yourself with mature leaders to consult not only when you are going through a crisis, but also in good times and times of decision-making.

> Where there is no counsel, the people fall; But in the multitude of counsellors there is safety. (Proverbs 11:14)

> For by wise counsel, you will wage your own war, And in a multitude of counsellors *there is* safety. (Proverbs 24:6)

Seek out wise counsel who have expertise and experience. Inquire of the Lord by asking the right questions. Recognize your enemies, and pursue them wisely and diligently.

Remember that your fight is not of flesh and blood, but of unseen forces of darkness in the spiritual and mental realms. The one fight you are called to fight is the good fight of faith, not the fight of fear, worry, and anxiety.

The Apostle Paul says in 1 Timothy 6:12: "Fight the good fight of faith, lay hold on eternal life, to which you were also called and have confessed the good confession in the presence of many witnesses."

The recommended scripture readings that we do not fight against flesh and blood is Ephesians 6:10–17. Knowing, understanding how to operate in the spiritual, mental and physical ream will help you to live a victorious and a fulfilled life.

Important Questions to Ask Yourself

Who is your enemy? For David, it was the Amalekites. Who are the Amalekites in your life and your family's life? Maybe ignorance or the lies of the enemy are your enemies. Discover the truth.

David recovered all that the Amalekites had taken. What have your Amalekites taken from you? Perhaps they have taken your health, good relationships, finances, peace, joy, or hope. Find out.

What steps are you willing to take to overtake your Amalekites? Rise up from the inside out, and take stock of your life. Ask the Holy Spirit to show you and help you. "Call to Me, and I will answer you, and show you great and mighty things, which you do not know" (Jeremiah 33:3).

How do you pursue and overtake your enemies? You do so through study, knowledge, understanding, wisdom, faith, God's guidance, and with the help of the Holy Spirit of the Lord. "This also comes from the

Lord of hosts, Who is wonderful in counsel and excellent in guidance" (Isaiah 28:29). The Lord of hosts is able to speak to you, counsel you, and give you excellent guidance.

No matter what you are going through, know that you are not alone. The Lord has promised never to leave you alone nor forsake you. Whatever the enemy meant for evil, God will turn it for your good.

Fight the good fight of faith. Many times, believers fight a bad fight of fear. "For God has not given us a spirit of fear, but of power and of love and of a sound mind" (2 Timothy 1:7). What has God given you? Power, love, and a sound mind. He has not given you a spirit of fear.

How do you overcome fear? You overcome by acknowledging God's love in your heart and by feeding your faith with the Word of God. Take quality time to offer thanksgiving, praises, and worship unto the Lord. These are strong spiritual weapons to use against your enemies.

Strengthen yourself in Him, and inquire of Him. Take strategic steps as led by the Holy Spirit, and trust the Lord to give you total restoration. Never give up. Victory is yours. May the Lord richly bless you! You are destined for greatness, and you are a transformational leader!

※

CHAPTER 17

A MOTHER'S INFLUENCE AT HOME AND IN THE FAMILY

Mothers play a significant role in families, communities, cities, and nations. Without the influence of good mothers, we could not achieve much in life. We need to recognize the importance of mothers and to honour and appreciate them.

When God wanted to bring life to the earth, He thought of a woman, Eve. In Hebrew, the name Eve means "source of life"; it also means "mother of all who have life." Eve was created from Adam's rib. She was named by Adam in Genesis 3:20. She is the only woman in history who never experienced childhood. She was supernaturally created by God.

Satan knew how powerful and influential this woman would be. When he wanted to bring deception into the world, he devised a plan to plant his evil nature into Eve. He knew that once she was influenced, he could influence the entire world.

However, God had a master plan to reintroduce truth into the world. He used a woman called Mary to achieve this. She became the mother of Jesus Christ. Women, never forget that you are great influencers, whether for good or evil. Choose the former.

Without a woman, God's agenda for humanity could not have been accomplished here on earth. Women need to know how precious they are to the heart of God and learn how to be strong in the midst of all that they go through in life.

I would like to acknowledge and salute every woman, mother, and girl around the world. I give God the glory for my amazing and beloved mother, who is now in heaven. One of the greatest things she taught me was how to pray to God on my knees. She also taught me how to be kind to people. She was the kindest woman I've ever known. She led her children by example. I thank God constantly for the great work my sweet mother did. She was always there whenever we needed her. She did the very best she could, all the way to her last breath. We are all proud of her—and, more importantly, very grateful to the Lord for her life.

My beloved wife, Edith, has also played a major role in my life. The Lord introduced me to this amazing woman many years ago. She is a gift from God. She possesses many positive attributes. She is focused, determined, trustworthy, purpose-driven, disciplined, loving, kind, joyful, and beautiful to behold. Without her support, I could never have achieved what I have or reached where I am today. I am forever grateful to the Lord for her life.

Mothers, you are indeed great. It is time to realize, more than ever, how important you are and the potential you have to influence many lives. Everything you dream of you can achieve. That is the gift that God has graced you with.

Philemon 1:6 says to acknowledge "every good thing which is in you in Christ Jesus."

John 16:33 says, "But be of good cheer." Know that, no matter what you go through, you will make it in life.

> And Adam called his wife's name Eve, because she was the mother of all living. (Genesis 3:20, MSG)

> And they blessed Rebekah and said to her: "Our sister, *may* you *become The mother of* thousands of ten thousands; And may your descendants possess; The gates of those who hate them." (Genesis 24:60)

> Honor your father and your mother, that your days may be long upon the land which the Lord your God is giving you. (Exodus 20:12)

> Children, obey your parents in the Lord, for this is right. "Honour your father and mother," which is the first commandment with promise. (Ephesians 6:1–2)

Mothers Are Great Givers

The womb is the first gift a mother gives to her child. It is a source of nourishment and a place of comfort and security. She cocoons her child in safety as her pregnancy is carried to term. It has been documented that even if a woman is unwell during her pregnancy or finds it difficult to eat, her unborn child remains nourished in her womb and is typically born healthy. The unique nature of the womb provides everything the unborn child needs to grow.

Children should be thankful for the first home their mothers provide. If you have never taken the time to thank God for your mother, this is your chance to do so. Even in the natural world, accommodation is expensive. Mothers provide food and transport for their babies while in the womb. From the day the child is born, the mother continues to provide nourishment, comfort, and care.

The greatest gift a mother can give to her child is love. This love is not based on anything the child has done, but it is given simply because the child exists. This is God's kind of love. Through this love, the child receives confidence and assurance. This type of love moulds the child for greatness.

A wise mother speaks life and blessings to her child, even while in the womb. The child not only recognizes her voice, but also responds to her tone.

Mothers can influence their children for good or for evil. Just as the womb shapes and forms the child, wise mothers continue that process after birth, shaping their children by speaking words of life, love, and blessing. Mothers have the unique ability to provide their children with their initial outlook on life. How mothers respond to life will greatly influence how their children see life. Mothers can choose to be good teachers or bad ones.

Proverbs 22:6 says, "Train up a child in the way he should go, and when he is old he will not depart from it." There is a Kiswahili saying which says, *"Asiye funzwa na mamaye hufunzwa na ulimwengu."* It is translated as "He who is not taught by his mother is taught by the world."

Mothers are their children's first teachers and are anointed to mentor and train them lovingly, wisely, and respectfully. As such, mothers are their children's first language teachers. This is where the phrase "mother tongue" comes from. That's why the first word a child speaks is often "Mama" and not "Papa." Most children have close bonds with their mothers.

Scripture tells us that every child is a gift from the Lord, on loan to us for a season. Mothers are tasked to raise children to be a blessing to their generation. Each child is likened to a gift wrapped in paper. Even though the child is given to both parents, God entrusts mothers to unwrap that package skilfully and carefully and present it to the world. You may be raising a president or prime minister without realizing it. Give the very best to that son or daughter. Time will soon reveal the rewards of your labour.

Fathers also play a key role in providing discipline and guidance to their children. "And you, fathers, do not provoke your children to wrath, but bring them up in the training and admonition of the Lord" (Ephesians 6:4). Fathers and mothers are both responsible for raising their children together lovingly and wisely.

What Makes a Great Mother

Women can learn skills and master certain habits to turn them from inexperienced mothers into extraordinary ones. The most important lesson is to develop a personal relationship with God through Jesus Christ. This is cultivated through times of prayer, meditation, and reading the Word of God. Acts 6:4 emphasizes the importance of giving oneself continually to the Word and to prayer. If this is lacking, a mother will fail to realize her full potential as well as the spiritual resources she has been given to fulfil her godly calling.

Healthy Bodies, Relationships, and Finances

It is important for every mother to be healthy, both physically and mentally. Carrying a pregnancy to term, going through childbirth, and nourishing a newborn baby are physically and emotionally draining tasks. Mothers need to take good care of their health and mental well-being both before and after pregnancy. They may also need to take care of other children during this time. As such, a healthy body and mind supported by a nutritious diet is essential in this stage of her life.

A mother's inner circle of friends will shape and determine how she develops. Proverbs 27:17 says, *"As* iron sharpens iron, so a man sharpens the countenance of his friend."

The word *sharpen* refers to questioning, encouraging, coaching, and challenging. These relationships can get a mother through challenging times, provide a sense of well-being, and make her the best parent she can possibly be.

A constant source of income helps to provide for the needs of the family as she raises her children. This reduces stress and helps maintain harmony in the home.

A strong, spiritual, and godly husband is also important. Ecclesiastes 4:9–12 says that two are better than one because they have a better reward for their labour. If either of them falls down, the other can help them up. If you are down, your partner can support you. Additionally, each partner brings strengths to the relationship. This allows the child to be raised in a balanced environment.

The attributes of the virtuous woman described in Proverbs 31 are admirable and help to provide a strong spiritual foundation. This woman's heart, her home, and the works of her hands were undeniably influenced by her fear and reverence of the Lord. This is important for each woman, as it will help her to understand who she is in Christ and what she has been called to do. She will then be able to receive a clear vision of her mission and purpose for her family.

In Proverbs 31, the woman is always ready to gain knowledge in the skills required to run her home effectively. She is well-balanced and looks for ways to improve and provide for the physical, spiritual, and emotional well-being of her family. Possessing these qualities helps her use her resources wisely.

The Support of Her Husband and Children

A wife's husband and children can motivate her to excel at home by responding positively to her homemaking skills. The children of the virtuous woman rise up and call her blessed. This is one of the greatest rewards of motherhood.

Spiritual Leadership

To help mothers mature in their role, they must be part of a good local community under strong spiritual leadership. Activities such as hearing the Word of God, fellowshipping, and praying are all essential to a mother's spiritual growth and well-being.

The Challenges of Being a Mother

Some problems, such as lacking love, respect, or emotional support from her husband and children, can keep a woman from reaching her full potential and fulfilling her destiny. She may also lack protection from her mother-in-law or other relatives. Furthermore, illiteracy and a lack of financial support can greatly limit her potential.

Poor Mother/Child Relationships

When a mother abandons her children, the children will often grow up and do the same. This cycle is repeated in many cultures and nations.

Other unrighteous traditions keep women in bondage. The worst thing a father can do is abuse or disrespect his child's mum. Those fathers need help. Both physical and sexual abuses by a husband introduces violence in the home. Women are often are afraid to speak out. Some are not allowed to speak out. If they do, they may be beaten to death. Women also often experience loneliness as a result of emotional abuse, mistreatment and other painful experiences. These are just a few of the challenges that can keep them from realizing their potential.

A Word of Advice to Children

If you have a good relationship with your mother, be grateful and thank the Lord. Some mothers received great love from their own mothers; thus, they are in a good position to pass it along.

However, others were not well-mothered and instead are poorly equipped to raise their own children. You cannot give to others what you do not have yourself. Therefore, if you did not receive love from your mother, a good spiritual mother may compensate for that. Most importantly, the Holy Spirit is capable of helping you and raising you up.

It is important to understand that mothers are not perfect. They do make mistakes. No matter what your mother has done to you, remember that she is still your mother. You only have one mother. Choose to forgive her, bless her, and move on, remembering that how you treat your mother will likely determine how your children treat you.

It is important that you guard your heart with all diligence. Do not be bitter against your mother; rather, be better. Proverbs 4:23 (MSG) says, "Keep vigilant, watch over your heart; that is the place of your influence and where all life starts."

Some daughters change their behaviour when they realize that what they have done to their mothers will someday be done to them by their own children.

> Therefore, you have no excuse or justification, every one of you who [hypocritically] judges and condemns others; for in passing judgment on another person, you condemn yourself, because you who judge [from a position of arrogance or self-righteousness] are habitually practicing the very same things [which you denounce]. (Romans 2:1, AMP)

I have been a counsellor for more than sixteen years. I have learned that those daughters who say they never want to be like their mother end up being just like them, simply because by judging others, they allow that same judgement to come upon themselves.

You can be set free by denouncing what you have said. Ask the Lord to forgive you. Reach out to your mother if she is still alive. Bless her, and trust God to restore your relationship. If she is no longer alive, ask for her forgiveness for all the things you said anyway. Then forgive her for anything she did to you. This simple act will release grace and power in your heart.

What Does God Say about Mothers Today?

> Then Jesus said, "Come to me, all of you who are weary and carry heavy burdens, and I will give you rest. The Lord is more than enough for you and for your family." (Matthew 11:28–30)

Accept the invitation and go to Him for inner rest, healing, and restoration.

According to Philippians 4:19, "And my God shall supply all your need according to His riches in glory by Christ Jesus." Make God your ultimate Source, and make use of the many resources He has given you.

Psalm 23:1–6 says, "The LORD *is* my shepherd;

I shall not want. He makes me to lie down in green pastures;

He leads me beside the still waters. He restores my soul; He leads me in the paths of righteousness For His name's sake. Yea, though I walk through the valley of the shadow of death, I will fear no evil; For You *are* with me; Your rod and Your staff, they comfort me. You prepare a table before me in the presence of my enemies; You anoint my head with oil;

My cup runs over. Surely goodness and mercy shall follow me

All the days of my life; And I will dwell in the house of the LORD Forever."

Proverbs 3:5–6 says, "Put your total trust in Me, and depend completely on Me. Trust in the Lord with all your heart, And lean not on your own understanding; In all your ways acknowledge Him, And He shall direct your paths."

Call upon My name, and I will answer you. "Call to Me, and I will answer you, and show you great and mighty things, which you do not know" (Jeremiah 33:3).

Joel 2:25–27 says, "So I will restore to you the years that the swarming locust has eaten, The crawling locust, The consuming locust, And the chewing locust, My great army which I sent among you. You shall eat in plenty and be satisfied, and praise the name of the LORD your God, who has dealt wondrously with you; And My people shall never be put to shame. Then you shall know that I am in the midst of Israel: I am the LORD your God And there is no other. My people shall never be put to shame."

Conclusion

All women young and old you are loved, accepted, and celebrated by the One who created you: the Almighty God. You must therefore celebrate yourself. Celebrate your uniqueness, your talents, and your gifts. Know that you are your first and best friend. You cannot give what you do not have. Love and accept yourself, receive the love of God, and give it away joyfully. Do not hate or reject yourself as some have done out of immaturity, ignorance, or a lack of guidance. Love yourself unconditionally, accept yourself joyfully, and acknowledge that while there are things you cannot change, you can change your attitude and your quality of thinking. As a result, your circumstances will begin to change.

> For the Lord your God has arrived to live among you. He is a mighty Saviour. He will give you victory. He will rejoice over you with great gladness; he will love you and not accuse you.' Is that a joyous choir I hear? No, it is the Lord himself exulting over you in happy song. I have gathered your wounded and taken away your reproach. (Zephaniah 3:17–18, TLB)

A Short Message to All Men

To all men, young and old: Wherever you are on Earth, I salute you! You are amazing, powerful, dynamic, and exceptional leaders – one of a kind! When God wanted to begin the work here on the earth, He thought of a man first. Then He put his wife and children in him. From my deep studies of men and my many years of counselling and coaching, I have learned that a man will never fully know himself until he studies the first man God created before the fall: Adam.

Here is a brief profile of Adam: He was supernaturally created out of the earth. It is not written how old he was when God created him. I can only guess maybe 30 years old. He lived to be 930. He was never a child or a teenager. He did not have earthly parents. He did not have siblings or relatives. He had a rich heritage given to him by his Creator, the Lord God Almighty. He was upright and handsome!

God was Adam's Father, and He loved him dearly. In Adam were seeds of life. In him were his wife Eve, his children, and the rest of the human race. Let us not forget that God created Adam on the sixth day. On the seventh day, Adam spent quality time with God. They needed to know each other. God had to reveal and unfold His plans, purposes, and priorities to Adam. Adam was ushered into a very beautifully designed home that had been prepared for him. These are lessons to learn as men: God plans and prepares ahead of time!

God entrusted Adam with managing the entire earth, with all its riches and resources. Adam was given the top office, chosen and appointed by his Creator. We could say he was the founder and CEO of the earth. We can surely say he was an excellent, exceptional, and transformational leader. He was destined for greatness, and he lacked nothing. God had equipped him in every way, and Adam had what it took to make his way prosperous and achieve good success.

Adam was incorruptible and practiced timeless principles. He was the seed that God had created: upright, just, and righteous. He knew his purpose, priorities, vision, and mission in life. He operated on a higher level of revelation knowledge, understanding, and wisdom. His greatest secret weapon for winning was total dependence on the Lord God, his Creator.

What Adam needed was within him. His darling wife Eve was taken out of him. He had carried her over all the years he was single. Likewise, what you are looking for is within you. It is waiting for you. The solutions you are looking for could be in the problems you are challenged with.

Adam knew the principles of life, and he applied them on a daily basis. That is why he was successful and prosperous before the fall.

Adam had a very good start, and he continued very well. But he did not finish well. Beginning, continuing, and finishing well is the secret to being a transformational leader. I will analyse Adam's end in my next book, *Born to Lead*.

> The greatest enemy of man is ignorance of self. Nothing is more frustrating than not knowing who you are or what to do with what you have. It is debilitating to have something but not know what it is for or how to use it. Even more frustrating is to have an assignment but not know how to fill it.

This statement is made by Dr. Myles Munroe in his book *The Fatherhood Principle*. I recommend it to every man to read.

Hunger and thirst to know your Source, the Creator of your life. Know who you are. Chapter 2 in this book talks about knowing yourself. Know your purpose, priorities, vision, and mission in life. Take full responsibility for yourself and your family, profession, business, and ministry.

You are loaded with potential to make a difference in our world! When you support and honour your wife, there is a promise from God for you. Your prayers will be answered. You will walk and work continually under open heavens. Your wife is a precious gift from God to you. Your gift back to God is to love, honour, and respect her. Treat her like a princess, and watch the blessings begin to flow like rivers into your profession, business, ministry, and everything else you do!

Remember this: When things went wrong in the garden, the home of Adam and Eve, God did not ask Eve, "Where are you?" No. He asked Adam. When things go wrong in your home, God will ask you, "My son so-and-so, where are you?" Men, while we have the opportunity, let us rise up and shine for the glory and honour of our Creator, God Almighty!

I leave you with some great words from Dr. Myles Munroe:

> One of the greatest tragedies in life is to watch potential die untapped
> (Myles Munroe [2011]), "Purpose for Living." p. 16, Destiny Image Publishers).

> Our life is the sum total of all the decisions we make every day, and those decisions are determined by our priorities. (Brainy Quotes)

> The greatness of a man is measured by the way he treats the little man. Compassion for the weak is a sign of greatness. (Brainy Quotes)

Men, see the greatness that is in both yourselves and others, and remember that God longs to use you in a big way.

CHAPTER 18

FROM NOTHING TO SOMETHING

In this chapter, we talk about a woman who went from nothing to something—from lack to abundance, from very little to more than enough. A great lesson to learn from this chapter is "do not despise the little things" that you could be having in your house or in your life. The little oil which seemed to this widow as nothing was used to solve her major financial problem and relationship situation.

> A certain woman of the wives of the sons of the prophets cried out to Elisha, saying, "Your servant my husband is dead, and you know that your servant feared the LORD. And the creditor is coming to take my two sons to be his slaves."
>
> So Elisha said to her, "What shall I do for you? Tell me, what do you have in the house?" And she said, "Your maidservant has nothing in the house but a jar of oil."
>
> Then he said, "Go, borrow vessels from everywhere, from all your neighbors—empty vessels; do not gather just a few. And when you have come in, you shall shut the door behind you and your sons; then pour it into all those vessels, and set aside the full ones."

So she went from him and shut the door behind her and her sons, who brought *the vessels* to her; and she poured *it* out. Now it came to pass, when the vessels were full, that she said to her son, "Bring me another vessel."

And he said to her, "*There is* not another vessel." So the oil ceased. Then she came and told the man of God. And he said, "Go, sell the oil and pay your debt; and you *and* your sons live on the rest." (2 Kings 4:1–7)

What We Learn from This Text

Looking at this from the spiritual side, the woman was the wife of a prophet who had died and left her in debt. Although the family feared and were devoted to God, they were in financial bondage and unable to redeem themselves.

Looking at this from the business side, the creditor was a businessman who had lent money to the prophet and now wanted it back. He was not interested in the widow's plight but threatened to sell her two sons to redeem his debt. That is the harsh reality of life.

What does one do when faced with debt and death in their family? The creditors are writing, calling, and threatening to repossess the car, the business is not doing well, the house bills are not yet paid, and there are many other things that need your attention.

Proverbs 22:7 says, "The rich rules over the poor, And the borrower *is* servant to the lender."

This can be a painful, heart-breaking experience. The woman in the story had it all. In times like this, one can easily make wrong decisions and thus deepen the problem or crisis. What did she do?

She chose to turn to God and the prophet Elisha who solved her problem by asking two great questions: "How can I help you?" and "What do you have in your house?"

Surprisingly, the woman could not see the source of wealth within a single jar of oil. The prophet helped her to see what she had missed seeing.

Many look around and see nothing. Very few look up and see

something. Elisha saw plenty of oil. The widow saw nothing but very little oil. The little amount of oil was used to clear the woman's debt and sustain her throughout the famine. When God begins to help you, He does so completely. "He who calls you *is* faithful, who also will do *it*" (1 Thessalonians 5:24).

As the prophet spoke, the widow listened carefully to his instructions and learned how to generate wealth and pay back her debts. She eventually experienced the supernatural intervention of God.

We often downplay our gifts or see them as insignificant, but God uses them to solve our problems. Could you be overlooking your gift? Let the Lord bless and multiply that little thing He has given to you. Never despise the little things in your life. God often uses them to be a tremendous blessing to you and others.

Always seek God's clarity of direction when life gets difficult. The Holy Spirit has been given to you to lead you out of depressing situations similar to the widow's. He will show you what to do and who to speak to.

For as many as are led by the Spirit of God, these are sons of God. (Romans 8:14)

I will instruct you and teach you in the way you should go; I will guide you with My eye. (Psalm 32:8)

Despite the challenges of life, never give up. A challenge indicates that it is your turn to receive a miracle. God's instructions are simple, so follow them. If you do not heed His first instruction, don't expect Him to give you a second one.

Know that our God is the God of miracles. He can solve all spiritual, personal, family, ministry, business, and other problems you might be faced with. What He did for the widow and her two sons He can do for you, too. He never changes.

"For I am the LORD, I do not change; Therefore, you are not consumed, O sons of Jacob" (Malachi 3:6).

For Jesus doesn't change, yesterday, today, tomorrow, he's always totally himself." (Hebrews 13:8, MSG)

Do not give up in whatever you have been trusting the Lord for. In whatever circumstances you find yourself in, know that God's timing is the best. He makes all things beautiful in His time. He will perfect all that concerns you. He loves and values you greatly.

God is never in a hurry, He is never too late. He is always right on time.

Dr. John Maxwell, in his commentary on page 454 of the *Maxwell Leadership Bible*, says:

There is something about "nothing" that moves the hand of God. He loves to lead us to empty places where we can lean on nothing except His provision.

If we are not experiencing God's presence and provision, could be that we aren't empty enough? Could we be distracted and dependent on ourselves? This story teaches that...

1. Emptiness is a gift from the Lord.
2. Emptiness tells us that we have a need.
3. It is possible that we may not be empty enough.
4. We must admit our emptiness.
5. Only God can truly fill us.

As you reflect on this widow's situation and her painful challenges, come before the Lord with an empty heart and mind and ask Him to fill your cup until it's overflowing.

Thanksgiving, praises, and worship could be the little oil you may be having. Your positive attitude could be the little oil you may be having or ignoring. He will turn the little into more than enough.

I love the following quote from author Charles Swindoll:

The longer I live, the more I realize the impact of attitude on life. Attitude, to me, is more important than facts. It is more important than the past, than education, than money, than circumstances, than failures, than successes, than what other people think or say or do. It is more important than appearance, giftedness or skill. It will make or break a company...a church...a home. The remarkable thing is we have a choice every day regarding the attitude we will embrace for that day. We cannot change our past...we cannot change the fact that people will act in a certain way. We cannot change the inevitable. The only thing we can do is play on the one string we have, and that is our attitude...I am convinced that life is 10% what happens to me and 90% how I react to it. And so it is with you...we are in charge of our attitudes.

CHAPTER 19

THANKSGIVING, PRAISE, AND WORSHIP

We give thanks for what God has given and because He promises to always be with us. We praise Him for what He has done. And we worship God for who He is.

Prayer brings God's blessings. In prayer, our focus is on our needs. But praise brings God Himself. In praise, our focus is on God's benefits. In worship, our focus is on who God is.

The importance of thanksgiving, praise, and worship can be better understood once we realize that the Bible is a book of thanksgiving, praise, and worship.

Why do we give thanks?

- *Because God is good.* "Give thanks to the Lord, for He is good; his Love endures forever" (1 Chronicles 16:34).
- *It is fitting for saints.* "Neither filthiness, nor foolish talking, nor jesting, which are not convenient: but rather giving thanks as is fitting for saints" (Ephesians 5:4).
- *We are rooted in Him.* "Rooted and built up in Him and established in the faith, as you have been taught, abounding in it with thanksgiving" (Colossians 2:7).

- *His peace rules in our hearts.* "Let the peace of Christ rule in your hearts, since as members of one body you were called to peace. And be thankful" (Colossians 3:15).
- *It glorifies God.* "All this is for your benefit, so that the grace that is reaching more and more people may cause thanksgiving to overflow to the glory of God" (2 Corinthians 4:15).
- *It shows our devotion.* "Devote yourselves to prayer, being watchful and thankful" (Colossians 4:2).
- *It's our response to good deeds.* "This service that you perform is not only supplying the needs of the Lord's people but is also overflowing in many expressions of thanks to God" (2 Corinthians 9:12).

Praise

Praise is something we do on a regular basis. For example, we praise our children when they do well, we praise people for their work or philanthropy, and we praise athletes when they excel in competitions. So, praise comes naturally to us, but even more so, praise is something that we direct toward God or express to others about God.

According to the *Collins English Dictionary*, praise is the act of expressing commendation or admiration, rendering homage and gratitude to the deity. To commend someone highly. It also says, adore, bless, exalt, glorify, and magnify.

The Biblical Definition of Praise

"We praise God directly "by extolling him or expressing our admiration to Him." "O Lord, our Lord, How excellent is Your name in all the earth, Who have set Your glory above the heavens!" (Psalm 8:1).

We praise God indirectly by commending Him or magnifying Him to others based on

Psalm 33:1–3, which says:

> Rejoice in the LORD, O you righteous!
> *For* praise from the upright is beautiful.
> Praise the LORD with the harp;

Make melody to Him with an instrument of ten strings.
Sing to Him a new song;
Play skillfully with a shout of joy.

Praise is:

- *A garment.* "To console those who mourn in Zion, To give them beauty for ashes, The oil of joy for mourning, The garment of praise for the spirit of heaviness; That they may be called trees of righteousness, The planting of the LORD, that He may be glorified" (Isaiah 61:3).
- *A weapon.* "Let the saints be joyful in glory; Let them sing aloud on their beds. Let the high praises of God be in their mouth, and a two-edged sword in their hand, To execute vengeance on the nations, And punishments on the peoples; To bind their kings with chains, And their nobles with fetters of iron; To execute on them the written judgment—This honor have all His saints. Praise the LORD!" (Psalm 149:5–9).
- *A fruit.* "Therefore by Him let us continually offer the sacrifice of praise to God, that is, the fruit of our lips, giving thanks to His name" (Hebrews 13:15).
- *A sacrifice.* "Whoever offers praise glorifies Me; And to him who orders his conduct aright I will show the salvation of God" (Psalm 50:23).
- *God's will.* "In everything give thanks; for this is the will of God in Christ Jesus for you" (1 Thessalonians 5:18).

The Sacrifice of Praise

Praise is discussed in Hebrews 13:15; 1 Peter 2:5; Psalm 27:6, 50:23, 54:6, 107:22, and 116:17; and Job 1:21.

Sacrifice speaks of something costly: the giving of something that is dear to you (1 Chronicles 31:15, 24).

In the Old Testament, a sacrifice calls for the death of something. In the New Testament, a sacrifice of praise calls for death, too—not physical death, but death to our comfort zones, selfishness, to our self-pity, to our ego, and to our desires.

The Cost of Praise

Praise is energetic. We expend energy by lifting our hands, dancing, and singing with loud, joyous voices. We often complain that we do not have the energy for it.

Praise requires preparation.

> Who shall ascend into the hill of the Lord? Or who shall stand in his Holy place, He who has clean hands and a pure heart; who has not lifted up His soul unto vanity nor sworn deceitfully. We prepare ourselves spiritually before coming into a time of praise. Can the King give us time to prepare and seek the Lord? (Psalm 24:3–4)

Praise requires time, which we spend with the Lord.

Things Begin to Happen as We Praise the Lord

> But at midnight Paul and Silas were praying and singing hymns to God, and the prisoners were listening to them. Suddenly there was a great earthquake, so that the foundations of the prison were shaken; and immediately all the doors were opened and everyone's chains were loosed. And the keeper of the prison, awakening from sleep and seeing the prison doors open, supposing the prisoners had fled, drew his sword and was about to kill himself. But Paul called with a loud voice, saying, "Do yourself no harm, for we are all here." Then he called for a light, ran in, and fell down trembling before Paul and Silas. And he brought them out and said, "Sirs, what must I do to be saved?" So they said, "Believe on the Lord Jesus Christ, and you will be saved, you and your household." Then they spoke the word of the Lord to him and to all who were in his house. And he took them the same hour

of the night and washed their stripes. And immediately he and all his family were baptized. Now when he had brought them into his house, he set food before them; and he rejoiced, having believed in God with all his household. (Acts 16:25–34)

As Paul and Silas praised God, God showed up to enjoy their worship and fellowship. Then His presence shook the foundations of the prison. Everything that had stood in Paul and Silas's way was removed. Similarly, when we praise God, negative attitudes, evil imaginations, discouragement, unforgiveness, bitterness, fear, poverty, sickness, and curses are driven away.

As they continued to praise, all the prison doors suddenly opened, and everyone's chains were broken. Salvation came to those in authority and their families. The jailkeeper began to minister to Paul and Silas as he recognized the power of God. Death was prevented. The jailkeeper then asked a good question: "Sirs, what shall I do to be saved?" And the glory of God filled the building.

When this happens in our services, our programmes get reorganized and are replaced by His programmes.

> And it came to pass when the priests came out of the *Most* Holy *Place* (for all the priests who *were* present had sanctified themselves, without keeping to their divisions), and the Levites *who were* the singers, all those of Asaph and Heman and Jeduthun, with their sons and their brethren, stood at the east end of the altar, clothed in white linen, having cymbals, stringed instruments and harps, and with them one hundred and twenty priests sounding with trumpets—indeed it came to pass, when the trumpeters and singers *were* as one, to make one sound to be heard in praising and thanking the LORD, and when they lifted up their voice with the trumpets and cymbals and instruments of music, and praised the LORD, *saying:* 'For He is good, For His mercy *endures* forever' that the house, the house of the LORD, was filled with a cloud, so that the priests could not continue ministering because

of the cloud; for the glory of the LORD filled the house of
God. (2 Chronicles 5:11–14)

Worship

Worship is the passionate cry of our surrendered and cleansed hearts
to the Lord. It is our pure and naked response to a holy and loving Father.
It begins as we come into a deep place of intimacy with the Lord.

While praise is loud and thunderous, worship leads us into a place of
quietness and stillness before Him. True worship comes from the heart, is
inspired by the Holy Spirit, and is acceptable to God.

How Is Worship Carried Out in Scripture?

In scripture, worship is carried out in spirit and in truth. "Yet a time
is coming and has now come when the true worshipers will worship the
Father in Spirit and in truth, for they are the kind of worshipers the Father
seeks. God is spirit, and his worshipers must worship in the Spirit and in
truth" (John 4:23–24).

Worship is done through the following:

- *An offering.* "Ascribe to the Lord the glory due his name; bring an
  offering and come before him. Worship the Lord in the splendour
  of his holiness" (1 Chronicles 16:29).
- *Musical instruments.* "The whole assembly bowed in worship,
  while the musicians played and the trumpets sounded. All this
  continued until the sacrifice of the burnt offerings was completed"
  (2 Chronicles 29:28).
- *Lifted hands.* "And Ezra blessed the Lord, the great God and all
  the people answered, 'Amen, Amen,' lifting up their hands. And
  they bowed their heads and worshiped the Lord with their faces
  to the ground" (Nehemiah 8:6).
- *Bowing down.* "Come, let us bow down in worship, let us kneel
  before the Lord our Maker" (Psalm 95:6).

- *Songs.* "Worship the Lord with gladness; come before him with joyful songs" (Psalm 100:2).
- *Reverence.* "Therefore, since we are receiving a kingdom that cannot be shaken, let us be thankful and so worship God acceptably with reverence and awe, for our God is a consuming fire" (Hebrews 12:28).

We are commanded to worship God only. Luke 4:8 says, "Jesus answered, 'It is written worship the Lord your God and serve him only.'"

In conclusion, thanksgiving, praise, and worship are three powerful spiritual tools through which we can please God, touch Him, and experience His tremendous power. Let us therefore arise in our hearts to continually thank, praise, and worship the Lord.

CHAPTER 20

UNDERSTANDING THE FAVOUR OF THE LORD

Favour is an act of kindness beyond what is due or usual. It demonstrates delight. It is tangible evidence that a person has the approval of the Lord. "'For all those things My hand has made, And all those things exist,' Says the LORD. 'But on this one will I look: On him who is poor and of a contrite spirit, And who trembles at My word'" (Isaiah 66:2).

Favour is the supernatural ability given by God to enable a person to complete the assignment he or she has been given here on Earth. Favour is closely connected to blessings, mercy, and grace. They are not the same, but they are related.

Scripture Readings on the Favour of God

> And he came to her and said, Hail, O favored one [endued with grace]! The Lord is with you! *Blessed (favored of God) are you before all other women!* ... And the angel said to her, Do not be afraid, Mary, for you have found grace (free, spontaneous, absolute favour and loving kindness) with God. (Luke 1:28, 30)

> And the Child grew and became strong *in spirit*, filled with wisdom; and the grace (favour and spiritual blessing) of God was upon Him. (Luke 2:40)

And Jesus increased in wisdom (in full understanding) and in stature *and* years, and in favor with God and man. (Luke 2:54)

Constantly praising God and being in favor *and* goodwill with all the people; and the Lord kept adding [to their number] daily those who were being saved [from spiritual death]. (Acts 2:47)

But the Lord was with Joseph and showed him mercy, and He gave him favor in the sight of the keeper of the prison. And the keeper of the prison committed to Joseph's hand all the prisoners who were in the prison; whatever they did there, it was his doing. Genesis 39: 21-23 The keeper of the prison did not look into anything that was under Joseph's authority, because the Lord was with him; and whatever he did, the Lord made it prosper.

(Genesis 39:21, 23)

And I will give this people favor *and* respect in the sight of the Egyptians; and it shall be that when you go, you shall not go empty-handed. (Exodus 3:21)

And the Lord gave the people favor in the sight of the Egyptians. Moreover, the man Moses was exceedingly great in the land of Egypt, in the sight of Pharaoh's servants and of the people. (Exodus 11:3)

Important Things to Know about God's Favour

Favour is found. "So Joseph found favour in his sight, and served him. Then he made him overseer of his house, and all *that* he had he put under his authority" (Genesis 39:4).

Favour is given. "And I will give this people favour in the sight of the Egyptians; and it shall be, when you go, that you shall not go empty-handed" (Exodus 3:21). "But the Lord was with Joseph and showed him mercy, and He gave him favour in the sight of the keeper of the prison" (Genesis 39:21).

Favour brings satisfaction. "And of Naphtali he said, 'O Naphtali, satisfied with favour, and full of the blessing of the Lord, possess the west and the south'" (Deuteronomy 33:23).

Favour brings the blessings of the Lord into our lives.

Favour enables you to possess the things God wants you to possess for His glory and honour.

Favour can be received or rejected.

Favour can be shown and demonstrated to a person, family, church, or nation.

Favour brings victories, promotions, and the right people into your life. It sets you on your way.

Favour can perform miracles, such as the multiplication of food:

> Then a man came from Baal Shalisha, and brought the man of God bread of the first fruits, twenty loaves of barley bread, and newly ripened grain in his knapsack. And he said, "Give it to the people, that they may eat."
>
> But his servant said, "What? Shall I set this before one hundred men?"
>
> He said again, "Give it to the people, that they may eat; for thus says the Lord: 'They shall eat and have some left over.'" So he set it before them; and they ate and had some left over, according to the word of the Lord. (2 Kings 4:42–44)

What Does Favour Do?

Favour supernaturally opens closed doors while paying off all your debts. It takes away sadness and brings in gladness (2 Kings 4:1–7).

Although favour does what no person can do, it can be lost in a moment and therefore has to be protected carefully. It can bring comfort and encouragement after tragedies that occur in life.

Favour helps to bring you to the right place at the right time. It connects you with the right people and enables you to do the right things in the right way.

Favour goes beyond what academic qualifications and credentials can do, as it's gained before God and others. "And the child Samuel grew in stature, and in favour both with the Lord and men" (1 Samuel 2:26).

Favour can affect everyone who interacts with you, both great and small.

> Now when the turn came for Esther the daughter of Abihail the uncle of Mordecai, who had taken her as his daughter, to go in to the king, she requested nothing but what Hegai the king's eunuch, the custodian of the women, advised. And Esther obtained favour in the sight of all who saw her. (Esther 2:15)

Favour makes people love you more than others. "The king loved Esther more than all the *other* women, and she obtained grace and favor in his sight more than all the virgins; so he set the royal crown upon her head and made her queen instead of Vashti" (Esther 2:17).

However, you must realize that regardless of who shows you favour, favour first comes from the Lord. "You have granted me life and favour And Your care has preserved my spirit" (Job 10:12).

Favour from the Lord lasts for a lifetime and surrounds us like a shield. "For You, O Lord, will bless the righteous; With favour You will surround him as *with* a shield" (Psalm 5:12).

I strongly believe that the Lord wants to show His favour to individuals, families, churches, cities, and nations. The time to favour you has come. "You will arise *and* have mercy on Zion; for the time to favor her, Yes, the set time, has come" (Psalm 102:2).

Ways of Experiencing the Favour of God

To become acquainted with the Lord's favour, I suggest that you take time and as you will be led by the Holy spirit to declare and decree His favour by acknowledging that you have it and are operating in it. Speak these words out as the Lord leads you in all areas of your life.

Derek Prince was a Bible teacher whose daily radio programme, *Derek Prince Legacy Radio*, is broadcast around the world in various languages. One day, as I was listening to him, I heard him say that a blessing is not a blessing until it is spoken out, either inwardly or audibly.

Words are like seeds. As you speak them out, you plant them; hence, you will ultimately collect their harvest. Those who confess and decree the favour of God over their circumstances experience His abundant blessings.

I declare and decree that I have favour and success not because of my works but because I believe that Jesus made me righteous and earned it for me, in Jesus's name.

I decree that from this moment forward, I will see myself the way God sees me. I am highly favoured by the Lord. I am crowned with glory and honour. I am the righteousness of God in Christ and reign as a king in life through Jesus Christ, the Messiah, in Jesus's name.

I declare by faith that I walk in divine favour. I have preferential treatment, supernatural increase, restoration, increased assets, great victories, recognition, prominence, petitions granted, policies and rules changed, and battles won. I do not have to fight or struggle because the blessing and favour of God is in my life, in Jesus's name.

Every morning when I arise, I expect divine favour to go before me and surround me like a shield, with goodwill and pleasures forevermore. All doors once closed now become open so that the things people once said are impossible become possible for me. No obstacle can stop me, and no hindrance can delay me, in Jesus's name.

I am honoured by my Father, as I receive genuine favour that comes directly from Him. I am special to Him. I am the object of His affection. I am blessed and highly favoured by the Lord, in Jesus's name.

Here are some scripture passages to back the declarations you will make. It is written in 2 Corinthians 1:20, "For all the promises of God in Him *are* Yes, and in Him Amen, to the glory of God through us." In Jeremiah 1:12, it is written, "Then the LORD said to me, 'You have seen well, for I am ready to perform My word." Many times, we are not using God's promises in our prayers and our confessions. In standing and using God's promises, we are in agreement with Him and His word. When you have no one to stand and agree with you, know that you are not alone.

Jesus has promised to be in our midst and with us always, even to the end of the age.

Here are very powerful and wonderful promises from Him which says: "Again I say to you that if two of you agree on earth concerning anything that they ask, it will be done for them by My Father in heaven. For where two or three are gathered together in My name, I am there in the midst of them." (Matthew 18:18-20)

The favour of God is producing supernatural increase and promotion in my life. (Genesis 39:21)

The favour of God is restoring everything that the enemy has stolen from me. (Exodus 3:21)

The favour of God is giving me honour in the midst of my adversaries. (Exodus 11:3)

The favour of God is increasing my assets and real estate. (Deuteronomy 33:23)

The favour of God is producing great victories in the midst of great impossibilities. (Joshua 11:20)

The favour of God is producing recognition, even when I seem the least likely to receive it. (1 Samuel 16:22)

The favour of God gives me preferential treatment. (Esther 2:17)

The favour of God grants me petitions, even by ungodly civil authorities. (Esther 5:8)

The favour of God causes policies, rules, regulations and laws to be changed to my advantage. (Esther 8:5)

The favour of God is winning battles that I won't have to fight because God will fight them for me. (Psalm 44:3)

You will arise *and* have mercy on Zion; For the time to favor her, Yes, the set time, has come. This is my season of walking and working in the favour of God. (Psalm 103:13)

The Favour of God is all over me, all around me, all under me and all ahead of me. It has brought to me victories that no money or man can give me. To God be all the praise and honour.

(Ephesians 3:18–20)

One day of favour is worth a thousand days of labour- Dr. Mike Murdock

More Confessions and Declarations of the Favour of God

I have studied God's Word concerning the topic on favour, and it is amazing what favour can do for you when you understand it. Favour is a seed God gives to His people for the good harvest. If you sow it, protect and water it diligently the harvest will be of great joy. One way God will visit you is through His favour. God wants to visit you through His blessing and His favour. It is written in Romans. 15:29, "I know that when I do come to you, I will come in the abundant blessing of Christ". Romans 10:10 says, "For with the heart one believes unto righteousness, and with the mouth confession is made unto salvation."

First, you must believe in something with your heart, and with your mouth, you make confession. What you believe and confess confidently with understanding and knowledge will serve you well. Unfortunately, what you don't believe in your heart or confess with your month will not serve you. Believing in something, confessing it with your mouth, and taking the right actions will give you undebatable and unquestionable results.

Mark 11:22–24 says, "So Jesus answered and said to them, 'Have faith in God. For assuredly, I say to you, whoever says to this mountain, "Be removed and be cast into the sea," and does not doubt in his heart, but believes that those things he says will be done, he will have whatever he says. Therefore, I say to you, whatever things you ask when you pray, believe that you receive *them,* and you will have *them."*

I would like to challenge you, if you can, to make these confessions as you are led by the Holy Spirit of the Lord and see what the Lord will do for you. These confessions are all based on the Word of God and are His promises.

Know that God has your best interest at heart and longs to bless you abundantly. All He has is yours! We read from Luke 15:31, "And he said to him, 'Son, you are always with me, and all that I have is yours.'"

Your confessions determine your possessions

I believe in Jesus. I confess that He is my Lord. I am justified by faith. I have been declared righteous in Christ Jesus.

I am destined for greatness, for I have obtained God's favour forever. "For His anger *is but for* a moment, His **favor** *is for* life." Psalm 30:5

I have what it takes to succeed by God's favour, grace, and mercy. I can do all things through Christ who strengthens me.

God's favour empowers me with knowledge, understanding, and wisdom to have good success, which brings glory to God, blesses God's people, and brings joy and peace into my heart.

God's favour gives me hunger and thirst to seek His kingdom and His righteousness first. The Lord Jesus has assured me that all the things I need in life to serve Him efficiently and effectively shall be added unto me as I follow His instructions. God's kingdom and righteousness are His priorities and strategies for blessing us as His people. I am a kingdom seeker, and His righteousness is His gift to me to receive it freely by faith.

God's favour locates me and positions me to see, think, and communicate wisely and effectively for better and greater results. Jesus said, I will have what I say. (Mark 11:22–24)

My destiny is accompanied by God's favour, mercy, and grace. I have faith that it is well, and it shall be well with me, my family, and the household of faith. Isaiah 3:10 declares: "Say to the righteous that *it shall be* well *with them,* For they shall eat the fruit of their doings."

God's favour causes me to grow up and increase wisely for better and greater results. And Jesus increased in wisdom and stature, and in favor with God and men. Luke 2:52.

God's divine favor is sufficient for me. When I am weak, His divine favor makes me strong. (2 Cor.12:7-10)

God's favour is a secret weapon that works on my behalf; hence, I am destined for greatness and with joy inexpressible in the Lord my God.

1 Peter 1:8 says, whom having not seen you love. Though now you do not see *Him*, yet believing, you rejoice with joy inexpressible and full of glory.

God's favour positions me to listen, hear, understand, and know His voice and take the necessary actions. My sheep hear My voice, and I know them, and they follow Me. John 10:27

I am blessed and highly favoured of the Lord! His favour assures me of His presence, provision, and protection. "And having come in, the angel said to her, 'Rejoice, highly fa*vored one,* the Lord *is* with you; blessed *are* you among women!'" Luke 1:28.

As Mary, Jesus, and the early church obtained favour before God and in the sight of man, so I have obtained the same favour before my Father in heaven and man. I rejoice greatly in the Lord, for He comforts and strengthens me in every area of my life with gladness, love, and care. "The LORD YOUR GOD IN YOUR MIDST, The Mighty One, will save; He will rejoice over you with gladness, He will quiet *you* with His love, He will rejoice over you with singing." Zephaniah 3:17.

My Father in heaven constantly thinks of ways of demonstrating His favour towards me, my family, and all those around me. I rejoice greatly in the Lord, for He comforts and strengthens me all around with gladness, inner rest, and singing. To Him be the glory.

In whatever circumstances I find myself in, God's eyes of favour and mercy are upon me to provide and protect me because He loves and cares for me. What a Mighty God I serve! "But the Lord was with Joseph and showed him mercy, and He gave him favour in the sight of the keeper of the prison". Genesis 39:21

As God demonstrated His favour to his people of old, Abraham, Isaac, Jacob, and Esther, so is He demonstrating His favour towards me now and forever.

I am destined for more and more of God's favour in all He has called me to do for all the days of my life. He is my shepherd and I shall not want, for He has supplied all my needs according to His riches in glory by Christ Jesus. He is my El Shaddai. "Not that we are sufficient of ourselves to think of anything as *being* from ourselves, but our sufficiency *is* from God." 2 Corinthians 3:5.

There will never be a time that I will come from the presence of God empty-handed. He is "the total Source of every good and perfect gift for me. Exodus 3:21 says: "And I will give this people favor in the sight of the Egyptians; and it shall be, when you go, that you shall not go empty-handed."

God's favour provides for me all the resources that I need and much more naturally and supernaturally as I keep remembering that He is the total Source of all my abilities, capacity and capabilities to get wealth that expands God's kingdom and blesses His people. "And you shall remember the LORD your God, for *it is* He who gives you power to get wealth, that He may stablish His covenant which He swore to your fathers, as *it is* this day." Deuteronomy 8:18

God's favour in my life causes people who do not know me to serve me cheerfully with good things, all for the glory of God. What a Mighty God of favour I serve!!! "And people will come from all over *to serve you*: Outsiders will tend your flocks, plough your fields, and prune your vines." Isaiah 61:5. This is what favor does when I understand, declare, and mix it with faith and actions.

There is no day in my life I will walk and work without the favour of God because of His love and care for me forever. "For You, O Lord, will bless the righteous; With **favor** You will surround him as *with* a shield." Psalms 5:12.

As a citizen of the kingdom of God, I have found and obtained favour in the sight of the Lord. "For whoever finds me finds life, And obtains **favor** from the Lord." Proverbs 8:35. "He who finds a wife finds a good thing, And obtains **favor** from the Lord." Proverbs 18:22.

God's favour works on my behalf constantly even when I am not aware of it because of God's love for me, my family, and those I am called to serve. His favour and His outstretched hand redeemed me from the house of bondage and brought me into the house of freedom that I may worship, serve Him and honor Him in everything I do.

"The LORD did not set His love on you nor choose you because you were more in number than any other people, for you were the least of all peoples; but because the LORD loves you, and because He would keep the oath which He swore to your fathers, the LORD has brought you out with a mighty hand, and redeemed you from the house of bondage, from the hand of Pharaoh king of Egypt". Deuteronomy 7:7-8

The blessing of the Lord makes me rich and He, the Lord, adds no sorrow to it. Yes, God's favour also opens for me and my family doors that no one can close. He is the door to all other doors. He leads me into green pastures and gives me inner rest at all times.

I am the door. If anyone enters by Me, he will be saved, and will go in and out and find pasture. The thief does not come except to steal, and to kill, and to destroy. I have come that they may have life, and that they may have *it* more abundantly. John 10:9-10.

God is working out right now how to favour me to be more productive and efficient in my calling and assignment. "For I will look on you **favor**ably and make you fruitful, multiply you and confirm My covenant with you." Leviticus. 29:9.

"Then he said to Him, 'If now I have found **favor** in Your sight, then show me a sign that it is You who talks with me.'" Judges 6:17. God's favour positions me to fellowship with Him, as He gives me clarity for my calling and purpose.

God's favor opens my eyes and enables me to find life and truth. For whoever finds me finds life, And obtains favour from the Lord. Proverbs 8:35. We read in John 14:6 which says: Jesus said to him, "I am the way, the truth, and the life. No one comes to the Father except through Me. Favour gives me a good life here on earth and everlasting life.

God's favour brings encouragement and comfort to me in good and challenging times.

At the right time, God's favour brings me to the great and the right people to serve each other. "Now, God had brought Daniel into the **favor** and goodwill of the chief of the eunuchs." Daniel 1:9.

God's favour makes me a saint of the Most High and brings me into God's kingdom to rule and reign with Him. To Him be the glory and praise. "Until the Ancient of Days came, and a judgment was made in favor of the saints of the Most High, and the time came for the saints to possess the kingdom." Daniel 7:22.

God's favour causes me to be recognized and gives me timely promotions when I least expect them, even in foreign lands. "So she [Ruth] fell on her face, bowed down to the ground, and said to him, 'Why have I found favor in your eyes, that you should take notice of me, since I *am* a foreigner?'" Ruth 2:10.

God's favour grants me life and care and preserves my spirit. You have granted me life and favour, and Your care has preserved my spirit. Job 10:12.

"And the Lord had given the people favor in the sight of the Egyptians so that they granted them *what they requested.* Thus, they plundered the Egyptians". Exodus 12:36.

From the previous confessions of favour, you can see what happens when you operate in the favour of God. Purpose to study and read books of God's favour and learn how it works. Jesus operated in the favour of God and had extraordinary miracle upon miracle. What about you? Favour is spiritual, and it controls the mental and physical realms.

I recommend Dr. Jerry Savelle's book entitled *God's Favor.* Check it out if you can. It will open up the eyes of your understanding concerning favour.

This was the prayer of King David, and may it be your prayer too. "Let the favor of the Lord our God be upon us. Establish the work of our hands for us—yes, establish the work of our hands." Psalm 90:17.

"Remember, it is written: You will also declare a thing, And it will be established for you; So light will shine on your ways." Job 22:28.

I have a sister in-law who was going through a very difficult time financially and struggling with other challenges. I sent her some confessions of favour, and she took those confessions very seriously. She confessed them again and again. Suddenly, she began to experience blessing after blessing and favour after favour. You are next on line for abundant blessings as you walk and work in the favour of God!

Start decreeing and declaring these confessions as the Holy Spirit of the Lord leads you, and watch and see God's favour overwhelmingly come upon you.

A prayer: Father God, in the name of Jesus, I come to you with these confessions that I have made based on your Word and promises.

It is written that what I decree will be established unto me, so Lord, I decree these confessions and declare them done in Jesus' Name.

Help me walk and work uprightly in righteousness and humbly seek You daily. You are the giver of every good and perfect gift. I thank you for your great love for me. I am forever grateful. You are My Father and I am your son/daughter forever.

Increase my faith and my capacity to receive all You have in store for me and those around me. I love You, and I thank You for being my great heavenly Father. In Jesus' Name, Amen!

CHAPTER 21

SEE AND SEIZE THE OPPORTUNITY

The word *opportunity,* according to the *Collins English Dictionary,* means "favourable, appropriate or advantageous combination of circumstances. It is a chance; the real moment or a prospective." It is the current moment, an open door, or a window that may close at any time.

Here are some observations about opportunity from John Maxwell:

> When you find your spiritual gift, God will give you an opportunity to use it.
> (AZ Quotes – Author John C. Maxwell)

> Might you be missing opportunities because you have been too quick to ask how instead of why?
> (John C. Maxwell quotes from Quotefancy.com)

> When you know your why, you will find your way, and when you find your way, you will find the wings to fly to your destination where opportunities could be waiting for you.
> (John C. Maxwell quotes from AZquotes.com)

> Adversity is an opportunity for self-discovery.
> (John C. Maxwell quotes from AZquotes.com)

The time to prepare isn't after you have been given the opportunity. It's long before that opportunity arises. Once the opportunity arrives, it's too late to prepare. (Craig Impelman)

Legendary UCLA basketball coach John Wooden once said, "When opportunity knocks, it's too late to prepare. You never know when a great opportunity in business or life will present itself. The person who is prepared—who is ready—is able to take full advantage of it."

Albert Einstein once said, "In the middle of difficulty lies opportunity."

It is important to note that opportunities may not always make sense. You will need discernment and humility to recognize and go through with them. But one thing is certain: Opportunity comes with new relationships, provisions, and protections.

There are different types of opportunities around us, including personal, professional, spiritual, mental, political, social, and economic opportunities.

Personal and Professional Opportunities

Personal growth guarantees you a better tomorrow. To grow, you require mentors who can guide you through the knowledge and experience they have accumulated.

"Most people who decide to grow personally find their first mentors in the pages of books." (John Maxwell quote from Quotefancy.com)

Personal growth starts in your spirit. Luke 1:80 says, "So the child [referring to John the Baptist] grew and became strong in spirit, and was in the deserts till the day of his manifestation to Israel."

In Luke 2:40, we read, "And the Child [referring to Jesus Christ] grew and became strong in spirit, filled with wisdom; and the grace of God was upon Him."

Both John and Jesus prepared themselves well before the opportunities for their respective missions manifested.

Once you grow spiritually, all areas of your life are affected.

And Jesus increased in wisdom and stature and in favor with God and men. (Luke 2:52)

> Now there was a long war between the house of Saul and the house of David. But David grew stronger and stronger, and the house of Saul grew weaker and weaker. (1 Samuel 3:1)

You can experience healthy growth, like David, or unhealthy growth, like Saul. Choose the former, and you will make a difference. Know and focus on the things that make you stronger, and avoid the things that make you weaker.

Professionally

You need to discover what you do well. Then you need to become so good at it that you are irreplaceable. This will help you take advantage of the opportunities around you. You need to focus on your gifts, be both diligent and excellent at them, and maintain your integrity. In Proverbs 18:16, King Solomon, the wisest man of his time, said, "A man's gift makes room for him and brings him before great men." In other words, your gifts will usher you towards good and great opportunities.

Dr John C. Maxwell said,

- Make a commitment to grow daily.
- Value the process more than events.
- Don't wait for inspiration.
- Be willing to sacrifice pleasure for opportunity.
- Dream big. Plan your priorities.

What great advice. Give up to go up."

John Maxwell – Quotes

Spiritual and mental opportunities are available to everyone. Those who can see and seize them will be blessed forever.

Spiritually

You have an opportunity to know and connect with the One who created you. The longest prayer Jesus ever prayed in public was in John 17. In Verse 3, He invites his listeners to receive spiritual life: "And this is eternal life, that they may know You, the only true God, and Jesus Christ whom You have sent."

Knowing the One who created you gives you eternal life. "But the people who know their God shall be strong and carry out great exploits" (Daniel 11:32).

Knowing God and having a relationship with Him through His Son, Jesus Christ, is the greatest opportunity that has been given to us. When we say yes to the Lord Jesus Christ, it is the greatest miracle we can ever experience.

If you have said yes to Jesus, congratulations. If not, don't worry; it's not too late to make that decision. You will have the opportunity at the end of this chapter to experience new birth.

Mentally

You have an opportunity to renew your mind every day. Most of the challenges that people deal with occur on the inside. We often want our circumstances to change on the outside, but we are not willing to change from the inside.

Your mind is the greatest asset the Lord God has given you. It can imagine, conceive, and achieve great and mighty things. Whatever you can imagine, you can achieve, and no one can stop you. Read Genesis 11:1–9. Your mind is the battleground for all the challenges you will ever experience. It is the control tower for your emotions. Failure to know how to manage your thoughts and emotions can lead to regret, frustration, and disappointment. Your mind is like a garden. Whatever you sow in it will grow.

Learn to walk in a renewed mind. What does that mean? Intentionally feed your mind with the truths of God's Word and not the lies of the enemy. Feed your mind with faith based on God's Word and not the doubts that come to you. Feed your mind with good pictures and not unhealthy pictures. Feed your mind with good sounds from good music or healthy meditations.

Isaiah 26:3 says, "You will keep *him* in perfect peace, *whose* mind *is* stayed *on You*, because he trusts in You."

We also read in Philippians 4:6–9:

> Be anxious for nothing, but in everything by prayer and supplication, with thanksgiving, let your requests be made known to God; and the peace of God, which surpasses all understanding, will guard your hearts and minds through Christ Jesus. Finally, brethren, whatever things are true, whatever things *are* noble, whatever things *are* just, whatever things *are* pure, whatever things *are* lovely, whatever things *are* of good report, if *there is* any virtue and if *there is* anything praiseworthy—meditate on these things. The things which you learned and received and heard and saw in me, these do, and the God of peace will be with you.

These verses can be summarized as follows: Do not be anxious for anything. Bring your cares and burdens to God in prayer. Be of a grateful heart and mind. If you practice that, you will begin to experience the inner peace of God, which surpasses all understanding. That peace of God will guard your heart and mind. What a great opportunity to grab with the two hands.

The Apostle Paul made a list of the things you and I should focus on: "Finally, brethren, whatever things are true, whatever things *are* noble, whatever things *are* just, whatever things *are* pure, whatever things *are* lovely, whatever things *are* of good report, if *there is* any virtue and if *there is* anything praiseworthy—meditate on these things."

We often meditate on things based on our past mistakes and present circumstances. We become anxious about the future. Do not fear and do not be anxious.

Fear and anxiety can lead to heart disease, mental illness, panic attacks, depression, and phobias. (Shared from page 86 of the book *What You Don't Know May Be Killing You!* by Dr Don Colbert, M. D.)

Anxiety in the heart of man causes depression, But a good word makes it glad. From the reading of the scripture, one of the causes of depression is anxiety. Feed your heart with good news. (Proverbs 12:25)

As cold water to a weary soul, so is good news from a far country. (Proverbs 25:25)

Based on the scripture we have read, God's Word is from a far country. It comes from the heart of God to us, from heaven to the earth. It has all that you need to make you whole.

Political, Social, and Economic Opportunities

Political
We can be involved and make a difference in our nations. We can be light in the darkness and the salt of the earth. We have opportunities to intercede and pray for those in positions of authority.

"Therefore I exhort first of all that supplications, prayers, intercessions, *and* giving of thanks be made for all men, for kings and all who are in authority, that we may lead a quiet and peaceable life in all godliness and reverence. For this *is* good and acceptable in the sight of God our Saviour, who desires all men to be saved and to come to the knowledge of the truth." (1 Timothy 2:1–4)

"Obey those who rule over you, and be submissive, for they watch out for your souls, as those who must give account. Let them do so with joy and not with grief, for that would be unprofitable for you." (Hebrews 13:17)

Our prayers and intercessions can make a difference in our nations.
As we pray, God will give our leaders knowledge, understanding, and wisdom to lead well with godly fear. That will be good, acceptable, and pleasing before the Lord, who desires all men to come to the knowledge

of the truth and be saved. God loves all people unconditionally, but He serves them conditionally.

We are also instructed to obey those who rule over us, as they watch over our souls. They must give an account of our souls. Our obedience and willingness will bring joy and not grief into their hearts, and that is profitable for us. There are many opportunities to work together with governing bodies to ensure that it will be well with us in the land.

Social

You have opportunities to connect with great people and make a difference. However, a word of caution with social media platforms: You can easily find yourself spending too much time on them and forgetting your priorities in life.

It is important to find the right balance in life socially, professionally, and in ministry and business. Otherwise, you may end up losing your family, your inner circle of good friends, and your relatives because you are too busy.

Be wise and diligent to do the right things with the right people in the right places at the right times and in the right ways. I received this advice from both my natural father and my spiritual father. It has always kept me on track and protected my time, energy, and finances. Both these men told me that there is direction, provision, and protection in these things. These fathers were amazing mentors to me and my family, and we are forever grateful to the Lord for their wisdom.

Economic

What is economy? It is the careful management of resources.

According to Merriam-Webster, economy is the process or system by which goods and services are produced, sold, and bought in a country or region.

It is careful use of money, resources, etc. It is something that makes it possible for you to spend less money.

The economy of Christ is seen in John 6:11–12, which says, "And Jesus took the loaves, and when He had given thanks He distributed *them* to the disciples, and the disciples to those sitting down; and likewise of the fish, as much as they wanted. So when they were filled, He said to His disciples, 'Gather up the fragments that remain, so that nothing is lost.'"

We should avoid the wasting of time, energy, money, food, water, space, electricity, etc. Let us be good managers of the resources that have been given to us. Jesus had to teach His disciples to make sure that nothing would be lost. Heaven never wastes anything. Do some reviewing and see where you need to improve and change.

What does the Lord say about the economy?

> And you shall remember the LORD your God, for *it is* He who gives you power to get wealth, that He may establish His covenant which He swore to your fathers, as *it is* this day. (Deuteronomy 8:18)

> Beloved, I pray that you may prosper in all things and be in health, just as your soul prospers. (3 John 3:2)

God wants you to prosper. This prosperity begins in the soul, the inner being. The soul refers to your intellect, conscious mind, emotions, and will. Those are the areas you should begin to work on. Your soul's prosperity determines your outer prosperity.

What is prosperity? It refers to the supernatural abilities that the Lord bestows upon you to enable you to accomplish the assignment He called you to fulfil on Earth.

We can also define prosperity as the natural and supernatural ability to meet your personal needs and the needs of others through the resources God has made available to you. It's God's peace and inner rest, the Shalom, the all-inclusive package. (The word *shalom* is a Hebrew word meaning peace, harmony, wholeness, completeness, prosperity, welfare and tranquillity and can be used idiomatically to mean both hello and goodbye. The word *shalom* is also found in many other expressions and names.

To experience God's prosperity, make Him your total Source. It is His will to bless you in all the areas of your life.

He says you shall remember Him—that He gives you the ability to make wealth. He swore and made a covenant with our fathers to do so. All the wealth He gives to you is to honour Him and bless His people; it should bring joy and peace into your heart and mind. His wealth may come through ideas, creativity, and innovation. See and seize the opportunity of those promises.

Part of your heritage in this society is the opportunity to become financially independent. Jim Rohn said, "Learning is the beginning of health. Learning is the beginning of wealth. Learning is the beginning of spirituality. Searching and learning is where the miracle process all begins." (Fancy Quotes)

Peter Drucker said, "The entrepreneur always searches for change, responds to it, and exploits it as an opportunity." (BrainyQuotes.com)

Train your eyes to see and seize the great opportunities given to you. Don't focus your heart, mind, and eyes on the obstacles. Focus on the opportunities. Be solution-oriented and not problem-oriented.

> And the LORD said to Abram, after Lot had separated from him: 'Lift your eyes now and look from the place where you are—northward, southward, eastward, and westward; for all the land which you see I give to you and your descendants forever. (Genesis 13:14–15)

> When you go, you will come to a secure people and a large land. For God has given it into your hands, a place where *there is* no lack of anything that *is* on the earth. (Judges 18:10)

Before God created Adam and Eve, He prepared for them a very beautiful home called Eden.

Eden means "pleasant," a place of good pleasure. Here is the description of its garden:

> The Lord God planted a garden eastward in Eden, and there He put the man whom He had formed. And out of the ground the Lord God made every tree grow that is pleasant to the sight and good for food.

> The tree of life was also in the midst of the garden, and the tree of the knowledge of good and evil.

Now a river went out of Eden to water the garden, and from there it parted and became four riverheads.

The name of the first is Pishon; it is the one which skirts the whole land of Havilah, where there is gold. And the gold of that land is good. Bdellium and the onyx stone are there.

The name of the second river is Gihon; it is the one which goes around the whole land of Cush.

The name of the third river is Hiddekel; it is the one which goes toward the east of Assyria.

The fourth river is the Euphrates.

Then the LORD God took the man and put him in the garden of Eden to tend and keep it. (Genesis 2:8–15)

Verse 10 says, "Now a river went out of Eden to water the garden, and from there it parted and became four riverheads." The four rivers created by God were economically and strategically placed in Eden to sustain the garden. Water plays a major role in any growing economy.

I like the following words: "Now a river went out of Eden to water the garden." The main purpose of this one river was to water the garden, and from there, it parted and became four heads. Rivers never stop flowing. One river went out and became four rivers.

The blessing of the Lord was on this one river, and as it went out of Eden, the Lord blessed it and multiplied it into four rivers. That is what the Lord does. He will give you a gift, a profession, a business, an organization, a church, or a ministry, and if you let it flow out of you faithfully, God will breathe His blessing into it and multiply it into many more streams of income. Ask the Lord to bless that one thing He has given you and let it go out and split into four rivers.

Here are the modest beginnings of five tech companies worth billions today. Google, Apple, HP, Microsoft, and Amazon all claim to have started in garages. They are now present all over the world. Each one of them started with one idea, and that idea parted into numerous ones.

Most of us use some of the products and services of some of these companies every day. We should be grateful and celebrate those who have made life easier and given employment to many around the world.

Could it be that you have an idea to start something but are afraid to step out? Once you have clarity of that idea, bring it to the Lord in prayer. Ask for wisdom, guidance, provision, protection, and the right timing regarding when to begin, continue, and finish. Aim to finish well, and give all the glory and honour to the Lord. Many people begin and continue but never finish—or if they do finish, they don't finish well. Be a good finisher.

Figuratively and spiritually, the rivers represent the presence of God, Christ Jesus, the Holy Spirit of God, the peace of God, and the prosperity of the saints. We need all these rivers in our personal lives, in every nation, and in all that we have been called to do.

Based on what we have read about the garden of Eden before the fall, nothing was missing, and nothing was broken.

The sin that entered into Adam and Eve broke down everything in their lives and all that was in the garden. That is why Jesus Christ came to the world: to restore us back into God's Kingdom. Jesus said that if we seek God's kingdom and righteousness, all these things shall be added unto us.

God is concerned about the economies of every nation on the earth. He wants us to make use of the resources that He has given that have not yet made use of.

One of the best ways that leaders can begin to grow their nations' economies is to grow their people with growth mindsets; this will enable citizens to think outside of the box. A growth mindset will challenge individuals to make that inner shift to think, believe, see, and do things differently, and it will grow a stronger economy. Let us take the responsibility to grow ourselves first; then we can grow others. You cannot give what you don't have.

Jesus said that out of your heart shall flow rivers of living water. Those rivers can include spiritual, personal, economic, or community development. For us to have any impact on the world, we must be intentional to impact those around us and around the world. Be innovative and creative in all that you do. Out of your heart shall flow rivers—not a single river, but rivers—of living water.

The Lord is the land-giver. He gives out land with love and promises. Know what land He has given you. The word *land* here refers to your calling in ministry or in the marketplace. Land could be your profession, career, business, politics, education, music, or sport. Your talents and gifts are large lands. Develop them. Whatever your land is, go in and possess it. Develop it to the best of your knowledge.

Strive for excellence, diligence, and integrity. This will keep you on the top floor, and you will never lack any great opportunity for the rest of your life. "Therefore, as we have opportunity, let us do good to all, especially to those who are of the household of faith" (Galatians 6:10).

Opportunities are always available; they are given to us, and they can be either received or rejected. Through innovation, creativity and with the help of the Lord; one is able to see those opportunities and take advantage of them. A simple prayer: Lord open my eyes that I may see the opportunities that are available and extended to me and help me to receive them with joy and gladness. Amen! Great opportunities come with great responsibilities. Take the right action now and think and meditate on what you can do without any fear or doubt that you will fail. Trust the Lord to help you. Opportunities also have an expiry date. They are not there forever.

I would like to conclude with the story of the two thieves who were crucified with Jesus Christ. This story depicts how Jesus, in His hour of death, extended His hands of grace and mercy to the thieves on either side of His cross. This final invitation seemed to declare, "I am the way, the truth, and the life to the Father of all spirits. Come and take this golden opportunity."

Listen to the thieves' responses:

> Then one of the criminals who were hanged blasphemed Him, saying, "If You are the Christ, save Yourself and us." But the other, answering, rebuked him, saying, "Do you not even fear God, seeing you are under the same condemnation? And we indeed justly, for we receive the due reward of our deeds; but this Man has done nothing

wrong." Then he said to Jesus, "Lord, remember me when You come into Your kingdom." And Jesus said to him, "Assuredly, I say to you, today you will be with Me in Paradise." (Luke 23:39–43)

Opportunity can be lost. The first thief did not perceive the opportunity extended to him in his dying hour; he despised it and lost his life forever. The other thief saw the opportunity extended to him and responded positively. Both thieves had the same opportunity, but only one saw the moment and seized it. It takes diligence and humility to perceive and grasp opportunities. Pride and negligence can be very costly, as they can lead to us failing to see and seize the opportunities presented to us. This can result in painful and regrettable experiences. May the Lord help us all to recognize and seize our opportunities as they come our way.

Here is your chance to make that switch. As I mentioned earlier, I would like to give you an opportunity to invite into your life the One who will give you eternal life. His name is Jesus Christ, the Son of the true living God. He is the way, the truth, and the life. No one goes to the Father in heaven except by Him. He is the same yesterday, today, and forever. All you need to do is to believe in Him, according to John 3:16, which says, "For God so loved the world that He gave His only begotten Son, that whoever believes in Him should not perish but have everlasting life."

This is the greatest opportunity of all the opportunities you will ever receive. If you believe in Him, you can pray the following prayer with me:

Dear Lord Jesus, I know that I am a sinner, and I ask for Your forgiveness. I believe You died for all of my sins and rose from the dead. I turn from my sins and invite You to come into my heart and life. I want to trust and follow You as my Lord and Saviour. Amen!

Congratulations. There is a great celebration in heaven for your response to the heavenly invitation. We read in Luke 15:10, "Likewise, I say to you, there is joy in the presence of the angels of God over one sinner who repents."

The Passion Translation says God responds every time a lost sinner repents and turns to him in this way: "He says to all his angels, 'Let's have a joyous celebration, for that one who was lost I have found!'" (Luke 15:10)

Now you have eternal life, and you are a new creation: "Therefore, if anyone *is* in Christ, *he is* a new creation; old things have passed away; behold, all things have become new" (2 Corinthians 5:17).

Here are some important things you should do for your personal growth:

- Learn to talk to God in prayer.
- Read your Bible (start with the Gospel of John).
- Find a good church to attend.
- Be the light and salt of the earth.
- Know that the Lord is always with you.
- Be of a grateful heart continually.
- Stay hungry and thirsty for righteousness and His kingdom.

You have given me a most precious gift—your time and attention—and I appreciate that greatly. Thank you. Should you have any further questions or testimonials to share with me, please do get in touch with me. I would be more than delighted to hear from you. Keep walking and working with the Lord. Remember that you are greatly loved, forgiven, accepted, highly valued and celebrated. You are destined for greatness. You have what it takes to succeed. Believe it. You are a transformational leader! My love and great appreciation goes out to you! You are my friend, sister or brother, in Christ Jesus! Abundant blessings!

Contact me through email:

daniel@tdclife.org
https://www.johncmaxwellgroup.com/danielogetoondieki/
Visit my coaching and mentoring website.
Remember to ask for your free gift in the website.

AMAZING TESTIMONIALS

The testimonials shared here are from various people who have been helped by the lessons that I have taught. They may make references to topics that are not in this book. Some may describe how they were helped during my counselling, coaching, or mentoring sessions with them. Some testimonials have been edited with permission from the owners for clarity purposes, but the content remains the same. Testimonials are very powerful. They inspire, motivate, and challenge us to change the way we see and do things. They also take us out of our comfort zones. Revelation 12:11 says, "And they overcame him by the blood of the Lamb and by the word of their testimony, and they did not love their lives to the death." They (the believers) overcame him (the enemy of God's people) by the blood of the Lamb and the word of their testimony. There is power in the blood of Lamb and the word of our testimonies. Our testimonies are based on God's written word in the Bible.

The main purpose of these testimonials is to bring glory and praise to the Lord, to inspire someone who could be challenged in one way or another, and to bring readers hope, comfort, and encouragement, especially during these difficult times. Remember, what you are going through is common to all men and women. Struggles are not new or uncommon. In 1 Corinthians 10:13, we read: "No temptation has overtaken you except such as is common to man; but God *is* faithful, who will not allow you to be tempted beyond what you are able, but with the temptation will also make the way of escape, that you may be able to bear *it*." Our God is faithful to see you through.

You are welcome to share your testimonial as well if you have been touched by this book. It will be used for the glory of God and for the edification of readers. I am forever grateful to all who have shared their testimonials. I greatly appreciate the time you took to write. It means a lot to me. You have added more value to this book and those who will read it. May the Lord richly bless you in every way.

Testimonial 1

I moved to a new city in a new country on a new continent. Its people spoke a language that I did not speak. But I knew that God's people can be a refuge. So I asked for a reference to a church that had meetings in English.

At the end of the service, I waited for the opportunity to speak with Pastor Daniel and tell him about all the uncertainties that had surrounded my life. He heard me, held my hands, and told me, "Monica, the miracle is in your mouth. From now on, you are going to speak what you want to happen. You are going to speak solutions."

I didn't fully understand what he meant, but I went home and started writing in a notebook. On the first page, I wrote, "The miracle is in your mouth." I changed my way of praying. I began not only asking God for his will in my life, but also reflecting on what I desired and speaking it out. Without knowing the *how*, without telling God how I expected Him to do it, I was declaring what I wanted to see happen in my life. And it started happening.

Through the teachings and mentoring of Pastor Daniel, I learned to actively participate in God's miracles. If I don't speak them, I am holding back the creative power that God gives us through words. Speaking is so important that it makes you start changing the way you normally talk. When someone asks me how I am doing and I am having a bad day, I am now very careful not to declare a "final verdict" that condemns my day. When I feel stressed or irritated, I check my inside communication and speak kind words to myself.

The power of words is a treasure of wisdom that Pastor Daniel reveals to us in a clear and practical way. I can't stop experiencing the benefits of this truth and revelation. Now, whenever I don't like what I am going through, I know that I need to change my speech, because the miracle is in my mouth.

Monica E.

Testimonial 2

It was mid-May 2019 when I called Pastor Daniel from an ambulance cruising at a high speed in the great city of Athens. My five-months-pregnant wife was in an emergency situation and fighting for our unborn baby boy. Pastor Daniel was keen to remind us of God's promises. He said a prayer with us and gave us divine assurance of God's great plan for us and our child.

A few days later, our son was born prematurely (three months early) and stayed in the intensive care unit for ten weeks. Pastor Daniel taught us and walked us through this crisis. His insight and wisdom were crucial to getting us through.

We were later transferred to Germany. Sixteen months later, our son is now doing great. He is a divine gift, a miracle indeed, and we thank God for the great man of faith who helped us to lift our eyes unto Him, from where the help we needed came.

The chapter titled "How to Go through Crises with God" will help you overcome any crisis that may come your way!
David Thuku Kamau, MD

Church Elder and Medical Doctor

Testimonial 3

My journey to know myself is very much connected to the seasons of life. Whenever I found myself in a challenging situation, I always searched for shortcuts and believed that my problems were then solved, only to realize that they would come back even more complicated than before. These complications affected my relationships and my finances. To say the least, I was in a total mess. I tried to change my situations in many ways, from reading books to following different life coaches and mentors. I even attempted to join meditation groups. But nothing worked to improve my life until I was taught and coached to "know myself." Like many of us, I had thought I already knew myself. However, I discovered that I had no clue of who I was when I started the true journey of discovering my identity with Pastor Daniel.

Every season of my life challenged me to reflect on the inner me. The deeper I went, the more painful it became. This reality check pushed me to see my life clearly. I knew that my challenges would only change if I was willing and intentional about that change. This meant that I needed to renew my way of thinking, my lifestyle, my companions, and my spiritual life.

One of my greatest problems was saying yes to everything, even when I should have said no. The renewal of my mind gave me confidence to say no at the right moments. And of course, my lifestyle changed as a result. I became selective with friends and other people. I started to enjoy my spiritual life.

Now I know and understand myself better. Whatever season I experience in my life, I choose to go through it, even if it will be a long journey. Today, I am a transformed woman because of my coach and mentor, Pastor Daniel, who constantly insisted on working on the inner me. He emphasized inside-out transformational leadership. He taught me to know the true me because that is who God wants to have a relationship with.

I thank God for sending me a mentor who helped me to find my true identity. With this identity, I am now able to face the challenges of the seasons of life. I believe this book will touch whoever is willing and intentional about living a life of abundance and greatness. May God continue to use Pastor Daniel and his ministries to reach out and touch many more souls.

Stella K.

Testimonial 4

I did not know how powerful our words are until Pastor Daniel taught and showed me in the Word of God. Words are seeds, and they can change our world. Since then, I have changed not only my words, but also my way of thinking. I do not allow any negative voices to speak into my life anymore, because death and life are in the power of the tongue.

I thank God for Pastor Daniel. He is a great mentor and coach, and he has a big heart that has touched many people. His passion is to help people grow in every area of their lives. Pastor Daniel lives this passion with patience and the wisdom of God.

Maral N.

Testimonial 5

In John 15:1, we read that God is the gardener and Jesus is the true grapevine. Regarding my life, God has used the author, Pastor Daniel, as a heavenly gardener to put many seeds of faith in my life. Not only did he sow them, but he also watered them with care and candour through personal coaching and praying together.

I want to give testimony that all the teachings I received from Pastor Daniel have blessed me so much in finding my identity in Jesus Christ. Through his teachings, led and guided by the Holy Spirit, my life was built up in the one and only right direction: towards God Almighty. I am very thankful that other people will also have the chance to be transformed by reading this book. Be encouraged to find God speaking to you in each chapter, and realize the profit from it for your personal life and growth.

I don't have the right words to say thank you for being my spiritual father. Your teaching and prayers are like medicine. My first prophetic calendar is the fruit of your coaching!

Charlotte L.

Testimonial 6

I had been in crisis with God for many years simply due to obliviousness and my lack of knowledge of God. Pastor Daniel reconciled me with God by illuminating my understanding of God and how He works on us, through us, and with us. Thanks to Pastor Daniel's wisdom and teachings, I came to understand that God was working on me and through me, but I was not working with Him. I understood that I was living in darkness simply because my relationship with God was one way: my way. The ways in which I was communicating with God and interpreting His messages were also not right.

Pastor Daniel transformed what I thought was a burden in my life into a blessing. He made me realize that my purpose in life is to bring light, purpose, and hope to those in need. He appreciated my love for my extended family and my persistence in supporting them, and this can be used to rethink the value and role of families as the nucleus of society.

I appreciate Pastor Daniel's work, and I am really happy that he is teaching and touching hearts, transforming minds, and healing souls. This is the beginning of a long journey, and I hope to continue working under Pastor Daniel's mentoring and coaching.

Dr. Miriam L. H.

Testimonial 7

One thing that we can all agree on is that God's timing is always perfect. Some months before I gave birth to my firstborn son, the Lord sent Pastor Daniel into my life through his personal coaching and mentoring (PCM) platform.

It was through PCM that I began to learn how to speak words and life over my unborn child. It is through PCM that Pastor Daniel taught me to anoint my children, even before their birth. Pastor Daniel taught me that even before a child is born, their spirit is already alive and needs to be fed with words of affirmation and life. Pastor Daniel taught me the power of the tongue—that you are what you speak, not what you eat, as many would say.

Through coaching and mentorship, I have understood and embraced the true calling of motherhood. I have learnt that a mother is the first mentor of her child. As a mentor, I have the power and ability to build my child's inner self or to destroy it with my words and actions.

Over the years, I have also witnessed growth in the way I relate to my husband, my children, my other family members, and my friends. I have learnt how to build my home and how to thank God for the things that are currently unseen.

What I really appreciate about Pastor Daniel's approach to coaching and mentorship is that he does not judge you; instead, he accepts you the way you are. He concentrates on your strengths and makes sure that you grow to the next level. With him there is no stagnation allowed.

I am forever grateful to God that I have a personal mentor and coach like Pastor Daniel. He has changed not only my life, but also my surroundings. I am now proud to say that I mentor other mothers and sisters around me.

Maggie N.

Testimonial 8

There comes a point and time in life that a man needs a mentor. For some men, their biological fathers automatically take this role at a young age. Unfortunately, however, for many young men, this is not the case. I belong to the latter group. Growing up without a father figure or male mentor made me realize how much I missed out during my youth.

I have made wrong decisions in life. Luckily, I have learnt from most of them. It was later in life and, by God's grace, shortly before becoming a father myself that God delivered His humble servant, Pastor Daniel Ondieki, into my life. I cannot even describe in words what impact Pasi, as we call him, has had on my life and my family.

The first time I was ministered to on 16 June 2012, I took notes on three key points that have become the foundation of where I am today as a man:

One: Why did God choose you to enter this world?

Two: What is God's purpose for your presence?

Three: What is the culture of the kingdom?

Together with his teachings over the years, Pastor Daniel has mentored me to become a man of accountability in all aspects of my life. He taught me on that very first day, during one of his seminars ("Times of Refreshing"), that God's promise to me in this world is to give me the keys of the kingdom of heaven. We are accepted as citizens in the kingdom of God, but only if we accept Jesus Christ as our Saviour. To integrate into the kingdom of God, you have to learn to have faith. You must not forget that doubt works as faith works. God can use the most neglected and the most vulnerable. God can use you to touch your family.

God used Pastor Daniel to mentor me so that I could touch my family. I'm proud and honoured to call him my spiritual dad, for he has never left my side since I was born again. To God be the glory, honour, and praise!

Angelo N.

Testimonial 9

"The Power of Words" (Chapter 1), "You Are Gifted" (Chapter 5), and "Understanding Your Assignment" (Chapter 8) spoke to us during our coaching and mentoring sessions.

It has been a great blessing to know Daniel Ondieki in various capacities as a father, pastor, coach, mentor, and counsellor. His words of wisdom have guided us spiritually and professionally. His teaching on the power of words shed light on something we had struggled with for years in our home. His coaching and leadership gently nudge you to realize the potential that is already inside of you. This is not another motivational book, but teachings that can transform your destiny and help you fulfil your assignment! Coach Daniel helped us to prioritize family, work, and business, and to understand the seasons and lanes of life. The knowledge and insights shared in this book are filled with power. We highly recommend it!

Dr. Osianoh and Ibukun Aliu

Testimonial 10

Words are indeed very powerful—this we had always heard but really hadn't given much consideration. Rather, we underrated the statement until we heard Pastor Daniel's emphatic teachings. The Bible says in Proverbs 18:21, "Death and life *are* in the power of the tongue,

And those who love it will eat its fruit."

The stakes are high. Your words can speak either life or death. Our tongues can build others up or tear them down. We have chosen the former.

During our six years of marriage, this teaching came in handy in our early days. We look back and think that we would not have made it this far if we hadn't crossed paths with Pastor Daniel and his wonderful teachings. May the Lord continue to bless him. As a newlywed couple, many were the times we found ourselves at loggerheads, angry and frustrated because we had not been mindful of our choice of words towards each other. In moments of disagreement, we found ourselves worse off due to a poor choice of words said at the height of anger. When piled up, those words slowly turned into resentment.

Over the years and under the influence of Pastor Daniel's teachings, we have learnt to be mindful of our words with each other in both the good and bad times. This is not to say we are in a perfect place, but, by the grace of God, we keep learning and re-learning every day. It's in the little things. When words and tone are well packaged, they go a long way. We reflect back and say, "The Lord brought us to Europe for our studies, but little did we know of how much more He had in store for us through Pastor Daniel's powerful seminars and teachings. The Lord has really kept us together and spoken to us through Pastor Daniel. To God be the glory and honour and praise!"

Dr. Georgina and Dr. Oliver

Testimonial 11

My name is Julieta. I met Pastor Daniel in September 2018 through my cousin, who invited me to a special seminar conducted by Pastor Daniel. I had just lost my job after working for twenty-three years, which was a very difficult time. This invitation came at the right and perfect time for me to seek the Lord for direction. The seminar was quite inspiring and motivating. It challenged us to go to the next level.

These were my takeaways from the seminar: When building your life, family is the sure foundation. When the storms of life come your way, you will be able to stand strong. The number one killer in the world is ignorance. As scripture says, God's people are destroyed for lack of knowledge. It is also written that God's people have gone into captivity for lack of knowledge.

One specific question was asked throughout the seminar: What do you see in your life in the past, present, and future? This was an eye-opener for me. What you see will determine what you constantly think about and act upon. We were challenged to work more from the inside out. Many times, we want to see the changes on the outside, but we are not willing to work on the inside of ourselves. Working on the inside enables us to work with renewed minds, which helps us to know what is good and acceptable according to the perfect will of God!

Proverbs 18:21 also spoke to me. It says, "Death and life are in the power of the tongue, and those who love it will eat its fruit." Words can work for us or against us. Jesus said that you will have what you say. We should speak out words of faith and not words of fear.

It has taken me discipline to be consistent, intentional, and careful in my speech in the midst of all kinds of life challenges. I have achieved and gradually become successful, as Pastor Daniel's coaching and mentoring has helped me to stay focused and on course. My faith has grown, and I am more aware of God's presence, knowing that I will never be alone. Thanks, Pastor Daniel, for your coaching and mentoring; I feel excited about my future. "What no eye has seen, what no ear has heard, and what no human mind has conceived, the things God has prepared for those who love him" (1 Corinthians 2:9).

Julieta G.

Testimonial 12

"You are gifted." Those three words became a reality to me when I listened to my coach, Daniel, speak on this topic. I had known Daniel for many years, but it was when he became my coach that I first tapped into the gifts of God that reside in him. Before I started my coaching journey with Daniel, my life could be likened to that of a person with a deep desire to build a house who has gathered all the materials and other resources necessary to build the house but lacks the skills to organize the materials into a house. A few sessions into the coaching programme, not only did my eyes begin to see my ability to identify the different materials, but my mouth began to speak things into being. Order and supernatural function were brought into my life by the help of the Holy Spirit, who is the gift of God freely given to us.

Hearing Daniel say that "the nine gifts of the Spirit help us to see, speak, and do" was very empowering. We all have been given gifts by God. All we need to do is receive them by faith. By identifying my area of gifting, I am more focused and productive as a coach and counsellor.

Anne N. O.

Testimonial 13

Daniel, thank you for the bold step you have taken to become an author. Congratulations! This is a true demonstration of the power of the spoken word. What you are today has come about through a continuous proclamation of the Word of God, as it is written in Romans 4:17 ("I have made you a father of many nations") in the presence of Him whom he believed—God, who gives life to the dead and calls those things which do not exist as though they did.

I have seen you grow up both spiritually and in other areas using your faith and actions and by trusting God at all times. Thus, the Lord has brought you this far and helped you!

You have been and continue to be an inspiration to me, my family, and many others. Your life has been a book we can read and draw principles of life from. I am looking forward to reading your book. God bless you, and good day.

Kennedy O.

Testimonial 14

I've known Daniel Ondieki for ten years. He has made a tremendous difference in my life, and I am forever grateful to know him as my spiritual father and mentor. The topics in this book will challenge and change your life for the better. Daniel is the one person who saw my gifts and continuously encouraged me to operate in those gifts. Due to my growth, I have finally seen the gifts myself and thus was able to bring them to another level. Today, I am confident in my gifts, and I can encourage others to see their own natural gifts.

Mentoring is one of Daniel's pillars and his daily bread. I was privileged to be mentored by him and developed exceedingly. He was there for me in the deepest crisis of my life. He advised as well as corrected me in my ways of going forward. I got to the point (after many bad things followed one after another) at which I asked myself, "Why should I live anymore?" As Daniel is a very good listener with a strong level of dedication and passion, this question vanished immediately when he addressed my burdens.

His advice has often helped me to go forward, and the results have been extraordinary. Now I am truly blessed in all areas of my life. I know my purpose as well as my root source of joy, peace, and wisdom. My heart runs over with thanks for Daniel's help, support, and trust. To God be the glory and praise!

Benjamin M.

Testimonial 15

Thank you, Coach. I honour you and appreciate you for directly mentoring and coaching me. As ambitious and optimistic as I am, after the uncertainty, stress, and disappointment of 2020, I wasn't really sure what the unique factor of the year would be for me. As a result of all the confusion, I struggled with my work-life balance and a lack of enthusiasm for my purpose.

Then, in late October, I was introduced to you, and that's how my year and my life changed. Teachings such as "The Lanes of Life" and "The Global Stage"—which are not shared in this book but were shared with me during my coaching and mentoring sessions—have helped and shaped my attitude, character, hunger for knowledge, and time management. Your knowledge has given me understanding, and this understanding has given me the faith to put into action everything I'm learning. I have set myself up for exponential growth and good success.

I am a testimony of the power of mentoring and coaching, which you outline in Chapter 9. Thank you, Coach Daniel. You are a blessing and the best.

Munene Githira
CEO, ORAC Branding

Testimonial 16

We are students studying in Germany. In the course of our studies, we fell in love with each other. Having confirmed the will of God concerning our relationship, we went to see Pastor Daniel for counselling and marriage preparation. He took us through the necessary premarital steps, which was really great. But when it came to finances, we only had 400€, which was not enough to organize a wedding in Europe. In our customary celebrations where we come from, everything has to be big.

Pastor Daniel's advice was to "make it simple." You don't have to host a big wedding to impress everyone and end up in debt as a newlywed couple. He said, "If you wish, I will conduct a wedding ceremony on Sunday morning and bless you. After the service, you can gather a few close family members and friends and have a small, good celebration." With those words of wisdom and encouragement, our faith grew and we started to organize the wedding, believing God would give us His favour and blessing.

We spoke with our family and friends in France and Germany. To our surprise, they were ready to support us. They were able to raise our budget from 400€ to 4,000€ in less than two months. We were left speechless! God's favour can get you from less to more! With this budget in place, we were able to have a very beautiful civil ceremony in Denmark, followed by a Christian wedding in France in a very beautiful atmosphere on 26 September 2020.

We are indeed grateful to our God for His favour and blessings to us. Thanks, Pastor Daniel, for your wise counsel and guidance. We are very thankful for the support of our family and friends. "For with God nothing shall be impossible" (Luke 1:37).

Nadine and Abel

Testimonial 17

I met Pastor Daniel in 2010 at one of his seminars called "Times of Refreshing." I was quite new in faith at that time. During that period, we were going through very tough and challenging times as a family. My mother and I sought to attend another very special seminar that focused on inside-out transformation. As my mother went through the instructions of the seminar, her marriage was restored, and my father came to faith. He was water baptized, which was a very special and great thing for us as a family. We experienced healing and restoration through prayers and God's supernatural intervention.

After the seminar, I registered for Pastoral Care Ministry and Counselling (PCM/C).

During the PCM/C sessions, I was greatly impacted. My marriage was enriched, I began to raise my children with godly principles, and my ministry with the children in my community was very blessed. I applied the same principles in my place of work, and I saw good fruits. I was able to manage my time well. Above all, I found my purpose in life! That is the power of coaching and mentoring. "You learn more in less time, and you become more to do more."

Over the past ten years, I haven't met a teacher and spiritual father as patient and full of love as Pastor Daniel! Indeed, I am forever grateful. What he invested in me I am still giving back to others. Thank you so much, Pastor Daniel and Edith, for caring for and blessing me and my family for all these years.

To God be the glory and praise!

J. Zei

Testimonial 18

When Pastor Daniel spoke in our church for the first time, he began his sermon with a clear structure: "First … Second …. Third …" Being a lawyer by profession, I felt immediately drawn to this well-structured path of loving thoughts.

This formal attraction was transformed into deep thankfulness when Pastor Daniel's coaching began to change my life. The key that opened the door for my professional success was his seemingly simple question, "What is your vision?" I had vainly asked the Lord for a vision and had waited for an answer for years. Being blind to the obvious, I had not seen the answer that was lying plainly in front of my hands. Instead of a spectacular revelation with lightning and thunder, it was just a question of knowing myself better.

In my case, the vision became very clear: helping elderly and sick people to finish well. Such well-selected words changed life's reality. This beginning to my coaching was as important as its ending: proper definition of the Holy Spirit's role.

After being around Jesus for years, one's head may be full of pious words. But at least in my case, those words did not sink into my heart. They swam like a wine cork floats on the surface of a pond. A solitary, self-employed person might not be motivated by correct sentences like "Everything belongs to the Lord, and you are just his trustee." This did not really inspire me to identify new projects and develop the necessary energy to overcome daily obstacles.

Then came Pastor Daniel's suggestion: "Let the Holy Spirit into daily business as your personal Senior Partner." That was it. Immediately, I was not working alone any longer. I had a partner's desk in my office, with the Holy Spirit sitting face-to-face with me, giving me advice, resources, and calmness.

Therefore, I am convinced that *Destined for Greatness* will boost many people's lives. It might lead to a breakthrough in a job or, even more importantly, the joy of the Lord's proximity.

Frederic S.

Testimonial 19

In 2020, South Africa went into hard lockdown, and all my contracts were cancelled from one week to the next. I had no work and was trying to pray. But I didn't hear the voice of God. I was trying to understand scriptures, but they were not making sense. I went through the Bible like it was a blank book. I asked the Holy Spirit to help me. He showed me things in the Word, and it still didn't make sense. I felt alone! When I prayed, yes, I did feel the presence of the Lord—but I didn't really know what to ask. Was it guilt? Surely.

I didn't spend good quality time with the Lord. The situation got worse, and wrong thoughts began coming to me. I fought them off as best I could. I spoke to my wife, Gloria; she encouraged me. She had been very hurt in the ministry, too. She didn't want to hear anything about ministry for some time. But Gloria was always praying and listening to the Lord, even through the darkest hour of our lives in ministry. She was very excited that tourism was working so well. She saw it as an answer to prayer.

I got worse day by day. I wanted to leave South Africa and go back to Germany. Being a German citizen, I could do that. Gloria said, "Don't run away from your problems." We had an argument. Nothing was working. I started to blame myself for wrong choices and wrong decisions, getting deeper into the valley. I even said to Gloria, "Maybe it would be better if I took an overdose of sleeping tablets and brought my life to an end."

She said, "And then leave me alone here to face all the problems?"

We more or less ran out of money and had no direction as to where to get another income. All avenues were closed!

I went to bed that night and asked the Lord to show me His way and His purpose for my life. I waited but heard nothing. I fell asleep. I woke up. I didn't see that my Bible was open (it was showing me Jeremiah 29 and Jeremiah 33:3). I didn't read it until later, after I had placed a call to Pastor Daniel from Germany.

I just said to the Lord, "I don't know You anymore. You don't even know me anymore! You don't know my number. It's best You take me now."

The day before, Pastor Daniel had tried to call me. I had met him in the ministry twenty-one years prior and had trained him to become a counsellor in South Africa. He sent me a text message, telling me that God had spoken to him and he needed to talk with me. I read it later the next day.

After I read it, I called Pastor Daniel. He was in a meeting. A few hours later, he called me back, and we spoke. He told me that God had spoken to him and showed him I was in a deep valley and a dangerous situation. The Lord had told Pastor Daniel to call me! We had not spoken for over a year. I hadn't even remembered that he had my telephone number.

Pastor Daniel said, "Ralf, God told me to call you." I started crying, because I had told the Lord that He didn't know my number anymore and that I wanted to die. I told Pastor Daniel the whole situation. He offered to counsel, coach, and mentor me. He wanted to bring me back to where God wanted me to be.

Over the next few months, Pastor Daniel took me by the hand and pulled me out of the valley. I got my vision back. I focused on the Lord. I listened to His voice. I spent time with the Father, the Son, and the Holy Spirit. We are working together now – helping people in need, doing counselling and entrepreneurship seminars, and soon offering leadership seminars.

God took me from the valley back to the mountaintop through the obedience of Pastor Daniel. Now I am on the mountaintop again, and I am helping other people to get out of the valley. My vision is still strong. I focus and hear what the Lord says to me. He directs me by His Holy Spirit.

Now I am preparing for what God has for me, running the race and fulfilling the calling on my life. God has anointed me to do what He has called me to do. I am looking forward to a closer and deeper walk with the Lord, my God!

Even as ministers, if we are not walking in the fullness of God, the enemy will try to ruin us. The enemy doesn't love us; he comes to steal, kill, and destroy us. That is his mission and purpose here on Earth (John 10:10). But Jesus has come that we may have life and have it more abundantly! We need to be on guard against the attack of the enemy of our souls all the time. We have the authority in Christ Jesus to fight and overcome him. Greater is He who is in us than he who is in the world. I can do all things through Christ who strengthens me. The same power that raised Jesus from the dead dwells inside of me. I am the temple of the Holy Spirit and an ambassador for the kingdom of heaven on Earth. He will call me home when my time comes!

Pastor Daniel coached and counselled me from the end of April to November. I had amazing encounters with the Lord. I received financial and spiritual blessings as I just sat back, being still. I praised and thanked the Lord for His glorious provision. In challenging times, shift into thanksgiving, praises, and worship, even when you do not feel like doing so.

In May 2019, I was taken in by Logos Global Vision, Korbach, to do ministry work for it in South and southern Africa. The Lord began to bless us financially; the most important bills, like medical aid, electricity, telephone, and food, could be covered. We praised the Lord for the income we received.

Suddenly, we also received a blessing from the Department of Tourism in South Africa. People who didn't even know our situation asked me for my banking details. One couple from Schwerin, previous clients of mine, asked how we were. They felt in their hearts that I needed some help. A couple from Bremen had the same inspiration, wanting to bless us. A lady from Johannesburg, South Africa, felt the same. Hallelujah!. Praise the Lord. God is good. He never leaves us nor forsakes us.

God is a God of the sudden. Sometimes we look to other sources, believing that those are the ones God will use. But if the Lord is not in them, then they won't be successful. He will come through and lead us by His Holy Spirit. He is the total Source of all that we need in life. I have learned and seen that during the months since I came back to the ministry and was restored and ministered to.

Could it be that you are going through a crisis or you are in a dead valley? Never give up! Don't take your life before your time comes, as I wanted to do. God loves you, and He wants to satisfy you with long life, according to Psalm 91:15–16:

> He shall call upon Me, and I will answer him;
> I *will be* with him in trouble;
> I will deliver him and honour him.
> With a long life I will satisfy him,
> And show him My salvation.

Praise the Lord!

Dr. Ralf Doepke, BTH, DMTH

Testimonial 20

I still remember it as if it were yesterday: my very first Personal Coaching and Mentoring (PCM) session with Pastor Daniel on 10 November 2017. Life hadn't gone as I expected, and I was in a crisis. God used that to bring me to where I am today.

During that first PCM meeting, Pastor Daniel asked me four questions: "Where are you spiritually? Mentally? Physically? Financially?" This helped me to see exactly what was right and wrong in my life. Pastor Daniel also said, "You are not a victim of your circumstances. You can only become a victim of your beliefs and the choices you make. Jesus says that you will have whatever you say."

I left the meeting uplifted and encouraged, knowing that there was healing for my brokenness. God had all the answers to my questions.

During the next twelve months, God used Pastor Daniel and PCM to teach me about our victory that has overcome the world: *faith!* Faith had helped me to work through my parents' divorce when I was a child. By faith, I overcame the fear of divorce in my own marriage. By faith, I was healed of a broken heart that had resulted from crushed hope and unfulfilled dreams when a promising relationship I was in at that time suddenly came to an end.

Pastor Daniel, through PCM, taught me to use the Word of God as a shield against any attacks on my mind, heart, and soul. I kept reciting 1 John 4:18: "There is no fear in love; but perfect love casts out fear, because fear involves torment."

One year after my first PCM meeting, I received a breakthrough. God's Word in Proverbs 29:18 suddenly became alive in my spirit: "Where there is no vision, the people perish." I realized I didn't have a clear vision, and as a result, I was lacking direction in life.

Daniel and I specifically prayed for a stable job, a new apartment, and a woman I might call my wife. I cried in my car on the way home, but those tears of sadness soon changed into tears of joy. God answered our prayer soon after. And here I am today, blessed with a stable job I love and living with my wonderful wife in our beautiful apartment.

God used Pastor Daniel through PCM to teach me another language in addition to the languages I had already learned to speak before: the language of *faith*, the most precious and powerful language of all. To God be the glory and praise!

Andreas E.

Testimonial 21

Pastor Daniel blessed and influenced me to live an intentional life throughout my time in Bonn, Germany. Whenever I think of Pastor Daniel, the first image that flashes into my mind is his gentle and wide smile with an expression that says, "Grow up to go up!" "Never stop growing" is his personal mantra. It has shaped who he is and his ministry. His approach to mentoring is effective. He is led by the Holy Spirit and is full of wisdom, speaking the truth in kindness and correcting me to the right path.

Since his Plumb Line seminar, Pastor Daniel has engaged me in Personal Coaching and Mentoring (PCM) and Group Coaching and Mentoring (GCM). This complementary approach to biblical teaching and personal mentorship has allowed me to grow both in the community and as an individual.

During my PCM/GCM with Pastor Daniel, we covered two topics: walking in a renewed mind and the power of your words. I was able to deal with some situations in my life that had been challenging me and overcame them. The second topic that changed my life was entitled: "Going from ignorance to knowledge" helped me to be more faith-filled, which brought spiritual and personal breakthroughs to my life. At some point, God pointed out the bondage I had been in since I was 16 years old due to my thought pattern. I have managed to have a breakthrough since then.

Pastor Daniel is the most consistent person I have seen in my life. He faithfully walks the talk. He is disciplined, loving, and anointed. He lives up to his calling with full, godly intentions. His life has impacted my life and inspired me. I strive to live a life of purpose and impact.

Pastor Daniel's approach, legacy, and personal convictions are the reasons why you should read his intentional book and have glimpses of his wisdom for your own life.

Beatrice S.

Testimonial 22

I thank God for the fathering and mentoring ministry I received through Pastor Daniel. At the time we got to know each other, I was joining a church; I had realized that I had come to the point in my walk with the Lord where I was stuck and needed help. I connected with Pastor Daniel, and we started to meet and have personal fellowship. He allowed me to share, listening patiently, and he also shared and taught me the Word of God. Through this regular fellowship, I not only learned to understand scripture in deeper ways, but I also had an example to follow of how to walk the walk of faith practically in everyday life. Every time we met, I was challenged to grow.

Especially in the beginning, it took discipline to stay faithful under Pastor Daniel's discipleship training. But in the course of time, I experienced the foundations of my personality being rewired for good under his spiritual fathering. I can say that much of what I am in Christ today is based on our spiritual father-son relationship. Had I not stayed in the relationship, I would not be able to face the challenges and the walk of destiny God prepared for me in the following years. I am still walking in it today.

Therefore, I am deeply thankful that God has given me a faithful mentor who saw beyond my limitations and failures, believed in me, and nurtured my growth until I matured. I am also deeply thankful to Pastor Daniel for availing himself to God for this intensive ministry. He was ready to consider a single person as precious as an entire nation.

As you read this book, with its different teachings about the kingdom of God and walking in it in a practical way, I pray that you may also find the person God has provided to nurture you and help you grow more into the fullness of Christ. I also pray that you will come to the place to avail yourself to God so that He can use you faithfully to father or mother others through you. All glory goes to the Lord in Jesus's name!

Christian S.

Testimonial 23

Knowing and walking with dear Pastor Daniel was one of our greatest treasures in 2020. After going through coaching and counselling sessions to deepen our walk with God, our lives were greatly transformed. The most remarkable session we went through during our couples coaching and mentoring occurred when we tackled the lanes of life. The eight lanes of life are what every Christian needs to implement into their walk with Christ. This topic is not in this book, but we all concluded that Lane 1 is the foundation of all lanes in life. If one does well in Lane 1, they will do well in the other lanes. If not, all the other lanes will be affected.

Pastor Daniel, it is a great honour and treasure to know you. We look forward to many more sessions, which we all need to maintain a sustainable relationship with God, spread the gospel, and be great role models, as Christ commanded us to be.

Shalom,

George, Carol, and the girls

"You Are Gifted" is a topic that spoke to me during a coaching session. I realized that I am not using many of the skills and talents God has given me.

Pastor Daniel, in his classes, has always empowered me through his words of encouragement and support. I have had the privilege of getting to know Pastor Daniel and the Plumb Line Ministry over the past ten years. I have been in his PCM courses. During my coaching sessions, he has shown me principles of the Word of God. The Word of God has ministered life, health, and restoration to me over the years.

I took a class called "Personal Development Plan," in which I learned that whatever I imagine I can achieve, as long as it is in line with the Word of God. For example, scripture says, "And the Lord said to Abram, after Lot had separated from him: 'Lift your eyes now and look from the place where you are—northward, southward, eastward, and westward; for all the land which you see I give to you and your descendants forever'" (Genesis 13:14–15). I, too, can develop a vision for my life and achieve it.

God has used Pastor Daniel to bring me forward. Pastor Daniel is always willing to listen to my personal challenges and mentor me, especially in the area of the soul. As you know, the soul is the conscience, mind, will, and emotions of a human being. Pastor Daniel taught me how to deal with various fears. We looked at scripture passages like 2 Timothy 1:7 ("For God has not given us a spirit of fear, but of power and of love and of a sound mind") and Psalm 124:7 ("Our soul has escaped as a bird from the snare of the fowlers; The snare is broken, and we have escaped").

I have grown up spiritually over the years of my personal coaching and mentoring sessions with Pastor Daniel. He has a great gift of counselling, too, and he is my spiritual father. He has encouraged me by telling me to never give up. Pastor Daniel believes in me and sees my potential.

I am also thankful for my family, who have supported me over the years in various ways. My thanks go as well to the ministers of my local church. I give glory to God for all He has done in my life through various people, especially through the Plumb Line Ministry of Pastor Daniel Ondieki. I bless Pastor Daniel and the team ministering to lost and hurt people. I am sure many more will be blessed through this ministry, just as I was.

Anjali R.

Testimonial 25

How many times have you used words that you later ended up regretting? My testimony is not one of regret, but one of hope and inspiration.

So, let me start at the beginning! I met Pastor Daniel and his wife Edith within the first few months after I arrived in Germany. And what a godly encounter that was. I met them by attending a seminar called Plumb Line, which they presented. There, Pastor Daniel first planted the seed of the power of words in my conscious mind and heart. That will stay with me. I have nourished and grown that seed in my life.

I have always known that words are simple, but what I probably neglected to comprehend was the incredible amount of power in words when used correctly. I have often forgotten that words indeed carry meaning, emotions, aspirations, ideals, and ideas. So what a revelation to me it was when, for the next year or so, I heard Pastor Daniel share this message with me on various platforms (GCM, PCM, CCM, etc.). It became like a mantra, a vortex, and a constant reminder of how I can transform my outlook on life, experiences, situations, and circumstances.

Utilizing the power of words was a decision. I look for opportunities every day to use the power of words to my benefit. I work to serve my best interests for my betterment and the betterment of those close to me.

I have learnt from Pastor Daniel that there is not only power in words, but also creative. For whoever believes in words, words will serve and work for them! Pastor Daniel has become my aha-verifier. Through the power of my words and my unwavering belief in that power, doors that were seemingly closed have been opened. People almost miraculously appeared to be of assistance to me. Systems known to be bureaucratic and rigid were seamlessly and smoothly unfolded in record-breaking time. And the list goes on.

The bottom line is that I chose to believe in the power of words!

So, next time that you self-talk or use words, make sure your words are positive, reassuring, kind, and constructive.

Romein S. V.

Testimonial 26

I vividly remember when I first met Pastor Daniel. It was back in October 2011, around five months after I had moved to the German city of Bonn. Although I was quite young then, about to turn 26, I had a lot of anxiety and worries about my future. This was because I hadn't been outside my home country before, and all my plans and dreams were there. I was in a new land with long-term prospects, adjusting mentally. To me, this was a big challenge.

While taking a stroll in Bonn one evening, I bumped into Pastor Daniel and his wife Edith in a shopping mall. After a brief chat, we exchanged contact information. That started a long and interesting relationship in which Pastor Daniel became a confidant, mentor, pastor, and friend to me. I soon signed up for an inner-healing seminar christened Plumb Line Ministry, which aimed at laying all fears, hurts, and anger at the feet of Jesus. It was a weekend session and very intimate. I revealed the skeletons in my closet to Pastor Daniel and an intercessor. After praying about those skeletons, I felt a weight lifted off my shoulders. I felt a fresh desire to confidently move on with life.

Thereafter, I signed up for a Personal Coaching and Mentoring (PCM) session with Pastor Daniel. We took time to read and understand the Bible better, focusing on revealing God's plan for me. I was indeed blessed by and grew during these sessions.

After some time, I got married. Due to work-related commitments, my wife and I had to live in different continents for three years. Although it was tough, we were blessed with the opportunity to sign up for Couples Coaching Ministry (CCM) with Pastor Daniel. These sessions, which took place every Thursday morning at 6:30 a.m. via Skype, addressed various pre-planned topics aimed at instilling heavenly principles in our marriage.

One of the topics we went through was "I Am Gifted." Speaking for myself, although I knew that God had given me some gifts and talents, I hadn't previously had the opportunity to take a deep dive into the topic.

Through our CCM study, I learnt that it was crucial for me to discover, nurture, and use my God-given gifts and talents. This is because God-given gifts and talents are good and perfect gifts given to each one of us. These gifts make room for us in the marketplace, bring joy to our hearts as we serve, and bless those around us by providing solutions to problems. Most importantly, using our gifts well gives God the glory, honour, and praise.

After taking some time to reflect, I discovered that God has given me the gift of always striving to find new ways to improve processes and make them more efficient. In addition to seeing this in projects that I undertake, I've been informed about this gift by my work colleagues and friends. I therefore continue to nurture this gift by taking self-development courses so that I can use my gift for the glory of God.

I have faith that, in the same way that God brought Pastor Daniel to my life, God planned to have you read this book. I believe this book has deep knowledge and wisdom from God to guide you as you go through the phases of life.

I'm therefore very excited for you as you read this book. I have no doubt that the chapter "You Are Gifted" will help you through the journey of discovering the beautiful and perfect gifts that God has given you.

God bless.

Hillary S.

Testimonial 27

The parable of the lost sheep that is found in Luke 15:4–6 shows us that we cannot view God's expression of love with our own eyes. For the sake of only one sheep, God can stop and turn everything around. And that is exactly what God did for me. I met Pastor Daniel Ondieki about ten years ago. At the time, I didn't know that God would use him to reach out to the one lost sheep. Since then, Pastor Daniel has been my mentor and coach.

In October 2012, I had an opportunity to go through Plumb Line, a weekend seminar that focuses on teaching the Word of God in plenary sessions and spiritual counselling in an individual session. The weekend seminar is intense; you get to examine yourself during the reflection sessions, interact with others, or just enjoy quiet moments with God. The highlight of the Plumb Line seminar is the one-on-one sessions with Pastor Daniel and an intercessor. During the one-on-one sessions, you start applying the lessons from the teachings. You slowly start uprooting negative roots (thoughts, behaviours, addictions etc.). You get into a moment of forgiveness, forgiving others and yourself, and plant good seeds—seeds that will bring forth the right harvest. I left the seminar feeling like a brand-new creation, ready to start life over again.

Following the Plumb Line seminar, I participated in the Personal Coaching Ministry (PCM) and the Group Coaching Ministry (GCM), and I later joined the Couples Coaching Ministry (CCM) with my husband. One of the topics we covered during the coaching sessions was the power of words. I learnt that words are powerful and have the ability to build or to destroy. As stated in Genesis, for instance, God created all things by His word. He simply spoke the word, and it was done. Therefore, words can manifest life and should be used to build, encourage, heal, and affirm.

A simple exercise that Pastor Daniel asked me to practice daily was to affirm myself by looking in the mirror and declaring, "Jackline, you are highly favoured. You are blessed. You are precious. You are beautiful." I was not mindful of all this before I understood how powerful words can be. I'm now more conscious when choosing my words.

After almost ten years of mentoring and coaching, Pastor Daniel has impacted my life positively and equipped me with knowledge that I am able to share with others, including my 7-month-old son and other family members. Isaiah 55 reminds us that God's ways and thoughts are not our ways and thoughts. God turned things around when I went astray and has been using Pastor Daniel as His vessel to draw me closer to Him. What a wonderful God we serve. He knows each of us by name and wants to have a relationship with us as His children.

God bless you, Pastor Daniel, for allowing God to use you as His vessel! To Him be the glory, honour, and praise! Amen!

Jackie S.

Testimonial 28

Understanding seasons in your life and transitioning through them are two different things. When I engaged in personal coaching sessions with my coach and mentor Daniel, clarity set in. I had reached a crossroads in my life and needed to move to a place of significance.

All my life I have been dedicated to success, and I have achieved it on many levels—at least success as I would have personally defined it. However, I found myself in this place where my personal success meant nothing and brought me no fulfilment. Coach Daniel made me question the meaning of life. Through the sessions, I came to understand why I did the things I did and why my definition of personal success was not enough. I have discarded beliefs, definitions, and habitual patterns that do not support fulfilment and significance. I learnt that I have the power to make different choices, and this time around I understand why I am making these choices.

Thanks to Coach Daniel, clarity, purpose, and significance are what my life is all about.

Wamaitha N.

Testimonial 29

It was a privilege to have Pastor Daniel around during my stay in Bonn in the early 2010s. I helped Pastor Daniel by being a translator for a group of Christians in the Chinese Fellowship in Bonn. Through Pastor Daniel's powerful yet easy-to-understand teachings, my heart and conscious mind were greatly enlightened about the richness and blessings from our Lord Jesus Christ, which I had never been able to experience during my previous twenty years of being a Christian.

I still constantly go back to the notes I took on the teachings shared by Pastor Daniel, especially on concepts like the power of words, understanding the favour of the Lord, and thanksgiving, praise, and worship, among others. I am really glad that I can now enjoy more freedom, be more grateful for and confident of our Lord's blessings and favours, and I have the knowledge and understanding to use words to bless myself and others in all circumstances.

I really can't wait to read Pastor Daniel's teachings again, along with new teachings! May our Lord use this book greatly to bless more people. To God be the glory, honour, and praise forever!

Brother Roy Fan

Testimonial 30

It's my great pleasure to honour you, Pastor Daniel, and thank you for your great contribution to my life through the leadership classes. You are a good teacher and a great leader. You are my inspiration in many areas. I am blessed by your teachings and guidance. The things I have learnt in leadership classes have reshaped me in my personal life as well as in our ministries. The three valuable and powerful words *knowledge*, *understanding*, and *wisdom* brought clarity and spectacular changes in me when I meditated deeply after hearing them repeatedly from you. Two other words that I have caught and received from you and am blessed with are *growth* and *seek*.

The labour and contribution you have given me in these three-and-a-half years won't go in vain. I am always ready to transfer your lessons to this generation and next generation. I would also like to thank Pastor Nihar and the Logos Global Vision team. You are always in my prayers and love.

Yours in His Kingdom,

Pr Pratus Ranjan Kumar

Testimonial 31

I thank God and Pastor Daniel for Pastor Daniel's leadership classes, which I have been attending since September 2017. I feel sad that the classes will be over in March 2021. Then the real challenge starts for us: to be fruitful and multiply what we have received. Perhaps we are sure of being fruitful because we are empowered already and have seen the results in our personality development and in our ministries and professions since the day we started the classes.

When we started, the classes occurred through WhatsApp video calls—that small screen! We did this for more than a year. But then, in

2018, we were blessed with a laptop by Logos Global Vision e. V. (E.V. is like TM in German)

All I would like to say is that it has been an awesome journey.

I would like to mention the following points to glorify God:

- We were truly only able to come this far by God's help, grace, and favour.
- I am grateful for Pastor Daniel's love for us. He was always patient and encouraging. He was also always there, an understanding man. He adjusted himself to fit our schedules. I remember that, on a few occasions during the winter season, we held the classes according to Indian time, which was 7:00 a.m. German time.
- During the leadership training, my eyes were opened as Pastor Daniel taught on the topic of "Who We Are in Christ Jesus." This topic shifted me, accelerated me, and lifted me into another dimension. His teachings on potential, growth, time management, leaders are readers, and many other topics truly empowered me. The tag line "knowledge, understanding, and wisdom" has been a great influence that has developed my sense of the importance of thinking.
- My self-empowerment in studying health, finances, and relationships has taught me many lessons. I would say that these lessons are assets to me.
- As a leader of the ministry, I have observed noticeable development among our leaders who took these classes. I have observed a transformation in their thought processes and approach to life with a kingdom identity. I am also truly excited for our leaders who are next in line to be trained by Pastor Daniel.
- The Logos scholarship accelerated the movement of our leaders. We didn't have a set-up of paid staff, but at the same time, all were facing some sort of struggle, which was a hindrance to their movement. The scholarships brought them release. I never thought they would be so blessed and so grateful in such a way for that.

- I remember God's presence connecting us and revolving through Germany to India. I remember how sometimes we had tears in our eyes during our reflections and prayer time.
- The Plumb Line Seminar that we did in November 2020 was empowering and eye-opening. "Christ is our security" was my greatest takeaway.

I want to close with the prayer found in 2 Timothy 2:2, which says, "And the things that you have heard from me among many witnesses, commit these to faithful men who will be able to teach others also."

Special thanks to you, to Pastor Daniel, and to the whole Logos team for making this possible. You have invested in us for a difference in eternity. Thank you, and God bless you.

Pr. Nihar N.

Testimonial 32

I would like to say thank you, Pastor Daniel. You always know how to make life brighter for everyone you know. Thank you for your invaluable mentorship over these past three years. I've had fun getting to know you better. I've learnt so much from talking with you and seeing how you work. You are amazing in what you do! I'm grateful and humbled to have had the chance to be your student.

The whole class blessed me beyond my imagination. I want to share the following few things I learned: who I am in Christ from the "In Christ Jesus" class, the power of declaration, how to balance every area of my life, and better reading habits. I learned from and was encouraged in the business class. I remember how you shared with us that our gifts, skills, and talents will help us to excel in our professions, businesses, and ministries. Quality and quantity brings growth in the business

I remember you asking us, "What would you say if you had one minute on the global stage?" That's challenged me, and I always think about it.

During the leadership class, you explained the difference between these three magical words: *knowledge, understanding,* and *wisdom.* Knowledge is gathered information; understanding is grasping or comprehension; and wisdom is the application of what you know and understand. These three words are treasures in life.

The leadership class was a real blessing for me. The lessons I learnt from Pastor Daniel transformed my personal life. With the help of this training, I can see better and grow up. Not only was I built up professionally, but I was also transformed from the inside out.

Thank you and may God bless you, Pastor Daniel Ondieki and Global Logos Vision. Thank you.

Mousumi N.

Testimonial 33

I am Avinash Kumar Hauman. First of all, I would like to thank Pastor Nihar Ranjan Nanda for introducing us to Pastor Daniel and his leadership class.

I believe that every end has a new beginning. Three years back, when I was enrolled in the leadership class, I wasn't sure what I would get in return. I was excited; however, at the same time, I was a little bit unsure of my ability to complete this leadership class. Pastor Daniel's leadership class was very useful in building a good personality that focuses on solutions rather than problems. It took me on the path towards a positive attitude in Christ and taught me the importance of knowledge, understanding, and wisdom in God. He explained to us that knowledge is gathered information, understanding is comprehension or having a grasp of something, and wisdom is the application of what you know and understand. Proverbs 3:19–20 says, "The Lord by wisdom founded the earth; By understanding He established the heavens; By His knowledge the depths were broken up and clouds drop down the dew." I'm 100 percent sure I will never forget these three words. I believe that, with these keys, we can reach the unreached people with the gospel of the kingdom of our God!

Pastor Daniel is really a great teacher; he taught almost every topic that we as believers must know and work on. He brought out and honed my spiritual life, positivity, attitude, potential, ability to learn, willingness, and punctuality. Now, on the edge of completing the leadership class, I can boldly say that in a world of anxiety, fear, perfectionism, and pressure, we can find rest. We can have the assurance that we are headed in the right direction—towards God's hand.

I pray to God that I will cherish this three-and-a-half years for the rest of my life. Thank you, and may God bless Pastor Daniel Ondieki and Logos Global Vision.

Avinash Kumar Hauman

Testimonial 34

Praise the Lord!. Thank you for the opportunity to share about the benefits I gained from the leadership class and Pastor Daniel. This class was really a great blessing in my life.

I would like to highlight some of the points from the leadership class that have added value to my life. One is learning how to select and delegate to a team. This helped me to change my leadership strategy. Another is the importance of having multiple sources of income. This lesson helped me learn how money works. Pastor Daniel taught us that Jesus was also a businessman. He did his work accordingly. What I learnt is to be more like Him.

I have grown in declaration prayers and am also seeing its results.

The humility and helping nature of Pastor Daniel have blessed me, and at the same time, these qualities have challenged me. The suggestions and advice of Pastor Daniel have transformed my life, especially when he arranged the Plumb Line seminar. Pastor Daniel has helped me to overcome many challenges.

Thank you again for everything that you taught us during the leadership classes. Thank you.

Daisy N.

Testimonial 35

I am so grateful to have taken the coaching and mentoring leadership classes with you, Pastor Daniel. I have gained and learnt a lot of things, more than I expected. I learnt how to use a positive attitude and positive energy to overcome stress. I learnt how to speak publicly. Now I am able to block out negative feelings more effectively than I have ever been able to. All the classes had an impact on my life. I am blessed by your personal testimony. Thank you so much for everything.

Shila

Testimonial 36

I thank God for this opportunity. I have been blessed and encouraged by all of your classes, Pastor Daniel. I was inspired by the following statement you made in the business class: "Begin small and dream big." I was also inspired to learn that Jesus was a businessman before He began His public ministry. I was encouraged and inspired to take a step of faith, bought a cow, and started my small business. This is how I am growing and using the teachings practically. Thank you.

Selvi

Testimonial 37

Thank you so much for such amazing leadership business sessions. These three months of learning shifted my thinking and personality for the better—towards being a great person. These classes have given me the confidence to speak up and share my ideas and views in front of other people. Thank you so much.

Lovely

Testimonial 38

Praise the Lord, Pastor Daniel! I want to thank you for your great contribution to us. Your humbleness and friendly nature really helped me to interact with you. I am learning many new things and am blessed by your teachings. From the "Relationship Journey" class, I learnt not to get trapped in any toxic relationships. Before these classes, I had been easily trapped into toxic relationships due to my lack of God's wisdom and knowledge. Through this class, I was greatly boosted and became more conscious about healthy relationships. I had unhealthy habits from my childhood which were difficult to replace. But since I attended your class titled "Develop Good Habits," I have tried to replace those bad habits with good ones. I am seeing good and great improvement. I am thankful and grateful!

Ankita D.

Testimonial 39

Thank you so much, sir. All the classes were extremely beneficial, enlightening, useful, and memorable. I have started looking at many things in a new way. I have learnt and practiced how to begin, continue, and finish well on work that I had initially given up on. I have started to see myself on a different level, and I have received many tools that I will definitely implement in my life. I would like to say I am excited to go to the next level of my life, family, career, and profession!

Ankita A.

Testimonial 40

I have been really blessed through these three months of leadership classes with you, Pastor Daniel. It was wonderful to learn many new things from you. I have never heard of or been taught in the way that you taught us. I thank you for all your efforts and the time that you gave us. Now I have knowledge of many new things, and I have started seeing things from a very different perspective. Thank you.

Usha

Testimonial 41

Thank you, sir, for these classes. Before these classes, I was an emotional girl who was always stressed out. But after attending the relationship class, I changed. I am not so affected by insignificant things anymore. I have started to trust God for the right partner and learnt to seek Him for guidance.

T. R. Florence

Testimonial 42

Before these classes, I was a person who always had doubts and was uncertain in my plans. But after the classes, I became a person who is able to execute plans and has more confidence. My way of thinking has totally changed in a positive direction.

Kalev

Testimonial 43

When I met Daniel Ondieki in Bonn Bad Godesberg, Germany, more than twenty-five years ago, I felt his joy of life and cheerfulness. I thought, "Look; this is how it can be to be a Christian." I was and am touched by his attitude, his approach to life, and his love for God and His people. Over time, he became a role model for me. I wanted to have a radiance like his, from the inside out! In the beginning, I was more interested in this than in Jesus's teachings.

Thanks to the many conversations I have had with Pastor Daniel, I now have a deep relationship with Jesus. He is my elixir of life today.

Honestly, in times of need or great matters of the heart, I call Daniel. All the wonderful things that have happened over the years after a simple request from the depths of my heart could certainly fill a book.

We need people in whom we can see the value of the spiritual connection.

Veronika P.

Testimonial 44

To my brother Daniel: I am very proud of your commitment to share your knowledge and wisdom with the world. In my formal and informal interactions with you, you have always displayed impeccable mastery in connecting with people on unique platforms that showcase how integrated human operations are.

Your ability to communicate with people about complex life issues, organizational structures, leadership, and many other areas has created a distinction that makes you a speaker who is always welcome for a second round.

Congratulations on your new book, and may God continue to use you to reach the masses.

Richard R.

Testimonial 45

My name is Leyre, and my husband's name is Carlos. We met when we were 15 and 16, respectively, on vacation in Almeria, Spain. We were young, but as soon as we saw each other, we knew we were made for each other! We only had a couple of barriers: distance and, on my side, very conservative parents.

In spite of everything, by means of phone calls and letters every week, we managed to maintain our relationship for three years. We only saw each other for fifteen days a year, during vacation.

Eventually, however, these difficulties and a lack of maturity on our part led to our relationship breaking up—but not our love.

Our paths took different directions. We both married different people. Carlos had no children, and I had three. Deep down, we both had something inside us that said we were not happy.

Twenty-two years later, thanks to technology, we got in touch again. Just as before, we embarked on numerous in-depth conversations in which we talked about everything as confidants. We could see again that, despite the time that had passed, our souls and our hearts were still united.

We decided to meet, and the connection was immediate. It had been twenty-two years since the last time we saw each other, but it felt to us as if it had been only five minutes—instant love again!

Already separated from our respective partners, we decided never to be separate from each other again. Our love was and is infinite.

But our pasts haunted us everywhere—we could not get over them. That put us in a permanent struggle with ourselves and with each other. It made us see all the mistakes we had made. We were unable to move forward.

Then we decided to take the reins of our lives and ask for help. We approached our saviour, the person who made our lives make sense and move forward: our dear friend Daniel.

I do not want to say that it was easy. On the contrary, we had a great deal of pain, rage, anger, and reproach. Without Daniel, we would not have been able to overcome those feelings. His first words after six hours listening to our pain were "I cannot help you, but I know Someone who will, and I will be His messenger."

Pastor Daniel led us to God through Jesus Christ, and we opened our hearts. Little by little and by the hands of both, we came out of the black hole we had been stuck in.

The hour-and-a-half drive home was very quiet (which was strange for us, since we are never silent). We needed to process everything that had happened during those six hours.

We were just beginning to be at peace with ourselves and with our past when the next deep divide appeared in our lives. It seemed that we would not be able to have children of our own. We were devastated. Medicine could do little for us.

After we told Daniel about this, he proposed that we take his seminar Plumb Line as a way to better understand what was going on in our lives, why it was happening, and how to make it change.

For a whole weekend, we absorbed a lot of wisdom and truths that in daily life almost nobody thinks about. We were taught to manifest our desires, to think about them, to desire them, and to give thanks for them. We learned that our minds and our energy are more powerful than we think. So began our path to be better, to live better, and to feel stronger.

During that same seminar, we wished to have a son—not only our son, but I also chose a name for him. I named him Apólo in prayer. Now we are accompanied by our miracle son Apólo, who is 3 years old at this time that I am writing this testimony . This the best and most unexpected thing that has ever happened in our lives. Forever we shall be grateful to God and give Him all the glory!

After that, we made a wall of wishes. We gave thanks every day for everything that was to come: new jobs, getting closer to our families, and having our own family. And here we are, almost five years later. We have our treasure, Apólo. We have the work that we described and put on our wish wall.

We are not yet in port, of course, but we are much closer.

Leyre and Carlos

Testimonial 46

As I went through the class on having a vision, I was so inspired to learn that the poorest person on the earth is not the one who doesn't have shelter, water, money, or clothing, but the one who does not have a vision. I also learnt that a vision has power to provide for its visionary.

Writing down your vision clearly and knowing the strategies for executing it are very important, as is sharing it with faithful people who will help you realize it. When you have a clear, God-given vision, you will be amazed at how fulfilled you will be. The most frustrated person on the earth is the person who has a vision and does not know how to execute it or bring it to reality. A vision will give you direction and protection. That is why you should write it down, make it known to others, and, if possible, publish it. Your resources are in your vision.

I am glad I attended Daniel's class, for I learnt a lot.

Caren M.

Testimonial 47

The author of this book, Pastor Daniel Ondieki, has written teachings which explain biblical principles and how to apply them in daily life. Pastor Daniel's personality excels in friendliness and love for people.

My husband, Horst, and I have been very blessed to follow his lessons, and we have learned a lot from them. May Pastor Daniel's book reach many people around the world, and may they be blessed as they, listen to the audio book, read, study it, memorize the scriptures given in the book, meditate on the teachings that are based on God's word, and be richly blessed.

Joke K. F.

Testimonial 48

A few years ago, we met Pastor Daniel Ondieki. He is a man of God, who unlike many others, always has a smile on his face.

His face radiates the love that expresses the divine that we as Christians should have. He preaches and teaches this in his seminars and services.

His passion is equipping believers with tools that help them discover their purpose in life. He aims to bring clarity of purpose as he explains biblical principles and how to apply them in our daily lives.

We bless him and his dear wife Edith, who actively supports him, with health, energy, and success in the name and love of our Lord Jesus Christ.

Horst F.

Testimonial 49

I went through these educational, illustrative and consultative coaching and mentoring classes with Coach Daniel. "The Power of Words" (Chapter 2) illustrates what words can do in your life, and I hereby testify that words have impacted my life. "You Are Gifted" (Chapter 5) shows you how you can link your spoken words with your identified gifts, thereby "Understanding Your Assignment" (Chapter 8). Chapter 8 vividly describes the importance of understanding your core purpose and mission in life and why you are here. This book will teach you these concepts and much more. As a result, you will achieve much more in your life and always deliver your services and products with excellence and beyond expectations.

Coach Daniel, during our coaching and mentoring sessions, you spoke so deliberately and passionately about the power of words, emphasizing the importance of using positive words to determine your life's path. It is clear that the lessons in this book have resonated with you as a coach. Your leadership and professional virtues are illustrated in this book. These lessons have left an indelible mark on my heart and have had a significant impact on me upon deep personal reflection and soul searching.

During these sessions, you also passionately underscored that "it is not too late to change your world with your words", and therefore, "nobody can say that it is too late to change, because most people regret this when they say, I wish I knew all these things ten or twenty years ago". I can indeed confirm that words have power over people's lives, including my own.

In one of your sessions you said quoting Dr. Bill Winston in one of his preaching saying: "Words are the highest authority in the world". That really spoke to me. You also quoted Matthew 12:37 which says: "For by your words you will be justified, and by your words you will be condemned." Another version PTP says: "Your very words will be used as evidence, and your words will declare you either innocent or guilty." The Apostle James also writes to exalt us to be diligent concerning the words. My dearest brothers and sisters, take this to heart: Be quick to listen, but slow to speak. "And be slow to become angry, for human anger is never a legitimate tool to promote God's righteous purpose". (James 1:19-20).

I can testify that the power of words has had a significant impact on my health, relationships, finances, and professional, spiritual and business life. I have learnt that most people do not want to do anything to change who they are; instead, they wish for their outside circumstances to change. Indeed, after participating in your coaching sessions, I took up the responsibility of ensuring that, if it has to be, it is up to me, and that means nobody will be responsible for my life other than my own self.

Your book also emphasizes that one should use positive words to change his/her life, as words are the thoughts spoken from the heart. Your heart and mind should therefore be in harmony with your thoughts, from which your reflections, words and deeds arise. This great and illuminating book will teach anyone that you can program your mind and tongue in such a way that it can chart the course of the rest of your life.

This great book also brings out so vividly the message that you are the pilot of your own life, no matter the rain, storms or wind you may encounter. You are responsible for directing your ship to wherever you desire through the use of positive spoken words. Pastor Daniel, your book also clearly illustrates that words are seeds because as soon as they are sown in one's heart and mind, the process of a good harvest or a bad one is begun.

If you want to reorganise your life to become more fulfilling and productive, this book is a must-read. Rest assured that you will experience significant growth – more growth than you have ever experienced in your life. As you read this book, your life will be completely transformed, and you will never be the same again. Many thanks coach Daniel for your wisdom, love and care for the many people you are reaching out to empower, inspire and equip for a better and greater tomorrow. To God be all the glory and praise!!!

Agnes Momanyi
Senior Counsel

CONCLUSION

My focus in this book is your personal, professional, and corporate growth. My understanding is that growth encompasses two sides of the coin: you can grow stronger and stronger, or you can grow weaker and weaker. Growth is a choice. Bear in mind that the choices you make will either make you or break you. My focus is to help you unlock the unlimited potential within you.

My challenge to you is this: Be at the right place at the right time with the right people, doing the right things in the right way. Stay within your strength zone, and keep growing where you are planted. You are destined for greatness and you have what it takes to succeed. Your transformational leadership journey begins where you are. When you focus on spiritual, personal, economic, and community development, you will make a difference, bring greater impact, and make the world a better place.

ACKNOWLEDGEMENTS

First and foremost, my acknowledgement and greatest appreciation goes to my beloved wife, Edith, who tirelessly made sure all went well during my writing. A trillion thanks are given for your love, care, trust, and endless support. You have supported me not only while I was writing this book but ever since we said, "I do" to each other. You are not only my darling wife but my dearest and great friend. May the good Lord continue to fill your cup to overflow. All my love to you. You are one of a kind. You are destined for greatness! Many have done well, but you have exceeded them all.

Second, I would like to acknowledge my parents and all my siblings. I would need to write another book to thank you for all the contributions you have made to my life. To my parents: Everything you taught me has remained with me. You raised us to love and have the fear of the Lord. A trillion thanks for your love, care, and discipline. To my siblings: You are an amazing and awesome team. A billion thanks.

From the depths of my heart, I would like to acknowledge all the teachers I had from primary level to high school. Time and space do not allow me to list all your names or describe what a difference you made in my school life. Many thanks, and may the Lord richly bless you and your families.

I would like to acknowledge all the lecturers and professors I had in my institutions of higher learning. You truly added value in my life, as you helped me to see the future positively and with the big picture in mind. I greatly appreciate you all. May the Lord richly bless you and your families.

I would like to acknowledge my spiritual fathers and mothers who heavily invested in my spiritual life and walk with the Lord. I am very humbled to be the man God has made me into today. To the apostle Harry Das, Mama Das, Pastor John Das, and family: Your spiritual impartation to my life and family is so special in my heart that I cannot explain it. That impartation is greatly treasured. The fivefold ministry anointing is making a difference in the lives of many. We love you greatly. As the apostle Das says, "The work continues."

I did not have a chance to meet Rev. Kenneth Hagan or his beloved wife, Sister Oretha, but their books, teachings, and videos have greatly helped me to grow up. One great teaching Rev. Hagan wrote in the little book *You Will Have What You Say* impacted me greatly: his four points, say it, do it, receive it, and tell it. This teaching tremendously transformed my life. Those are principles that work at all times for anyone. I am forever grateful to the Lord for Rev. Hagan and Sister Oretha. Your work continues.

I would like also to acknowledge the following great men: Rev. Oral Roberts, Rev. Reinhard Bonnke, Dr. Morris Cerullo, and many other generals of God who have been promoted to glory. You were my inspiration and role models. You led with love and wisdom. Time and space do not allow me to mention your contributions to my life and family. You deposited so much in me that I can never thank you enough. I greatly appreciate you, your families, and your ministries. Your works and ministries continue until the Second Coming of our Lord Jesus Christ.

I would also like to acknowledge Dr. Myles Munroe and Pastor Ruth Munroe. What a great teacher and a great apostle Dr. Myles was in teaching about the kingdom of God, visions, management, and leadership. You have made a difference in my life and family. Your voices are still loud here on the earth, and your work continues. Dr. Myles, you challenged me to write a book and showed me how to write it. Here it is, finally. I greatly appreciate you, your family, and your ministry.

I would also like to show my appreciation for Pastor E. A. Adepoye, the general overseer of the Redeemed Christian Church of God (RCCG). You are a great example to millions. You love God and His presence more than anything else. You wish and desire for the whole world to say yes to Jesus. To God be the glory! It was a great honour, sir, to serve under your ministry some years ago. You and Mama G. O. are amazing. May you continue to shine like the stars of heaven. We love you and appreciate you greatly.

I would like to acknowledge pastors Musa and Eunice Bako. We love and appreciate you greatly. When we arrived in Germany, you trusted us and handed over your ministry to us. That was my first pastoral ministry, and it brought us from one ministry to another. Thanks also for the wisdom and guidance that you have continued to give us. You are destined for greatness. You have what it takes to succeed and deliver beyond expectations.

I would like to thank Pastor Funbi Oni-Orisan for taking my manuscript and working on it for hours and hours. Many thanks, Pastor Funbi, for all the investment you put into my book. You are an amazing and committed leader on whom I can count for my next book project. You delivered beyond my expectations. Thanks, Pastor Agbo and children, for supporting Pastor Funbi as she worked on my book. You are a blessing.

I would like to acknowledge Dr. Boaz Olang, his dearly beloved wife, Jane, and their family. Dr. Boaz has been mentoring and coaching me for the last thirty years. Boaz, you are a friend indeed. Your wisdom and guidance are priceless. You have always challenged me to treat my wife like a queen. Boaz always challenges me to plan for a hundred years here on the earth, but to live as though Christ is coming in the next second. Thanks, Dr. Boaz, for believing in me. You have constantly unlocked the potential within me. This book is a result of your contribution and the support you have given me. Many thanks for the amazing foreword you wrote for me! You are a friend who walks the talk. I value you, your family, our friendship, relationship, and fellowship greatly. Many thanks!

Time and space do not allow me to mention all the spiritual leaders who have had an impact on my life. Please, if you do not see your names mentioned here, know that I love you, your families, and your ministries, and I appreciate you greatly.

I would like to thank my prayer team, which continually prayed for this book. You are some of my greatest role models. You have always challenged me to wake up early and begin the day with the Lord in prayer and the Word. You are an amazing team. Continue to call upon the Name above all names. Your reward in heaven will be great.

I would like to thank my church, CLW Bonn. What an amazing family you are. To our eldership, pastoral team, administration team, internationals, district leaders, members, and friends: A billion thanks are given for your love and care for each other. I am greatly humbled to be your international pastor. Together, we are making a difference in CLW, in our city, and in God's kingdom. My love and great appreciation goes out to you all. Special thanks to our senior pastor, Mario, and to Claudia, who welcomed us so warmly to the city and to the church when we came to Bonn. We love you and greatly appreciate you and your family.

I would like to acknowledge Dr. Heinrich (Heinz) Floreck, the founder and president of Logos Global Vision e. V.

In 2005, Dr. Heinz came to the church where I was pastoring in southern Germany and conducted a seminar called Plumb Line. During that seminar, the Lord laid it on Dr. Heinz's heart to train me. In July of that year, we flew together to Durban, South Africa, where he would train other pastors and spiritual leaders. During the seminar, I was super blessed and took the challenge to train others. Sixteen years later, my various teams and I have trained many people, and we have seen the Lord transform many of those lives! Many thanks, Heinz, for being obedient to the voice of the Lord. You are truly a man of God who walks and works with the Lord! You are my role model and a great example to me, Edith, and many others. Abundant blessings!

I would also like to acknowledge Helga, who is a great support to Dr. Heinz. Helga, you are an amazing and great woman of God. Not only that, but your cooking is amazing! Each time we visit you, we are blessed and refreshed. Thanks for your great hospitality ministry.

Thank you, Claudia, for being our great CEO. You lead by example, and you are a great blessing to many. Thank you, Kevin, for being a great support to Claudia and Logos. Thank you, Matthias and Caroline, for introducing me and Edith to your family twenty-two years ago. You are such a blessing. My recognition goes to all our Logos Global Vision leadership teams and partners. We are growing together, making a difference, and showing the needy and the helpless their value. Many thanks go to you.

I cannot forget to acknowledge Dr. John C. Maxwell and the John Maxwell Team (JMT). Dr Maxwell has given us a whole new dimension of how to be light and salt at home, in the church, in organizations, and in the marketplace. There are many things I have learned from Dr. John Maxwell. He emphasizes *personal growth*. In his book *Leader Shift*, he says,

"Improving yourself is the first step in improving everything else."
UNKNOWN *Leadershift*, page 41

Goals help you do better, but growth lets you become better. Leaders are growth oriented. Make growth your top priority and:

- you will be an example for others to follow;
- you will become more so you can do more;
- you will grow in humility and self-awareness;
- you will strengthen your values and abilities;
- you will feel good and great about yourself;
- you will unlock and achieve your potential; and
- you will see your level of success expand.

Many thanks, Dr. Maxwell, for being the person you are and a great friend to millions. You are my hero and a great leader I look up to in many different ways. Thank you, JMT coaches, mentors, and family! Together, we are adding value to each other and making a difference in the world. As we say in Kenya, "*asante sana*"—thank you very much!

Finally, I would like to show my great appreciation for Dr. Mike Murdock, a great man of God who God has used to touch millions of people around the globe. I know Dr. Mike as a man of wisdom. Whenever I read Proverbs 4:7–9, I think of him. This passage says,

> Wisdom *is* the principal thing;
> *Therefore* get wisdom.
> And in all your getting, get understanding.
> Exalt her, and she will promote you;
> She will bring you honor, when you embrace her.
> She will place on your head an ornament of grace;
> A crown of glory she will deliver to you.

I have read many of Dr. Mike's books and my life has changed as a result. His ministry has helped me to feed the people who are assigned to me. Thanks a million, Dr. Mike, for being the man you are. Whenever I want to sharpen my wisdom, I turn to Dr. Mike by reading his books. *The Law of Recognition* was the first of Dr. Mike's books I read. It helped me to recognize who I am, whose I am, and the resources at my disposal. Abundant blessings to you and your ministries, Dr. Mike!

On June 21, 1981, at the age of 18, I dedicated my life to the Lord Jesus Christ, and I have never looked back. More than a billion thanks to my Heavenly Father for sending Jesus Christ to come and save the world. More than a billion thanks, too, for sending us the most important Person to the earth: the Holy Spirit, who is our guide to the truth and our Comforter at all times. I am Yours, and You are mine. I am forever grateful to know You.

John 15:4–5 really speaks of my walk and work with the Lord over all these years. It says, "Abide in Me, and I in you. As the branch cannot bear fruit of itself, unless it abides in the vine, neither can you, unless you abide in Me. I am the vine, you *are* the branches. He who abides in Me, and I in him, bears much fruit; for without Me you can do nothing."

The secret to victorious living is abiding in Christ Jesus!

Without Him I can do nothing. With Him, I can do all things! He is my Hero.

> His peace, His example, His Word, and the Holy Spirit are our legacy. Let us take advantage of this great heritage that He has left behind. Shalom!
>
> A wise man/woman is one who surrenders his/her heart, soul, and body to God, the Creator of the heavens and the earth, and acknowledges the Lord Jesus Christ as the Lord of all.
>
> —Daniel O. Ondieki

AUTHOR BIO

Daniel O. Ondieki is a certified life coach, trainer, teacher, and speaker with the John Maxwell team. Daniel emphasizes that transformational leadership begins from the inside out. He reveals the secrets of prosperity and good success based on meditation on God's written Word and His promises. He also highlights cases from the Bible, revealing spiritual kingdom principles to help you navigate a world in crisis. "Become more to do more" is his emphasis in his leadership training sessions.

Besides being an author, Daniel is an international pastor, a motivational speaker and a business consultant. For over 21 years, Daniel has shared his wisdom, gifts, and talents through his seminars, workshops, and leadership trainings, challenging audiences to rise up from within and shine forth like the stars of heaven. Daniel's philosophy is, "What you are looking for is within you"! Daniel and his dear wife Edith live in Bonn Germany.

ABOUT THE BOOK

We all go through crises, be it in our health, finances, or relationships. We often feel like we have no way out. But there is always a way out. As you seek the Lord diligently, He will make a way where there seems to be no way. God is never in a hurry. He is never too late. He is always on time.

In this book, pastor and coach Daniel Ondieki will point you to your true Source of life and the resources at your disposal. Daniel brings hope, comfort, and encouragement, especially during challenging times, to those who may be considering giving up on life.

This book equips you with the tools you need, based on timeless kingdom principles in God's Word, to turn your life around, improve your spiritual relationship with God and those around you, and give you clarity about your vision in life.

Daniel reveals a blueprint for how to unlock your potential and become a transformational leader by:

- developing clarity of purpose in your life, profession, business, and ministry,
- positioning yourself strategically for God's blessings and victorious living,
- being at the right place at the right time with the right people doing the right things
- in the right way,
- equipping and empowering others to become more and to do more,
- discovering the blessings of the fear of the Lord,
- understanding that "your gift will make room for you" and learning to develop it and never give up.

Daniel addresses issues affecting individuals' social, spiritual, economic, and professional development. He emphasizes that some of the destroyers in the world today include ignorance and cluelessness. As it is written, God's people are destroyed by lack of knowledge. These enemies must be confronted with God's kingdom principles, the exact knowledge and study, which will raise the awareness and consciousness of who you are and the resources you have at your disposal, given to you by the Creator of heaven and earth.

Daniel emphasizes that transformational leadership begins from the inside out. He reveals the secrets of prosperity and good success based on meditation on God's written Word and His promises. He also highlights cases from the Bible, revealing spiritual principles to help you navigate a world in crisis. By applying the wisdom in this book, you can become the person God created you to be and make the world a better place.

The topics Daniel explores include inside management and leadership; creativity and innovation; the importance of beginning small, continuing, and finishing well; the need to become more to do more; clarity of purpose; a vision-guided life; the lanes of life; lack of joy and fulfillment; identity crisis; and much more.

Proverbs 25:25 says, "As cold water to a weary soul, so is good news from a far country." Destined for Greatness comes to you with good news and hope. There is greatness in you!

Ingram Content Group UK Ltd.
Milton Keynes UK
UKHW040645290323
419341UK00001B/1